D1591878

Draft Day Do's

➤ Start early.

➤ Be prepared for a long day.

➤ Have plenty of refreshments on hand.

➤ Try to keep your player information as concentrated as possible; the less paper shuffling the better.

➤ Keep track of everyone's roster and money as you go.

➤ Always start bidding at $1, no matter which player it is.

➤ Always bid $1 at a time; don't jump.

➤ Use poker techniques when bidding.

➤ Let the other guy rush into mistakes.

➤ Always have money left for the late rounds.

➤ Bring a draft assistant if your league allows them; they can help.

➤ Take frequent breaks.

➤ If it rattles the other guy, be annoying (tap fingers and feet, stretch, sigh, moan—anything to distract him).

➤ If you feel indecisive about a player, let him go.

➤ Have fun.

Draft Day Don'ts

➤ Never overspend on superstars in the early rounds.

➤ Never overspend on over-hyped rookies.

➤ Never get impatient.

➤ Never get outwardly excited over any player.

➤ Never bid more than you have to.

➤ Never use a "scare" or pre-emptive bid.

➤ Never let anyone influence your bids.

➤ Never listen to the devil on your shoulder.

➤ Never let anyone rush you.

➤ Never run out of processed food products.

➤ Never take an auction loss personally.

➤ Never underestimate the fatiguing effects of alcohol, caffeine, and nicotine.

➤ Never share your player information.

➤ Never forget your cash.

➤ Never let anyone ruin your good time.

alpha
books

Pick-Your-Own Stats

If you can find a stat service that carries them, any of these categories are fair game in fantasy:

Batting

Batting average (BA)

Home runs (HR)

Runs batted in (RBI)

Runs scored (R)

Stolen bases (SB)

Caught stealing (CS)

Games played (G)

At-bats (AB)

Hits (H)

Singles (1B)

Doubles (2B)

Triples (3B)

Walks (BB)

Intentional walks (IBB)

Hit by pitch (HBP)

Strikeouts—batter (K)

Grounded into double play (GIDP)

Sacrifice bunts

Sacrifice flies

Plate appearances

Total bases

Slugging percentage (SLG)

On-base percentage (OBP)

OBP + SLG (OPS)

BA with runners in scoring position

Pitching

Wins (W)

Saves (S)

Strikeouts—pitcher (K)

Earned run average (ERA)

Walks + Hits per Inning Pitched (WHIP)

Losses (L)

Won-loss percentage

Games pitched (G)

Complete games (CG)

Shutouts (SO)

Innings pitched (IP)

Hits allowed (H)

Runs allowed (R)

Home runs allowed (HR)

Walks allowed (BB)

Hit batters (HBP)

Wild pitches (WP)

Balks

Batting average allowed

Strikeouts per nine innings (K ÷ 9 IP)

Walks per nine innings (BB ÷ 9 IP)

Strikeout/walk ratio

Blown saves (BS)

Holds (H)

Pitches thrown

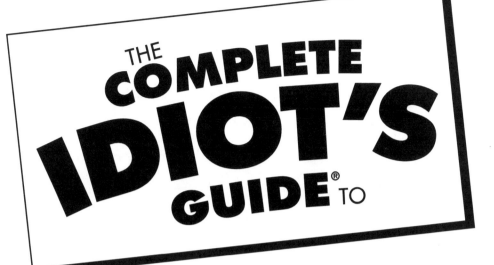

THE COMPLETE IDIOT'S GUIDE® TO

Fantasy Baseball

by Michael Zimmerman

alpha books

Macmillan USA, Inc.
201 West 103rd Street
Indianapolis, IN 46290

A Pearson Education Company

I dedicate this book to Visa. The check's in the mail.

Copyright © 2000 by Michael Zimmerman

International Standard Book Number: 0-02-863830-1
Library of Congress Catalog Card Number: Available upon request.

02   01   00   8   7   6   5   4   3   2   1

Interpretation of the printing code: The rightmost number of the first series of numbers is the year of the book's printing; the rightmost number of the second series of numbers is the number of the book's printing. For example, a printing code of 00-1 shows that the first printing occurred in 2000.

Printed in the United States of America

Publisher
Marie Butler-Knight

Product Manager
Phil Kitchel

Associate Managing Editor
Cari Luna

Acquisitions Editor
Randy Ladenheim-Gil

Development Editor
Joan D. Paterson

Production Editor
Christy Wagner

Copy Editor
Susan Aufheimer

Illustrator
Jody P. Schaeffer

Cover Designers
Mike Freeland
Kevin Spear

Book Designers
Scott Cook and Amy Adams of DesignLab

Indexer
Angie Bess

Layout/Proofreading
Angela Calvert
John Etchison
Cheryl Lynch
Gloria Schurick

Contents at a Glance

Contents

Part 5: It's a Long, Hot Summer   155

14 April and May: Opening Day Jitters and the Virtue of Patience   157

15 Things Heat Up: June to the All-Star Break   171

16 The Dog Days: July and August   185

Foreword

Who would have thought 20 years ago that Daniel Okrent's idea of rotisserie baseball in midtown Manhattan would turn a boyhood hobby into a multi-million-dollar industry?

Or that a group of young baseball fanatics in Niles, Ohio, in the late '70s, led by my own kid brother, Jim Foster, and our cousin, Rob Hinton, originating "boxscore baseball," playing against each other, and scouring the daily newspapers for the boxscores, would continue into the new millennium in what we call, affectionately, fantasy baseball?

My first exposure to fantasy sports was back in 1982 when I moved to Florida and joined a league with *Ultimate Fantasy Sports* with someone who is now one of my best friends in the industry, John "Dr. Z" Zaleski, a real promoter and leader in the fantasy baseball industry. He has been a fantasy pioneer in building his hobby into a successful business in one-year and lifetime leagues for baseball, basketball, football, and hockey.

Charlie Wiegert of CDM Sports, another pioneer and founding member of the FSPA, summed up his memories of how his hobby has turned into a profitable business this way: "The card in our P.O. box said to come to the counter; all of the responses won't fit in the box. I knew at that moment my life would never be the same, and the passion for playing fantasy baseball, which had been a hobby, just became a business. Fantasy baseball has become the chosen entertainment for over six million fans and a reason why Major League Baseball continues to be one of America's favorite pastimes."

Greg Ambrosius, editor of the first fantasy baseball publication at Krause Publications, is another offspring of turning his hobby into a career. "When I first began playing fantasy baseball in 1986, I never imagined that this passionate hobby that I was enjoying would one day be my profession. Three years after playing fantasy baseball, I saw an ad in the *Green Bay Gazette* stating that Krause Publications was looking for a fantasy baseball editor. Had I died and gone to heaven? What could be better than that? I landed the dream job of any lifetime baseball fan. To this day, I thank my lucky stars every minute I spend being a professional fantasy baseball writer."

Greg, Charlie, and Dr. Z are just a few of the many fantasy baseball diehards I've met over the years who have now joined together with nine other key individuals to form the basis of the Fantasy Sports Players Association, Inc. (FSPA), a nonprofit trade association, to be the voice of the fantasy industry and work to improve the quality of fantasy sports.

Major companies like ESPN, CBS SportsLine, CNN/SI, The Sporting News, Prime Sports, CDM Sports, Yahoo!, and many more are finding fantasy baseball to be integral parts of their revenue sources and business plans. The Internet has taken fantasy baseball to another level and catapulted the industry into cyberspace with millions of players globally.

The FSPA will be honoring the founding fathers of Rotisserie Baseball at their First Annual Fantasy Trade Show by inducting them into the FSPA Hall of Fame. The first-ever Fantasy Choice Awards will be announced with baseball great Gary Carter as the guest speaker. There are fantasy baseball radio and television shows, magazines, news-letters, and scores of Web sites for games, software, information, and stat services.

The Major League Baseball Players Association has recognized fantasy baseball as a great way for the players to interact with their fans. Just don't have a bad year, Albert Belle, or I'll trade your butt.

The FSPA fully endorses *The Complete Idiot's Guide to Fantasy Baseball* as an informa-tive, entertaining tutorial to get the novice or even the expert in full stride to become the next fantasy baseball champion of his own local backyard league, or if he wants, to venture out in one of the many national games now available.

It's the "Roto-Lennium" and what idiot wouldn't want to play fantasy baseball?

Even my wife's coming around after all these years.

Carl L. Foster
Vice President of Media and Fantasy Sports
United Sports Fans of America (UsFans.com)
President/CEO
Fantasy Sports Players Association, Inc. (FSPA)

Carl Foster is a Fantasy Sports Hall of Famer with over 18 years of playing competitive fantasy sports in local and national baseball, football, and basketball leagues. He turned his hobby and passion into career opportunities when he launched the na-tion's first live fantasy sports radio show on the Internet for CBS SportsLine. He cre-ated the Net's first fantasy sports search engine at www.usfantasy411.com and currently works as the Vice President of Media and Fantasy Sports for the nation's largest fan advocacy group, United Sports Fans of America. He is one of the founding members of the Fantasy Sports Players Association (FSPA) and was elected by his peers as the first President/CEO to bring the industry together with one voice as we head into the new millennium.

Introduction

A Book's Book

There comes a time in every book's life when it has to put up or shut up. Don't just be a book. Be a *real* book. I wanted all the other books on the shelves to take a look at this book and think, "Now there's a good-looking book. That book has his spine wired tight at all times. That's a book all books can be proud to know." All the guy books want to be it, all the girl books want to be next to it on the shelf.

Despite this obvious magnetism, you won't find this book hanging out on Hemingway's turf. You won't find it fending off femme fatales with the books written by Jim Thompson, James M. Cain, or Dashiell Hammett. You won't find it talking fastballs with David Cone's book, polishing pistols with Charlton Heston's book, or trading insults with Henny Youngman's book.

But it's still a book's book. It's real. It tells the truth, sometimes the painful truth. It tells you exactly what you need to know, because it knows exactly what you need to hear: *Fantasy baseball is one rocking good time.*

The Fan's Revenge

At last, there is a game that allows fans to put their money where their foot goes by drafting, managing, and—most important—*paying* for their own teams. You use real-life major leaguers. Actual pitching and batting stats are compiled during the regular season. And whoever has the best stats at the end of the year is champion.

Beginners will find it indispensable. Advanced players will find insights and strategies that they may not have thought of. But any fantasy baseball player—not necessarily just complete idiots—will find this book informative, entertaining, and a necessary addition to their pre-season research (which, believe me, is both exhaustive and exhausting).

At the very least, the rest of the books on your shelf will be envious: "Why doesn't he read me like he reads that silly orange book?"

Walk the Walk, Strut Your Stuff

Sad to say, not many women play fantasy sports. So chances are, you are a guy. Which means this book speaks your language. But if you do happen to be female, you're in luck. Not only have you just opened the best resource for starting up a fantasy baseball league, you may even find some insights into the male psyche, which will help you win not just the battle of your league, but the battle of the sexes.

Men do have minds. Corrupted, quick-witted, dirty minds. Maybe you'll finally come to understand why guys aren't afraid to show up on Draft Day without showering.

Why guys value good seats at the stadium more than good seats at their own wedding. Why guys like movies on TNT's "Movies for Guys Who Like Movies."

Stuff like that there. What can I say? We all try to be men's men and this book strives to be a book's book. The best way I can describe it is thus: If this book had tickets to a Yankees game, it would be sitting in the right-field bleachers.

Enjoy.

Daddy's Little Helper

Much like the way my infant son will help me with my upcoming draft, I've added little helpers throughout this book. These little boxes will jump out at you, so don't be alarmed. They're harmless, but helpful.

Strike Three

Classic "don'ts." If you miss these warnings, you'll look like a guy who just missed a fat fastball with the bases loaded. Let the reader beware.

Foul Tips

Classic "do's." These indispensable tips are the backbone of fantasy baseball knowledge. They'll emphasize the most important points in the book.

Trash Talk

You need to know the lingo if you're gonna speak the language. These sidebars will help.

Overheard in the Dugout

Everyone loves a story. These anecdotes from my own experience come with a bonus: morals. I mean the kind that make the stories relevant to the subject, not wholesome.

Acknowledgments

A book like this doesn't write itself (even if it reads like it did). It exists solely because these people wanted it to exist as badly as I did:

Jessica Faust, editor and friend, who suffered through many a fantasy baseball tale, and sent the fateful e-mail that pulled me down this Blair Witch path. Thanks for asking. Seriously.

Randy Ladenheim-Gil and Joan Paterson, who yanked this manuscript tooth by tooth from my stubborn literary maw. You know what they say about people who are always late. What a jerk! Thanks for your patience and generosity.

Charlie Wagner, the Furious Shepherd, who knows this game better than I do. Hey, dude, why not write your own book? Thanks for your help.

Leroy Boyer, Chief Wahoo, who probably never thought his expertise would be needed on such a severe level. I'm going to beat you next year, Leroy, so remember this thank-you. It's the only kind word you'll get out of me until next season is over.

Scott Savage, a great friend for many years, who one day asked me if I wanted to join a fantasy baseball league. "It's cool," he said. Ain't it though. I probably still owe you a beer for that.

And thanks to the rest of the poor souls who have endured season after season of our tortured league. They've all been a part of it at one time or another, and all unknowingly contributed to this book (for free!) in some form:

Jim Carriglitto (a god), Kerry and Ted Minner (champ and son), Tom Brennan (I hope you choke on Maddux), Mike Adam (he has e-mail!), Steve Bailey (Tampico or bust), Keith Sweigert (I would've given more for Vlad), Bob Ebling (why won't you trade me Ankiel?), Evan Jones (nice draft), Dave Myers (do even), and Frank Madeira (ever heard of birth control?).

And special thanks to my wife Elaine, who tolerated my long nights in the attic writing this monster, and who birthed a beautiful baby boy who will naturally become a major league pitcher (lefty) and who will support us in the manner in which we would like to become accustomed. Right? Riiiiiight.

Special Thanks to the Technical Reviewer

The Complete Idiot's Guide to Fantasy Baseball was reviewed by an expert who double-checked the accuracy of what you'll learn here, to help us ensure that this book gives you everything you need to know about fantasy baseball. Special thanks are extended to Leroy Boyer.

Leroy Boyer is in his seventh year as a full-time sportswriter with the Pottsville daily newspaper *Republican & Evening Herald.* A die-hard baseball fan and Sunday season ticket-holder with the Philadelphia Phillies, Boyer has been playing fantasy baseball for three years. His Sculp's Hill Seminoles have finished in the money every year of their existence, ending up tied for second place last season.

Trademarks

All terms mentioned in this book that are known to be or are suspected of being trademarks or service marks have been appropriately capitalized. Alpha Books and Macmillan USA, Inc. cannot attest to the accuracy of this information. Use of a term in this book should not be regarded as affecting the validity of any trademark or service mark.

Part 1

What's Your Fantasy?

You know who you are. You sit at the bar, or on your couch, or in the nosebleed section, and you guzzle your expensive cheap suds while your team gets bombed. You yell. You wail. You bark like an outraged dog that hasn't been fed a championship in years. Why does your @#+*%@! team lose so much? You know exactly why, and you'll let everyone who'll listen know that you know.

"The GM is an idiot. The owner is cheap. The scouts are blind. The farm system is foreclosed. No one wants to win." You laugh bitterly. "I could build a championship team. I could put a team on that field that would win 130 games!"

Well, maybe you could. Everyone thinks they can do it, in just about every sport. Guess what? Thanks to thousands of fantasy leagues across the country, they are *doing it.*

Now, for you, it's finally time. You're a fantasy baseball junkie waiting to happen. This part shows you the way.

Chapter 1

Get Into the Game

In This Chapter

➤ What is fantasy baseball?

➤ Hitting and pitching still count the most

➤ Do you choose National League, American League, or both?

➤ How to score points

➤ Using the Internet

Fantasy baseball is the greatest thing to happen to baseball fans since the box score. You become the person with all the power: owner, general manager, and manager of a baseball team—on paper. You draft real major league players. You form your own team. You use real stats from the upcoming season. You use your own money. You stop your own bucks. If you win, you own the right of all rights: bragging. And if you stink? You have only yourself to fire. But you won't stink. Nah, not you.

You're smart. You'll read this indispensable burning bush of a book before you do anything. It will take you step by step, day by day through one full year of fantasy baseball: forming a league, staging a draft, managing a team, and working the off-season. Along the way, I'll tell the tale of my team, the Fedora Brigade of 1999. How did we do? Hindsight is the best medicine; not all my moves were smart. You'll see the consequences firsthand. You'll learn all you need to know and then some.

Fantasy Baseball Is More Than Fantasy

Here's the first thing you need to know about *fantasy baseball:* You and a bunch of your buddies getting together the Sunday after Opening Day and drafting teams does not a fantasy baseball league make.

Fantasy leagues have to run. And run well. Trust me. If you want even a snowball's chance of actually finishing the season (let alone winning), you have to research a heck of a lot more than just Ken Griffey Jr.'s career home run total. If you don't properly prepare, your "league" will die violently by June 1 in a hail of arguments and a pool of bad blood. Like George Foreman and his mufflers, I guarantee it.

But done right, there is no sweeter thing. A fantasy league becomes the ultimate toy box. Picture a vintage T-Bird convertible, mint condition, driving down a beer commercial highway where all the cops look like Salma Hayek and require you to take mouth-to-mouth Breathalyzer tests every hour.

A great fantasy league is a living, breathing entity that thrives even in the off-season—an honest-to-God, 365-days-a-year playground for the die-hard sports fan. In fact, you won't even care if your favorite team wins or loses. Well, okay, you'll care, but you'll care less.

Trash Talk

Fantasy baseball allows an "owner" to draft his or her own baseball team using real players and their real stats from the up-coming season. Whoever has the best overall stats in the fantasy league at the end of the regular season wins.

It Takes Passion

The Philadelphia Phillies have been my team since birth. They haven't had a winning season since that magical, unshaven '93 World Series campaign. But my owning a fantasy team has taken the sting out of all the Phils' lopsided losses and blown saves. It will for you, too. You'll find yourself cheering for players on teams you used to hate. As a Phillies fan, who do I hate more than the Braves, right? Those disgustingly talented pitchers, those ridiculously gifted hitters, and that rich owner who foisted his team on an entire nation by airing nothing but Braves games on his cable station.

Well, guess what? For the last two years I owned Greg Maddux on my fantasy squad. And every time he went head-to-head with Curt Schilling at the Vet, you know exactly who I was pulling for. So, yes, your loyalties will be tested. But the passion you feel for the game of baseball will grow exponentially, as will your appreciation of just what a great dynasty the Braves have had for the past decade. Love 'em or hate 'em, you'll always want a couple of their pitchers on your fantasy squad.

It Takes Work

In creating a fantasy baseball league, there are few rules. In running a fantasy baseball league, however, there are many rules. The league I'm currently in has finished its third year, and we still have plenty of growing pains, sniping, crying, and hand wringing (all in a very macho way, of course). Imagine: a dozen hardcore fantasy baseball fans who know the game inside and out, and who still debate league policy and rules like overzealous senators.

Now imagine this: a dozen hardcore baseball fans (*your* friends) trying to put together a fantasy league from scratch. That's a Titanic waiting to happen; add a giant ice cube and you'll be on the rocks in no time.

Like it or not, guys (and some gals, too) have egos. Big egos. They all think it's their way or the highway. And if you get them on the highway? They own that, too. So before you build this delicate beer can pyramid known as a fantasy baseball league, take a gander at what lies within these pages. It'll save you hours of anger and years of blood pressure medication.

The best weapon against all strife is intelligence. And I mean that in every sense of the word. Smarts. Common sense. Information.

After reading this book, you'll know how, when, and where to tap into all these things. And if you take the time to do it right, I promise you, you'll have one of the best times you'll ever have with major league baseball.

Foul Tips

In creating a fantasy baseball league, there are few rules—after all, it's your fantasy. In running a league, however, there are many. Don't skimp on rules. The more common sense rules you have in place *before* you begin your league, the better.

Statistics Count

As in real baseball, statistics are the heart and soul of your game. But unlike real baseball, stats are the *only* thing that count. There lies the true difference between fantasy baseball and real baseball.

You can't make your players bunt. You can't call a pitchout. If a scrub infielder hits a two-out, bottom-of-the-ninth grand slam to win the game—and no one in your league owns him—no one wins. It's an *orphan stat*, no matter how heroic a homer it was.

Trash Talk

Orphan stats are statistics produced by players who aren't owned by anyone in your league, or are owned but not on the owner's active roster. Orphan stats usually cause great feelings of disgust, frustration, and helplessness—and spur beer sales.

Your job as owner—your only job—is to assemble the greatest statistical baseball machine ever put on paper. Numbers, numbers, numbers. That's it. You do that, you'll win every time.

If only it was that easy.

Overheard in the Dugout

True story: The most frustrating orphan stat I've ever seen happened just last season. On June 26, 1999, pitcher Jose Jiminez of the St. Louis Cardinals tossed a no-hitter. His owner in our league, who liked to rotate his pitchers to have the best ones active at any given time, had reserved Jiminez for the week. He fired himself the next day.

Choosing a Format for Your League

Let's talk about league formats, of which there are literally dozens. I'm not going to tell you there's a right or wrong format—this is fantasy, which means anything goes. The idea is to make yourself happy. You can get a bunch of friends together and form your own league. Or, if you have no friends, you can join leagues online. ESPN, *USA Today,* and other media run fantasy games in a variety of sports, but they're more like contests than leagues. There are early season leagues, mid-season leagues, and off-season simulation leagues. The options are many and the tastes can be as wide as a power alley or as refined as an inside strike. The point is, if you look, you'll no doubt find what you want.

The version of fantasy baseball that we'll talk about in this book uses 10 statistical categories—5 batting, 5 pitching—also known as a "5 × 5" league. You win the league by amassing the most points. You amass points by winning statistical categories. We'll use the model of a 12-team league, with 23-man rosters (13 position players, 10 pitchers).

Rosters break down like so:

> 2 Catchers
>
> 1 First baseman
>
> 1 Third baseman
>
> 1 Corner man (1B or 3B)
>
> 1 Second baseman

1 Shortstop

1 Middle man (2B or SS)

4 Outfielders

1 Utility man (qualifies at any position)

10 Pitchers

For AL-only leagues, the utility guy becomes the designated hitter (DH). This can become a sticking point since a utility guy ideally can play anywhere. However, there are some pure DHs who play no defense (think Jose Canseco). So you have to decide for yourself how a player like that would qualify. (We'll discuss position eligibility down the road.)

Now before you scream, "Hey, that's not the way my buddy/cousin/niece plays!"—relax. As I said, this is one version, probably one of the most common. As you learn to play and get more comfortable, you'll find yourself tweaking rules to make your league better and better. Leagues are evolving creatures. They can be anything you want.

You'll find that this particular format varies. Some leagues have more or fewer teams. Some leagues use only eight categories (4 × 4). Some might use twelve (6 × 6). You can use twenty for all I care, as long as you remember one important rule: Split the categories evenly between hitting and pitching. If you don't, player values in your league will be utterly skewed.

For example, say you go with three pitching categories and seven hitting categories. You would almost have to ignore pitchers and concentrate on dominating the seven hitting categories. This would render any outside player values (from magazines, books, and the Internet) totally useless. Stick with the 50/50 split.

Strike Three

Always split the categories evenly between hitting and pitching. If you don't, your league will be skewed towards the dominant stats, making any outside player values useless. Unless that's your evil plan.

Pledge Allegiance to a League

Now you have a big decision to make. Is your league a National League-only league, American League-only, or mixed? You can try mixing both leagues—a lot of people do—but I personally don't prefer it. See, the American League has this little feature called the Designated Hitter. No matter what your personal opinion on the subject—and there are millions of personal opinions out there—the only opinion right now that matters is the one belonging to the Major League Baseball Players Association. The DH is here to stay, at least for now.

Trash Talk

Reserves are players selected in the supplemental reserve draft, or any player who is not currently on the active roster during the regular season. In fantasy baseball, a **free agent** is any player not taken in the normal draft who remains unclaimed. During the season, he can be claimed to replace injured players or players lost in a trade to the other league.

Over in the NL, however, pitchers still have to bat. And on top of that, the Senior Circuit has two more teams than the AL, 16-to-14. So if you're interested in realistic balance, avoid drafting from both leagues.

On the other hand, this is fantasy baseball! You can do whatever you want. If you want to have a six-team league consisting of 23 players from both the NL and AL, knock yourself out. You'll have All-Star squads. But forget about using player values from other sources. And forget about realism.

Here's why: The league I'm in has 12 teams of 23 players using 10 categories. I like this version because with 12 teams, you're drafting 276 players. We also pick up five reserve players and eight minor league players in our supplemental drafts. That's a grand total of 432 National League players harvested on Draft Day. That's not quite pure … but it's close.

When you're taking that many players from one league, you have to do your homework. You'll have to know a little something about each team's 40-man roster. And you'll have to know a big something about each team's 25-man roster. There's no way around it. In this version of fantasy baseball, *reserves* and *free agents* are what separate winners from losers. You have to know Manny Ramirez from Manny Martinez. Kerry Wood from Kerry Ligtenberg. Greg Maddux from Mike Maddux.

Now you're goin' deep. Now you're talkin' realism.

Putting Points on the Board

Let's talk about scoring.

The point system works like this: In a 12-team league, teams get one point for each place they achieve in each statistical category. If you finish in first place in home runs, you get 12 points. If you finish in last place, you get 1 point. Using that system, if a team finishes in first place in all 10 categories, that team gets 120 points. That's almost impossible, but you should figure that it'll take 95 to 105 points to win this type of league.

In the event of a tie within a category, the teams take the total number of points between their places and divide by the number of teams. For example, say three teams have tied for first in runs scored. Take the top three positions in the category and add their point total together, like so:

12 (First place) + 11 (Second place) + 10 (Third place) = 33

That's 33 points split between three teams, or 11 points per team. As you can see, points are the lifeblood of your season. Just wait until you get into the dog days of August. You'll be squeezing every last point out of all 10 categories. That's the time when you separate the real owners from the wannabes.

I'll break down specific categories in Chapter 2, "Going Batty." For now, just understand that fantasy baseball is a game of balance. Ideally, you want to have a good showing in all categories. Plenty of speed. Good pitching. Lots of home runs. But that's a perfect world, and we don't live in a perfect world.

Look at the Colorado Rockies. Would you call their roster balanced between hitting and pitching? Not a chance. Because of that thin Rocky Mountain air, pitchers have a terrible time with their breaking stuff. The high altitude actually affects the spin of the ball. And once the ball leaves the bat? Forget about it. Knowing this, the Rockies have assembled one of the most potent offenses throughout the '90s.

Can you do the same thing in fantasy? Sure. But you'll probably have mixed results (much like the Rockies). In this game, you have to chart your own course based on what's happening around you. Do you want to dominate the offensive power categories for the first half of the year? Or do you want to nail down wins, saves, and earned run average (ERA), then trade pitching for power later on? Like a real major league hitter facing a hundred different pitchers, you must constantly adjust. Know your strengths and weaknesses. Stay active. Trade. Pick up free agents. And above all, stay informed.

Remember: balance.

For Love or $$$:
Why We Really Play

In this book, we assume you will play for money. Maybe you won't, but I'll bet good money that you will. If so, your league will probably accumulate a pretty little kitty by October (depending on how you handle the Decimal Debate, which we talk about in a minute). Hey, money is a good enough reason to play. After all, the players do it. In fact, so do the owners, the general managers, the managers, the coaches, the trainers, the broadcasters, the grounds crews, the beer men, and even the almighty Phillie Phanatic do it for money.

Strike Three

Most leagues play for money. It's your call. Just remember what money does to some people. Fathers turn on sons. Brothers turn on brothers. Spouses turn on their heels and walk out. Beware ....

But I'll bet 99.9 percent of them would do it for the love of it (well, maybe not the grounds crews, but you get my point). If you get into fantasy baseball like I think you will, the money will quickly become irrelevant. You'll do it for the passion. Be warned: If you're an addictive personality, you'll find yourself spending way too much time staring at your roster. Dreaming. Planning. Tweaking. Changing type fonts. Finding new ways to list the same 23 guys (by birth weight!).

Think I'm exaggerating? You'll learn. This newfound love of the game will be palpable. You'll know so much about the sport, the personalities, the pennant races, the day-to-day shuttling of minor leaguers back and forth between rosters that your head will spin. So will your spouse's head, having to listen to you bellyache about BA, SB, ERA, RBI, WHIP, and ESPN. (We'll discuss these terms later.) To her, you might as well be talking CIA, IRS, and LSD. You'll be mysterious ... mad ... a little frightening. Enjoy it.

Baseball is a wonderful game. And what fantasy baseball does is give you knowledge you never would've had by following just one team. When you play fantasy, you must follow not just every team, but *every player*.

If you aren't a Yankees fan, you probably hate them. That goes without saying. But if you owned a couple of Yankees in '98? Suddenly you were a part of that record-breaking march into baseball history. You were part of the winningest team ever. You were there. And suddenly your opinion of the boss and his boys doesn't require a bleep when mentioned on TV.

How do you think Mark McGwire owners felt that year? Sammy Sosa owners? Better yet, imagine what Kerry Wood owners felt on May 6, 1998, when he struck out 20 Astros. Then imagine how they felt on March 13, 1999, less than a year later, when he blew out his elbow.

That's the game, friends and neighbors. That's red-blooded baseball. A roller coaster that never stops. Sure, there's money to be won. But like those MasterCard commercials, some things are priceless.

Let's Talk $$$

Then again, everything has a price. And to find out what kind of tag your team will sport, you have to engage in the Decimal Debate. If you don't do it right, the only tag your team will sport is a toe tag.

The Decimal Debate

The Decimal Debate will determine just how much money you want to play for. First, start with number 26. In fantasy baseball leagues across the country, that's the base number in dollars that each team has to spend on Draft Day. Could be $2,600. Could be $260, $26, or $2.60. Could even be $2,600,000 (your cognac, Mr. Gates). All depends on where you put the decimal point.

Twenty-six has been the industry standard for 23-man teams for as long as the game has existed. Every player value that you'll run into out there—on the Internet, in books, in 'zines—will be based on that number. If you decide to go with some other number, those published values will become useless. It's best to stick with what works.

Each owner in my league ponies up 26 bucks on Draft Day. We're no Rockefellers (or Colangelos, for that matter). Just a bunch of working stiffs who love the game a little too much. But once you add up a season's worth of transactions (each of which costs some pocket change), you come up with a respectable pot. Something worth shooting for.

> **Foul Tips**
>
> You can experiment with more or less than a 23-man roster. Try adding a fifth outfielder and an 11th pitcher, while bumping your draft budget to $28. Remember, it's your game. How you play is up to you.

If $26 is too steep for you, knock it back to $2.60. Or better yet, play for nothing. Give each owner an imaginary allowance of 260 fake dollars and have yourselves a draft. That way, player values remain consistent, the draft remains competitive, and no one loses their beer money.

There are literally hundreds of options. Use 26 in all of its glory. Double it to $52 per team. Halve it to $13. Make yourselves happy. Do whatever works. Just remember to stick with 26, and make sure that all player values change accordingly.

In this book, when referring to hypothetical player values, I'll use straight dollars for simplicity, based on a $260 budget.

Splitting the Kitty

It's also imperative that you decide how the money will be split before you start the league. My advice is to spread as much cash around as possible. That way, more owners have a vested interest in the standings.

In our league, the winnings break down like this:

First place	50 percent
Second place	25 percent
Third place	10 percent
Fourth place	7 percent
Fifth place	5 percent
Sixth place	3 percent

Even a token bone of 3 percent is better than nothing. Finishing in the money is a lot like making the post-season. The winner is the de facto World Series champ. Again, it's all about bragging rights, but finishing in the money really does amount to a successful season. Split your kitty any way you like. But by spreading the money around, even sixth place becomes a dogfight.

Foul Tips

A man named Gekko once said, "Greed is good." Nowhere is that more apt than in fantasy baseball. The promise of $$$ is enough to keep even the nicest owners involved throughout the year. Greed can also eat you like a Phillies Phrank. If the $$$ becomes a problem—and it can—immediately refund each owner his fee and play for fun. Or beer.

Another way of spreading the cash around is to award small prizes to owners of players who achieve on-the-field greatness during the season. No-hitters, grand slams, hitting for the cycle, things like that. It's fun enough when Sammy Sosa hits three homers in a game. It's even more fun to get paid for it. For a sample list of achievements and what they're worth, see Appendix A, "A Sample Rulebook."

How the Internet Has Changed the Game

My friends and I first started a fantasy baseball league back in 1986. A simpler time. $15 million bucks would get you Mike Schmidt—for 5 years. We were psyched. Primed. Ready to go the distance and dominate the standings like they had never been dominated.

We did everything right. We had a good group of guys. We elected officials. We did our homework. Then came Draft Day. Wonderful. Stupendous.

Overheard in the Dugout

The first name called in our very first draft was Von Hayes. Remember him? Phillies outfielder, solid but he never quite fulfilled his promise. His final draft price? $67! Naturally, this was before individual player salary caps. We took full advantage of one owner's legendary love for the Phillies (no, it wasn't me). Remember, if you can find out which players a certain owner likes, you can bid him up to the moon.

My draft highlight was putting together the best middle infield in the league, bar none: Ozzie Smith, Juan Samuel, and Bill Doran. Not bad for a first-timer. Samuel went on to hit 28 dingers and drive in 100. Boy, were we happy that day. Then reality gradually sank in.

We had to keep stats. And when you move players around as much as we liked to, you have a lot of adding and subtracting and keeping track of dates. It soon became a logistical nightmare. Everything had to be done by hand. We fell behind in a matter of weeks. By June, the league was all but dead.

But now, life is different. One hundred eighty degrees different. Forget about Bonds, Griffey, and Maddux. Here's the true fantasy baseball star of the '90s: the Internet.

The Internet is responsible for the fantasy sports explosion in the past few years. These days, software and Web sites exist that will run your league for you: keep stats, record transactions, and update standings. Some of them for *free*. No kidding. You'll find many in Appendix B, "Useful Web Sites," in the back of this book.

It really is a renaissance in convenience. You can pick up John Frascatore as a free agent on Sunday, keep him on your roster for three weeks, then waive him, and the only stats that will appear on your page are the innings he logged for you. Talk about indispensable. (I mean the software, not Frascatore.)

E-Mail Is Easy

But just as valuable as the Internet is e-mail. E-mail has revolutionized how fantasy baseball owners meet and do business. Now you can negotiate a trade without picking up the phone. If you have a local Internet provider, you'll never have to make a long-distance call to another owner ever again. (Although people might begin to think of you as this pale, gaunt creature that doesn't come out of the basement … drinking dinner out of an old Big Gulp cup … grunting "trade, trade, trade" endlessly. But then, that's what you want them to think, isn't it?)

Foul Tips

Without e-mail and the Internet, our league wouldn't exist. We're a classic long-distance league spanning three states. Don't be afraid of distance when forming your league. Let technology be your best friend.

Make Contact in Chat Rooms

Chat rooms are a plus. You can get together with an owner in your own private room and pound out a deal. This kind of communication-on-demand has become the lifeblood of fantasy leagues everywhere.

If you haven't gotten the point yet, it is definitely to your advantage to have everyone in the league wired tight. A few guys in our league have been slow to join the computer age. They aren't necessarily out of the loop, but they get all of their information secondhand and a few days later than the online guys. In this game, you can't afford to be a few days late with anything.

Overheard in the Dugout

Last summer, an owner in our league without a computer didn't find out about Pittsburgh catcher Jason Kendall's season-ending ankle injury until three days after the fact. He missed the weekly transaction deadline and had to keep Kendall active for another week. He lost valuable production from his backup catcher as a result. Had he been wired, he probably would've known about the injury before Kendall even reached the hospital. Behold the power of techno-literacy.

So get wired. By now, you've got the basic idea. The planets are in line and the beer's on ice. Let's build you a fantasy baseball league.

Recommended viewing: Ken Burns's *Baseball.* If you can find a place that will rent you all nine tapes, do it. It's 18 hours long, but then so are some doubleheaders. You'll come away a better fan for it.

The Least You Need to Know

➤ A good fantasy team runs on smarts, common sense, and information.

➤ Keep the number of statistical categories evenly balanced between hitting and pitching.

➤ Stick with the number 26 when deciding how much money each owner will have to spend on Draft Day ($260, $26, $2.60).

➤ Let the Internet do the sweat work of stat keeping and bookkeeping.

➤ Use e-mail and chat rooms to propose trades and keep in constant touch with other owners.

Chapter 2

Going Batty

In This Chapter

➤ What is a five-tool baseball player?

➤ Batting average can be manipulated

➤ Home runs: overrated?

➤ Runs batted in: the blue-collar category

➤ The need for speed

➤ When normal categories are not enough

Swing and a long drive! Deep centerfield! Jones is back, back, back to the wall … it's outta here! Home run! Cubs win! Cubs win! Cubs win!

Now there's some fiction for ya. Well, not really. The Cubs have won a few games. And as for home runs, there's a guy named Sosa who has smashed a few windshields outside Wrigley Field. Even a Phillies fan can appreciate that.

Anyone who's watched baseball the past few years knows that we are in the middle of a no-bull offensive golden age. The home run record has fallen. Or risen, actually, to 70. Mark McGwire has been a one-man, record-wrecking crew. No one has hit more taters in one season than Mac. No one has hit more in the last three years combined than Mac. No one has reached 500 dingers faster than Mac. Complain all you want about baseballs being "juiced." Then watch Mac swat a few moonshots. He don't need no stinkin' juice. In fact, the greatest power hitter in the history of the game may be performing right now, in our time, every day. Savor it.

But as the superlatives pile up for Mr. McGwire, the reality is that Mighty Mark is not the greatest fantasy baseball player. In fact, he might not even be in the top ten. Here's why ....

The Five-Tool Baseball Player

Say a hot prospect is coming up through the minors. The newsies are buzzing, the fans are yapping, and the scouts go on and on about the guy's "tools." He ain't no plumber in the off-season, though. "Tools" are a player's athletic skills, and when you have a genuine *five-tool player,* you have a potential superstar in the making. Five-tool guys can ...

➤ Run.

➤ Hit for average.

➤ Hit for power.

➤ Throw.

➤ Catch.

Trash Talk

The **five-tool player** excels in every aspect of the game. In real baseball, he runs, throws, catches, hits for power, hits for average, and makes few mental mistakes. However, in fantasy ball, the five-tool player dominates the five major offensive categories.

Basically, they do everything well. Some ballplayers can do some of the things some of the time. But only the great ones do it all. The Mike Schmidts. The Willie Mayses. The Roberto Clementes.

But it's different in fantasy baseball. In our game, the five-tool player is simply an offensive juggernaut, an unstoppable statistical machine who seems to put up numbers even while shagging flies during batting practice. The five-tool fantasy player excels at the following categories:

Batting average	(BA)
Runs scored	(R)
Home runs	(HR)
Runs batted in	(RBI)
Stolen bases	(SB)

You want to draft players who pile up the most statistics—across the board—for the least amount of money. Therefore the ideal player hits in the heart of a good lineup with a high average, good power, and blazing speed.

You really must appreciate how rare and valuable the five-tool fantasy player is. Very few players do it all. McGwire doesn't. Ripken doesn't. Sosa has done it, but never in all five categories at the same time. Early in his career, he hit bombs and stole bases. But he never hit for average. Nowadays, he still hits bombs, hits for good average, but doesn't run anymore (mostly because he's too busy rounding the bases to steal them).

This might help put things into perspective: In fantasy ball, Barry Bonds in his prime is worth more than Babe Ruth in his prime. Even more telling, Dale Murphy in his prime is worth more than Hank Aaron in his prime. Let the Braves fans chew on that one.

Try Alex Rodriguez, Seattle's shortstop. Hits .300 or better. A 40-40 man (40 homers and 40 steals in the same year). Knocks in runs as fast as he scores them. And he's not even 25 yet. A true fantasy god. On your knees, dog. There's simply no one better.

Strike Three

Learn the lesson early: The Sosas and McGwires of the world will win you home run titles, but five-tool players will win you the whole league.

In the NL, Jeff Bagwell is the closest. He still steals quite a bit for a power hitter over age 30. Ken Griffey Jr. is another five-tool stud. And Larry Walker, when healthy. All are great players to build around. The problem is they'll be so expensive you might not have much left to build with.

As for some lesser-known gods, try Shawn Green, Chipper Jones, or Craig Biggio. Or to a lesser extent, Jason Kendall and Kevin Young. If you like your players temperamental, how about Raul Mondesi? You may not like him, but if you just hold your nose and buy the guy, he'll put up 30-30 numbers between pouting sessions.

Don't forget the five-tool veterans who still throw decent numbers up there: Barry Larkin, Ricky Henderson, and Gary Sheffield. Let's say you're interested in five-tool players-to-be. Remember the names J.D. Drew, Mike Cameron, Bobby Abreu, and Andruw Jones (if he could just get his batting average up there …).

The point of all this is that as historically relevant as guys like McGwire may turn out to be, they are largely one-dimensional players. Bottom line, the more categories a player dominates, the more he brings to your team.

Think of it this way: Would you want three players who hit 20 homers with 10 steals each for an average cost of $12 each, or would you rather break the bank on McGwire at $36? You'll get all those home runs from Mac, true. But you'll also get 60 from the three cheap guys, as well as 30 steals—all for the same money. If McGwire gets hurt (and he has in the past), you're out one expensive superstar. If one of your cheaper guys goes down, however, you still have two solid, healthy players.

This is just one strategy to consider—and no strategy is foolproof. Strategies are like opinions. And you know what opinions are like. Just make sure yours doesn't stink.

Basically, this chapter is meant to aid your analysis of a player's value, which is the key to your success in fantasy baseball. Granted, there are a lot of sources out there with player values figured down to the last RBI. But those numbers should be only the beginning for you. Know the categories. Know what players can help you the most in each. If you can't judge a player's value for yourself, you're fish food for your league's sharks. A little shakin', a little tenderizin', and down you go.

There's Nothing Average About Batting

Batting average. The most basic measure of a player's hitting ability. Calculated like so …

> Batting Average = Hits ÷ At-Bats

The accepted line of excellence is .300. The accepted line of misery is .200. But in fantasy, anything under .260 should be viewed with suspicion. These are the players who will hurt you.

Granted, these low-average dudes could be bringing other things to the party. Todd Hundley, Jeromy Burnitz, and Jose Canseco (when healthy) all struggle to hit .250, but their home runs make up for a lot of shortcomings.

Batting Average Is a Performance Category

The problem with batting average is that it's different than any other offensive category. It's a *performance category,* whereas home runs or RBIs are *volume categories.* What's the difference? Home runs are counted. Batting average is calculated.

Trash Talk

Performance category is a category that is mathematically calculated—batting average, earned run average, on-base percentage, for example.
Volume category is a category based on the accumulation of statistics: home runs, RBIs, runs scored, wins, saves, and so on.

You might ask why I call it a performance category, when even volume stats like home runs and RBIs are based on performance? That may be true. But performance in volume categories is in the eye of the beholder. Think of it this way: say Sammy Sosa hits 38 home runs next season. That's a lot of home runs. But is it a good performance based on his past triumphs? Not by a long shot.

Volume stats can pile up even if a player has a substandard season. Batting average, however, doesn't lie. A guy who hits .300 for the year is considered a good hitter no matter who he is or how much he plays. He has *performed*.

Performance categories can be manipulated. For example, say it's the middle of September. You're in the thick of a pennant race with a real shot at winning it all. You're tops in batting average by only a few hundredths of a point. You've got two shortstops on your roster, one who's hitting .220, and one who's out for the year with a wrist injury. If you put in the light hitter, you could lose the top slot in batting. But if you let the injured guy sit on your active roster, he won't do a darn thing. Meaning he can't bring your average down.

This strategy has been used in the majors before, to great controversy, when there's a tight race for the batting title. If a player's ahead by a few points, the manager sits him down the final weekend of the season to prevent any unsightly oh-fers that would kill his batting average. Not the most honorable thing to do, but it's been done.

Strike Three

For every injured player on your active roster, the more volume stats you lose. This comes into play more so in the pitching categories, which we'll discuss in Chapter 3, "The Perfect Pitch."

"Yeah, whatever, buddy," you might be thinking. "All I have to do is draft 13 .300-hitting studs and I'll win it all." Yeah, right. Try it. You'll be out of money by the fifth round of your draft. And we haven't even talked about pitching yet.

Be Suspicious of Batting Averages

When drafting hitters, your best bet is to look at batting average like gas mileage on a new car sticker. Is it really going to determine if you buy the car? Sometimes. Sometimes not. It's all about balance (there's that word again!). If you draft a couple of Sean Caseys, Tony Gwynns, or Bernie Williamses, your lineup will be able to tolerate a Punch-and-Judy hitter of a shortstop.

But there's a better way—and this is where the old performance categories can be manipulated. Do your research. There are veteran platoon players out there who don't put up great volume numbers. But because they're veterans, they know how to hit, and if platooning, they'll have the advantage of seeing only pitchers they can historically hit (right-handers). They'll give you that .275 to .300 average. Ask yourself what's more valuable: a full-time shortstop who'll hit .220 with 35 RBIs in 145 games? Or a utility guy who qualifies as a middle infielder who'll hit .285 with 35 RBIs in 80 games?

I know you're probably muttering, "I ain't gonna have to draft no lame-oid players. I'll have a starter at every position."

No you won't, dude. Not unless you're in a league with six teams or fewer. But if you're in a deep, 12-team league? Ha! Believe me, at the tail end of your draft when you have zilcho in the money pile, these questions become more relevant than contraceptives at Mardi Gras.

Think about these things as you formulate your draft strategy. The bottom line: Don't sacrifice batting average if you don't have to.

Getting the Runs

Runs scored is perhaps the most underrated statistic in fantasy baseball. If you have a 4 × 4 league, runs don't even count. The big problem is that no one drafts a player based strictly on the number of times he crosses the plate. Manly men seek out the manly stats: the home run kings, the batting champs, the stolen-base czars. What do you call the guys who score the most runs? The "run raconteurs"?

You see, runs are usually a by-product of a five-tool package. The guys who hit like madmen generally draw a ton of walks as well. Which means they're on base more, which means … yada, yada, yada, you get the picture. Look at guys like Bagwell, Bonds, and Griffey. They know how to get on base, period.

Therefore, if you draft one of those monsters, you kill five birds with one stone, runs included. But you can't draft 13 Barry Bondses. You have to squeeze all the runs you can out of lower-end players, especially late in the draft.

A good pre-draft strategy is to write down the projected leadoff hitter of every single team. For every Craig Biggio, there are lower-tier leadoff guys who play for worse teams. They may not steal a lot of bases, but they will score enough runs to make them valuable. If you can snag one of these guys late in the draft, he'll be cheap. And if he scores 75 runs? He's worth a ton more than that six-homer part-timer you have your eye on.

You might be asking yourself, "What do I want with a one-dimensional player who don't do nothin' but hit .260 and score runs?" Simple. If they break out—and some do—these players win you championships. They're *sleeper picks*—the players no one sees coming. And they're not just leadoff hitters. They emerge at every position across the board. We'll discuss sleepers and how to predict them in Part 3, "'Do You Feel a Draft?'" But you should be aware of what they are.

As for leadoff hitters, when you're doing your pre-season research, understand that these guys are a fickle lot. They are the offensive equivalent of bullpen closers. When they stink, they stink bad. And like closers, they'll be the first ones to lose their jobs if they fail.

So be warned: If a guy has a lousy career *on-base percentage* (OBP), he's going to be a substandard leadoff hitter, no matter how many times the manager says, "He's my man."

Yeah. He'll be the man for a few weeks. Then he'll be the man in the eight-hole picking at the offensive scraps. Or worse, he'll be butt-polishing the bench. Suddenly you've got a worthless player. So choose wisely from this crop. There are many unpolished gems. But there's a ton of fool's gold, too.

Don't be fooled by this category. It has the same importance as the "glory" categories such as homers. If you neglect it, some other industrious owner won't. So be industrious. No one is going to care if you're the home run champ, especially if your team comes in seventh. What kind of accomplishment is it anyway? You're not the one hitting the home runs.

Trash Talk

On-base percentage (OBP) is how many times a player reaches base divided by his total at-bats. This includes hits, walks, and hit-by-pitches, but not bases reached on errors.

I'll take Craig Biggio over Mark McGwire any day, any year. Ask a Biggio owner if he ever had run-scoring or base-stealing problems. Or how about Roberto Alomar? He does it all.

Overheard in the Dugout

To give you an idea of what a fine five-tool fantasy player Craig Biggio is, listen to this. In the first week of the '99 season, Biggio recorded his first run, his first RBI, and his first stolen base before he ever got his first hit! That's a man who knows how to work the base paths. And yes, I owned him. (The pitter-patter of excessive back-patting echoes through an empty room.)

The moral of this story is that in a beginner fantasy league, the more testosterone flowing at your draft will probably mean higher bids for power hitters. Don't get sucked in. Bid intelligently on players who do a little bit of everything—including scoring runs. Better to be in third place in five categories than first in three, last in the rest.

Make sense? Let's move on.

Did I Mention Home Runs?

Seems fitting that we go from the most underrated category to the most overblown. Hey, I won't argue: Everyone loves a home run. Ask your average Toronto Blue Jays fan about Joe Carter in the '93 World Series. Now that's a home run.

That was every Phillies fan's JFK assassination. We all remember exactly where we were when it happened. Me? Staring dumbfounded with my friends, beers in hand, at a hotel TV after a wedding. Our guts had been ripped out and thrown on the floor. I doubt the maids were able to get the stains out of the carpet.

Everyone remembers home runs. McGwire's 61st, 62nd, and 70th. His 500th. I distinctly remember Mike Schmidt's 500th. I was in the kitchen of my youth, staring at a new TV. Three-oh count. A Don Robinson fastball—*bam*—Harry Kalas goes berserk, Schmitty almost misses his hands trying to clap, and around the bases he goes: Phillies win!

There are dozens more: Hank Aaron's 715th, Kirk Gibson's limping World Series long ball, Carlton Fisk's body english blast, the list is endless.

Trash Talk

How many names for "home run" can you think of? Homer, bomb, blast, tater, jack, dinger, dong, slam, gone yard, parked it, left the building, round-tripper, four-bagger, four-base knock, moonshot, screamer, souvenir, and it must be a homer since the pitcher just said, "Doh!"

The glory heaped on the home run is justified. It's the ultimate victory against a pitcher. The batter states with a big exclamation point, "I win," even if his team loses.

Our society places its value on strength: Who can lift the most, hit the farthest, run the fastest, or throw the hardest. That applies to any sport. In baseball, they come to watch McGwire's batting practice. In tennis, it's Pete Sampras's aces. In soccer, Mia Hamm's cannon kicks. In golf, John Daly's unholy drives. In basketball, Michael's airborne slams. In football, Reggie White's quarterback slams. While we're at it, in pro wrestling, Stone Cold's body slams.

Name a sport, any sport, and I'll show you one player who captures the imaginations of every fan. These athletes rack up more of the stats we consider important than any other in their games: goals, touchdowns, points, fouls, sacks—you name it.

In baseball, it's home runs. This love of the long ball keeps butts in the seats, makes us cheer or curse, and makes us love the game even more. But in fantasy baseball, home runs have been the downfall of many an over-amped owner.

Don't Go M.I.A. in the Home Run War

Home runs are but one category. By their very nature, they also lead to runs scored and RBIs. Which is fine. I don't want you thinking that pure home run hitters are useless to your team. Quite the opposite: They're invaluable to a balanced squad.

All too often, however, inexperienced owners (and even some scarred vets), place too much value on these muscle-bound ball mashers. This is all part of that manly man hero worship. A severe case of home run fever.

Mark McGwire is a living, breathing immortal. He'll be remembered forever. I love what he does. It's fun to watch. But for our purposes, he is nothing more than a three-tool player. Granted, boomers like him will get you a serious chunk of home runs. But should you break the bank to get them?

Overheard in the Dugout

Halfway through the '99 season, I offered to trade first baseman Kevin Young to another owner for outfielder Andruw Jones, straight up. Their power and speed numbers were similar. But Kevin Young had the edge in runs scored by a nice margin. Plus, KY was hitting a cool 50 points higher than Andruw. I wanted to make the deal to cut salary. To me, KY was the better player, but Andruw was cheaper with stats comparable enough not to hurt me. The other owner said no way, no how. Why? "Andruw will get you homers." Right there is a prime example, ladies and gentlemen, of home runs taking precedence over runs scored and batting average.

Be careful on Draft Day, especially in the early rounds when you have all that money to spend. You'll be seduced by the names—Sosa, McGwire, Griffey—as they are bid up into the $40 range. Don't do it! Let someone else spend the money. Sure, you'll have the pleasure of owning Sammy Sosa. But owning Sammy Sosa doesn't get you any special privileges!

No velvet ropes will part at your local dive bar. No reporters will call you for comments on his performance. No VIP invitations will come for Britney Spears's high

Strike Three

In 1999, for the $40 spent on Barry Bonds—who was out most of the year—the owner could've had *20* Geoff Jenkinses ($2). Don't know who Geoff Jenkins is? Look him up. In '99, Jenkins was the kind of sleeper who won fantasy championships. He'll never go for $2 again in any league.

school graduation party. All you'll have is an over-priced ballplayer. Oh yeah, you'll also have a miserable late-round draft.

Use your head. If you can get a player like that for a good price, do it. They are definitely worth it. But when alarm bells go off screaming "Whoa! Too much money … but it's Mark McGwire!" take a deep breath and let him go.

Let the Other Guy Spend the Big Bucks

Doing this has two benefits:

First, you'll have saved up to $40 (or more) of draft budget which can buy you players at their real value or—even better—below value.

And second, The guy who forked over the money is now out $40. He'll have a hard time late in the draft when he has to fill out his final slots. With any luck, he'll be stuck with $1 bums who have little or no real fantasy value. Believe me, when you come up short in the draft, it's a long, hard road back to respectability during the season.

Can you win the league if you spend $40 to $45 on one player? Sure. But you'll have to have a fantastic draft. I mean, G-R-E-A-T. Give it a shot if you're feeling cocky. But I prefer balance (that word again!). With balance, comes depth. With depth, you always have options.

And if that doesn't convince you, try this: Chicks may dig the long ball, but league champions have more money for beer.

R.B.I. or R.I.P.?

If Mark McGwire is the modern-day home run champ, then Juan Gonzalez must be the poster boy for runs batted in. Sure, Juan-Gone hits his share of dingers. But every year he pursues what many consider to be an even more impossible record to break than 61 homers: Hack Wilson's RBI mark of 191.

Imagine that—191 RBIs in one season. Whew. Actually, no one's even come close yet. Gonzalez, Sosa, and Manny Ramirez have all given it a shot. But the strength-sapping dog days of August prove to be more powerful than even creatine.

The Working Man's Stat

RBIs are sort of middle "glory" ground between homers and runs scored. They get attention. But I don't think anyone remembers where they were when Fernando Tatis drove in eight runs in one inning in '99.

But in fantasy baseball, RBIs are the gateway to good value. Once you get past the big-name, big-ticket players of the first two draft rounds, you enter a second tier of talent inhabited by the players who can make or break your team's season.

Here you'll find players whose names aren't synonymous with glory. Rico Brogna. Kevin Young. Jermaine Dye. Matt Stairs. Richie Sexson. Never heard of them? All of them approached or passed 100 RBIs in 1999.

Guys like these are relatively obscure, therefore cheap. A smart owner will use the money he saved on McGwire to lock up two or three of these players.

Foul Tips

Every year, RBI-rich talent comes out of nowhere: Kevin Millar (67), Preston Wilson (71), and Bruce Aven (70) didn't make anyone's opening day roster in our league in '99. Yet all three drove in a bunch of runs for one team—the Florida Marlins. Imagine who else is out there. Do your research and root these players out. They emerge every single year, and they win fantasy championships.

RBIs are perhaps the most abundant statistical resource out there. As I've said before, expensive five-tool players will get you RBIs in their sleep. The real challenge is finding the unknown players who knock in a nice chunk without making the papers.

Remember Glenn Wilson in the late '80s? Not many do. He was a right fielder for the Phillies and his best asset was his rocket launcher of an arm. But before you can say "fluke," Glenn-bo drove in 100+ runs in two consecutive seasons. No one saw him coming.

These players emerge every year. Your job is to find them *before* they do it. No easy task, but the scouts are out there. If you do the right digging, advance reports exist for virtually every professional baseball player at every level. You don't have to know them all, but spend an hour scouring the minor league stats.

Finding Talent in Strange Places

One of my favorite strategies (not that my public admission of this will help anyone in my own league beat me—ha, ha, ha, ha, ha) is checking the AAA stats of every major league team's farm system looking for older players who have monster years but aren't considered top prospects. This is profitable for two reasons:

First, if they aren't top prospects, no one in your league is watching them closely. But you can bet your top-to-bottom dollar that the brass at the major league level is watching. If that team happens to have a hole, or needs help in a pennant race, that player might get a call.

And second, these players are usually over the age of 25, which means no rookie hype. But boy do these guys have something to prove. They're out to win jobs because their jobs have never been secure. They'll play like maniacs. Maybe become minor folk heroes. But best of all—they'll come very, very, very cheap.

Overheard in the Dugout

In our league's 1998 reserve draft (after the regular draft), I selected a little known player in the Marlins' farm system named Kevin Millar. No one at the table knew who he was. I spotted Millar while perusing minor league stats. He was 27, reportedly had no bat speed, and couldn't run. But one fact was overlooked: He was the Eastern League Player of the Year in '97. He was out with an injury for '98, but in early '99, first baseman Derrick Lee floundered. I pounced on free agent Kevin Millar, who replaced him, hit .285, and drove in 67. All it took was some patience and vigilance. (Again the alien sound of solo back patting can be heard.)

Seek out RBI production like you seek out free beer. It can be had, but you have to work at it. This category benefits the most from stubborn research. Anyone can draft Chipper Jones and get RBIs. But the tenacious owner drafts Chipper and four more guys who drive in 75 without one stinking headline to their names. You call that owner Champ. Or is it Mr. Champ to you?

The Real Thieves Are the Agents ... or Are They?

Back in the roarin' '80s, new stolen-base masters popped up like new sexually transmitted diseases, one after the other. You know about Henderson. Remember Vince Coleman? Willie McGee in his prime? Juan Samuel? Rock Raines? Eric Davis? Even the immortal John Cangelosi? Back then guys were swiping bags faster than a street thug in a supermarket parking lot on senior citizens double-coupon Tuesday.

But in the early '90s ... what happened? Other than conspiracy theories surrounding athletic shoe manufacturers and cement, no one can really explain why the stolen base went the way of the cassette tape.

One reason is that no proof has surfaced that stealing bases actually equates to more victories, namely because last-place teams steal bases about as much as first-place teams.

For fantasy baseball purposes, all this debating is moot. The only thing we care about is volume. Steal 'em, boys. Steal 'em now, steal 'em often, steal 'em when yer up 10–zip. Just steal 'em.

The year 1999 saw a resurgence in the stolen base, at least from a volume point of view. Roger Cedeno emerged as the new Prince of the Pilfer, taking his tutelage from the Supreme Ruler of All Thieves himself, Rickey Henderson. But others made away with their share as well: Tony Womack, Shannon Stewart, Luis Castillo, Eric Young, Mike Cameron, and many more.

Still, with all this running going on, the stolen base remains the most elusive fantasy stat next to the save (which we'll talk about in the next chapter).

Foul Tips

A good strategy is to draft players who tack on 10 to 12 steals to their other stats. The total is low enough that the players aren't considered base stealers, so their draft prices are unaffected. Yet the numbers pile up. You snag five guys like that, you have 50 to 60 steals without really paying for them.

As before, the five-tool guys will get you steals galore. Unfortunately, the steal specialists get real pricey real quick. Roger Cedeno came from nowhere last year, and will never be cheap again. Plus, you won't get Womack and company for less than $25 in most leagues. That's a lot for a one- or two-tool player. Unless a Cedeno comes out of the woodwork every single year (Not!), you'll have to cough up the green for steals.

As a rule of thumb, I try to draft players who will get me at least five steals (yeah, even catchers, although that's sometimes impossible). And if you have speedy guys on your reserve roster, try to rotate them into active duty now and then, for steals are the one category where you must avoid orphan stats at all costs. Bleed these guys dry.

Another useful strategy for finding steals is watching managers. Some skippers flash the green light more than others. Bobby Valentine of the Mets unleashed Cedeno and Henderson all over the league in '99. But Tony Muser of the Royals, Larry Dierker of the Astros, and Bruce Bochy of the Padres all had multiple players with double-digit stolen base totals.

If you're in a heavily competitive league (and I hope you are), you should always check out the schedule a week or two ahead of time. Why? Well, for pitching reasons that will be discussed later. But also because some catchers can't throw anyone out. This could be because of injury or a lax pitching staff that doesn't hold runners on first very well. If someone gets that reputation, teams run on them like fugitives run on Tommy Lee Jones.

In 1999, Todd Hundley was coming off a major surgery and the Dodgers pitching staff was underperforming. The league ran on poor Todd at will—successfully. The point being that your faster players should be activated when they're playing teams that can't stop the run.

Overheard in the Dugout

Roger Cedeno slipped through our 1999 Draft Day without a peep. Later, I wanted to add some depth to my outfield corps the week before Opening Day and picked him up as a free agent. I snagged him strictly for the dozen-or-so steals that I thought he'd get me as a part-timer. Well, I hit the lottery. I take no credit for predicting Cedeno's break-out, but this just goes to show you that when you're snagging a cheap free agent for his 12 steals, it's no heartbreak if he doesn't get them. But if he does—or gets even more—man, that's as sweet as cheap cherry wine.

We can only hope that speed demons continue to terrorize pitchers and catchers everywhere into the next century. But whether they're running or not, beware that year in, year out, the SB category is always a dogfight. My best advice is don't be the runt.

Hey, What a Cool Idea!

Who says your league has to be normal? The previous categories are simply the Big Five, the stats that fans and agents throw around in barrooms and boardrooms. But baseball is a cryptic sport. Stats are kept on just about everything from sunflower seeds consumed to foul balls per at-bat. How about number of cups adjusted per inning? Or profanities mouthed (readable to viewers at home, of course) by players and managers during day games?

Well, maybe not. But what follows is a list of official stats that most sites and software can keep track of in addition to the Big Five. Give 'em a try:

➤ **Doubles.** This gives line drivers like Biggio, Sean Casey, and Mark Grace a big boost.

➤ **Triples.** An interesting stat since you can't try to hit a triple. A pure lottery deal, though you can purposely draft speed. Use only if you're feeling lucky, punk.

➤ **Net Steals.** Like steals, only you're rewarded for the players who are the best at it. Hey, a fast guy can steal 50 bases, but if he's caught 25 times, he's not the best thief in the league even if he's the champ. Only 25 of his steals would count here (50 steals – 25 times caught).

➤ **On-Base Percentage (Hits + Walks + Hit-by-Pitch ÷ Total At-Bats).** Discussed earlier. Adds a new dimension to the leadoff hitter. But the players whose values really skyrocket in this category are the McGwires, Bondses, and Griffeys—the guys who walk more than 100 times a year.

➤ **Walks.** See on-base percentage. This rewards the guys who know how to take a pitch and get on base.

➤ **Slugging Percentage (Total Bases ÷ Total At-Bats).** Again, this benefits the big boppers.

➤ **OPS (On-Base Percentage + Slugging Percentage).** This stat is now widely recognized as the best barometer of a player's total contribution to offense. Just how many runs does Rafael Palmeiro create? Do the math.

Foul Tips

You may have noticed by now that defense isn't taken into consideration in fantasy baseball. That doesn't mean you can't do it. After all, this *is* your game. Errors make an interesting stat. You can count them two ways: most or least. If you rack 'em up, guys like Vladimir Guerrero take on a whole new value. If you reward the slicksters, Rey Ordonez becomes a sudden stud.

There's almost no limit to the flexibility you can add to your league when it comes to categories. If major league baseball keeps track of it, you can use it. Just remember the basics and know the talent. Everything you need to win your league is already out there. You just have to figure out the combination of players it'll take to do it.

Easy, right?

Recommended viewing: The joyous couple having sex in the upper deck during a baseball game. They were caught on camera and the video clip has made the rounds on the Internet. Haven't seen it? Oh dear. Once again, when it comes to fantasy baseball (or just plain ol' fantasy), owning a computer is imperative.

The Least You Need to Know

➤ Batting average can be improved by part-timers who hit well.

➤ Don't underestimate the value of runs scored—no category takes care of itself.

➤ Don't be seduced by the glory of home runs—they are only one category.

➤ Unknown players who bang out lots of RBIs emerge every year—seek them out for cheap.

➤ Stolen bases are a dogfight every year—draft lots of guys who steal 10 bases and watch the numbers pile up.

➤ Spice up your league by adding an obscure offensive category—just remember to offset it with a pitching category.

Chapter 3

The Perfect Pitch

In This Chapter

➤ Can there be a five-tool pitcher?

➤ Winning isn't everything

➤ Earning runs is hard work

➤ WHIP it good

➤ Ways to make pitching categories more fun

Pick up a baseball. Feel it. The perfect weight. The smooth, supple hide. The tight little stitches running in an endless ribbon around and around. There really is no other ball in all of sports that begs to be thrown more than the baseball. You know what I mean. You pony up a buck for three throws on a carnival radar gun, daring your rotator cuff to unravel. You spin the pill in your hand, warming up the palm oil of a hundred rubber-armed geeks before you. You stare down the fake batter painted onto the tarp about 40 feet away. He's thinking heat.

Well, that's just fine by me, you think. You want the cheese, meat, you got it. You set. You check the runner, who looks a lot like your bored girlfriend. You smirk. She's running on the pitch. Your eyes roll back to the target: a scuffed faux catcher's mitt boxed in by a strike zone of peeling electrical tape. The mitt calls for the heat. Yeah. Bring it, baby.

You rear back. You kick and twist like Luis Tiant in a Cirque de Soleil commercial. Your jeans bind and pinch. Your work boots crunch in the gravel. Your arm snaps forward. Your fingertips burn on the ball. It leaves, spinning so tightly that the air around it sizzles. Finally, you grunt: one last warning to the sports world that you are a cannon that has just fired, and your shell is on its way. A Nolan Ryan grunt. Possibly even a Monica Seles grunt.

A split second later, impact. The ball pounds the tarp with a loud pop, as if the mitt of Johnny Bench himself had just met with your best number one. A smirk creeps up your cheek. It's just enough to show up the stick, who's on his way back to the dugout as we speak. That was it. Your best pitch. Your best stuff. Your best location. You wink at your girlfriend, the stranded runner. Then you gaze up at the radar tally, prepared to chalk up another personal best. The florescent numbers shining down mock you like a dancer behind a Plexiglas window—and you're fresh out of quarters: *65 m.p.h.*

No Such Thing as a Five-Tool Pitcher

If batting is the science, pitching is the art. In no other team sport can one man on the field dominate a game the way a pitcher can. Sure, you have your quarterback. But he depends on the precise actions of his teammates. He can't make his center chop-block a 270-pound sack specialist.

But a pitcher? He has no one to blame but himself when that hung curveball lands in the right-field bleachers.

You could argue that a pitcher depends on his teammates, too. Sure, but when they fail it's called an error. Which does not effect the pitcher's *earned run average* (ERA).

So it's up to the pitcher to determine the momentum, the pace, and the outcome of every inning. Naturally, not all pitchers do well. Some do downright diddly. But every year, one or two guys emerge as unexpected aces, or dominating closers, or even premium set-up men (who have fantasy value, too, as you'll soon see).

So too, every year one or two aces or closers fall from grace and get knocked around harder than Joe Pesci in a *Lethal Weapon* movie. Like batters, you have to pick the right ones (he said confidently).

Your basic five pitching categories are …

Earned run average	(ERA)
Walks and hits per nine innings	(WHIP)
Wins	(W)
Strikeouts	(Ks)
Saves	(S)

Trash Talk

Earned run average (ERA) tells us how many earned runs a pitcher allows every nine innings. It is calculated by multiplying earned runs by nine, then dividing by innings pitched.

If you're running a 4 × 4 league, strikeouts drop out (usually). Naturally, there are a slew of categories that can be substituted to change the dynamic of player values. I'll go over them later.

Right now, let's begin where we began with batting. Sort of. See, in fantasy baseball, there is no such thing as a five-tool pitcher. Even a Cy Young winner will be a four-tool guy at best.

Why? Take Randy Johnson. He's one of the best fantasy pitching commodities this side of Pedro Martinez. The Big Unit will rack up unbelievable strikeouts. He'll flirt with no-hitters. He'll make you smile every five days. But he won't get you one stinking save.

Which makes drafting a pitching staff one of the most challenging aspects of fantasy baseball. It's grueling. It's ugly. It's expensive. And in the home run era, it's heartbreaking. But you have to do it.

So let's do it well, okay?

Counting Bert's Earnies

We'll start with the performance categories. Earned run average (from here on in referred to as ERA) is a good measure of a pitcher's overall performance. But don't be fooled. Just because a pitcher has a good ERA doesn't mean he's a quality fantasy pitcher.

Oh, How the Numbers Have Changed

Back in the old days (circa 1985), if a pitcher's ERA rose above 4.00, he wasn't very highly regarded. If it hit 4.50, a poor guy could be shunned.

Nowadays, 4.00 ain't too shabby. It ain't great, but it's a good threshold to judge fantasy talent. If you can achieve a sub-4.00 staff ERA, you'll probably be in good shape. Throw in a breakout pitcher or two and you'll be in phenomenal shape.

Then again, throw in a nightmare case, and you'll be sunk faster than Orson Welles on a jet ski. Which brings me to the curious case of the Colorado Rockies ....

I mentioned that Rocky Mountain air before. As good as it is to own a Rockies batter, it is equally bad to own a Rockies pitcher. I'm not knocking these guys as athletes. Darryl Kile, Pedro Astacio,

Strike Three

Owning Colorado Rockies pitchers may be hazardous to your mental health. They have been proven to cause enlarged ERAs, cracked WHIPs, and terminal ownership. Do not engage in firearm maintenance or knife sharpening after drafting a Rockies pitcher.

Brian Bohanon, and their cohorts are just as dedicated to winning as anyone in baseball. They go out there every five days and spill their guts in the name of victory.

Unfortunately, those guts usually get spilled by the third inning.

All I'll say is caveat emptor (let the sucker beware). These guys will get you strikeouts and wins. But the damage they can do to your ERA and WHIP is staggering. You'll be tempted late in the draft because they'll be cheap. You'll see those 200 strikeouts or those 15 wins and you'll finger your trigger, oh-so-tempted to pull it.

Don't do it! Drop the gun, back away, and put your hands above your head. It's not worth it. You'll just make things worse for yourself. My advice? Stare long and hard at that accompanying ERA of 5.50. And think of what owning a guy like that will do to you. Yeah. That's right.

Overheard in the Dugout

In '99, an owner in our league drafted both Darryl Kile and Pedro Astacio of the Colorado Rockies. Both came at good prices (for starting pitchers). But both finished with ERAs over 5.00. This owner made a good run at the title and finished in the money. But guess which categories betrayed him in the end? ERA and WHIP. Two starting pitchers were the difference between fourth place and a shot at the whole ball of earwax. 'Nuff said.

Foul Tips

A good league rule to have is a minimum-innings-pitched threshold. This prevents owners from stocking up on middle relievers.

The Middle Reliever Debate

By now, you may be saying to yourself, "Why spend so much time and money on starting pitchers who may or may not pan out? Why not just buy Randy Johnson, Greg Maddux, and eight decent middle relievers?"

Now there's a debate. Middle relievers are like those RBI guys I mentioned last chapter. Great ones emerge every year and they can help your team immensely. They'll pitch 70 to 100 innings, chalk up double-digit wins, snag a few saves, and sport a sub-3.00 ERA.

In '98, they were your Wayne Gomeses and your Dan Micelis. In '99, they were your Mike Remlingers and your Jeff Zimmermans (no relation to me). But predicting these breakouts is perhaps the hardest forecasting you'll do in this game.

Why? Middle relievers are *vultures*. They scarf up the leftover wins and saves (also known as vulching) that the aces and closers leave behind on their off days. All you can really do is keep an eye on a few of the better ones, wait for a starter to go down, and plug one in as a free agent.

Naturally, there will be a daring few who will actually use middle relievers as a legitimate part of their pitching plan. They'll try to draft a couple of these arms super cheap at the end of the draft and ride them into the ground. If you must go

> **Trash Talk**
>
> **Vultures** are the dozens of middle and long relievers populating major league staffs. These athletes rarely have Draft Day value, but can be very useful when one of your starters gets hurt and the pickings are thin.

this route, stick with the primary set-up men on playoff-caliber teams. These teams win more, which means they come from behind more. Which translates into vulture wins.

> ### Overheard in the Dugout
>
> Back in '98, I stocked my pitching staff with five starters and five middle relievers. It was great. No one could touch my ERA and WHIP. I struck gold specifically with Wayne Gomes and Dan Miceli. They both had nice ERAs and WHIPs, and they combined for 20 wins (and a handful of saves to boot). Most starting pitchers in the league couldn't match their numbers. But the bottom line was that I got killed in the volume categories (strikeouts especially). Remember: there's good and bad in middle relievers. The big thing is balance (that word again!).

The bottom line? Use middle relievers wisely, but don't depend on them. Onward.

WHIP Is a Snap

Perhaps the most frustrating category (other than saves) is *WHIP*, or more fancifully put, *walks and hits per innings pitched*. The formula is pretty simple:

WHIP = Total Walks Allowed + Total Hits Allowed ÷ Total Innings Pitched

Why is it so frustrating? Well, the quality of pitching in recent years—as any baseball fan knows—hasn't inspired many visions of Bob Gibson and his 1.12 ERA. Bottom line, with 30 teams you have more players on major league rosters than at any time in history. Do they all belong there? That's a whole 'nuther kettle of fish to fry.

In fact, let's line up some kettles just for laughs. Here are some other "maybes" why pitching isn't so great these days:

➤ **Umpires.** Has the recent labor situation affected their performance? Has the strike zone shrunk? Do umps hold personal grudges? Do the Braves pitchers get the outside strike more than any other staff? All questions that have been hotly debated on sports radio talk shows again and again and again.

➤ **Baseballs.** Are they wound tighter than Cosmo Kramer after three espressos? Do rabbits multiply inside them? Are they coated with a special Teflon cowhide to reduce air friction while in flight? Are they actually smaller, like the balls used in the '99 All Star Home Run Derby? Call your local congressman. Demand answers.

➤ **Pitchers.** Are they afraid to throw inside because most batters come to the plate wearing American Gladiator armor? Are they rushed through the minors because they have a 95 m.p.h. fastball (and not much else)? Or are they simply overmatched by batters fortified with andro, creatine, and intensive off-season kryptonite tolerance training? I digress. But you shouldn't.

The reality is, pitchers are getting shelled. Hammered. Pounded. It's amazing the grounds crew doesn't have to mop blood off the mound after each game.

We talked about ERA already. But WHIP is one performance stat that is as unforgiving as a mother scorned. Bottom line: If your pitchers give up walks, your WHIP will suffer. And boy, are pitchers giving up walks.

I know I sound very doom-'n'-gloom, but it's not all hopeless. Not to be obvious, but good overall pitching leads to good WHIP. Which means that the top 20 arms in the majors will give you solid WHIP numbers. But after those big—and pricey—names, your choices narrow considerably.

Overheard in the Dugout

Remember, WHIP is a performance category, and can be manipulated. As the season progresses, watch your opponents' WHIP numbers. You may think your staff stinks, but all the other owner's hurlers might stink, too. Such was our league's case in '99. Only 3 of 12 teams had staff WHIPs lower than 1.400. Still, the category was one of the tightest races of the year, with places being decided by *thousandths of a point*. Don't let anyone tell you that a pitcher's one bad outing doesn't mean anything. They all mean something.

So what should you do? Homework. Lots and lots of homework. Crack open some stat guides. Find the pitchers with the good strikeout-to-walk ratios. Find the unflashy veterans who pitch in good ballparks—they know *how* to pitch.

Most importantly, use any and all means available at your garbage disposal to avoid the big, young, hyper-hyped rookie phenoms. I mean it. Sure, they look nice on your roster. Sure, they make you look smart for drafting them. Sure, it'll hurt to let them go. But impact pitchers are a one-in-a-zillion shot.

For every Kerry Wood there are two dozen Todd Van Poppels. For every Scott Elarton, there are even more Sid Finches. They all throw hard, they all strike out a bunch of guys, but they can't throw a 3-1 strike to save their families. Mark my words: They will hunt down and kill your WHIP faster than Schwarzenegger.

Strike Three

Don't get sucked in by young pitching phenoms. They are enemies of WHIP. They may throw as hard as Nolan Ryan, but remember that even Nolan didn't have good command until he was 40.

Winners Win

Yes, winners do win. Sometimes. Whaddaya mean, sometimes? Easy. The Yankees won the American League East in 1999. Great team. Great pitching staff. But David Cone pitched all year long on that mega-team, enjoying that run support and contributing to the championship run as much as anyone else on the squad. Had an ERA of 3.44 and a WHIP of 1.314. But he won only 12 games.

In the real game, especially when it comes time to talk contract, wins are the barometer of any pitcher. But they don't tell the whole story. Some guys have ERAs over 5.00, yet they manage to win a ton of games because their team scores a ton of runs for them. On the other hand, you have some truly dominating pitchers who couldn't get runs if they drank Tijuana tap water out of a Grand Central Station mop bucket.

Overheard in the Dugout

In '99, Randy Johnson went through a truly tortuous stretch of nearly a month with no run support. I mean, *none*. He gave up less than two runs in each of five starts, and won absolutely nada. So who had it worse? The Unit, or the hundreds of owners who drafted him? 'Tis tragic that so many who will never play this game will never know this pain ....

Like any fantasy category, you can only make educated guesses about wins. Just be as educated as possible. Here's a no-brainer: If you draft an Atlanta Braves pitcher, you expect your fair share of Ws. But how do you know which Brave to draft? Glavine? Maddux? Smoltz? Nope. In '99, the smart money was on Kevin Millwood. He turned out to be the most consistent starter on the Braves staff. Whooda thunk it?

Wins are unlike any other stat in fantasy baseball in that they are tied directly into the quality of a given pitcher's team. See, in every game, there is *always* a winning pitcher, be he starter or reliever. The better the team, the more wins to be split among the pitching staff. Which means the better the odds that those pitchers will win more. Get it?

For example: The '98 Yankees won 114 regular season games. The '98 Royals won 72. That's 42 more wins split among Yankees pitchers. That's *huge*.

A Tribute to Greg Maddux

The Cy Youngs are meaningless. The division titles, the pennants, the World Championships—they mean diddly. They don't help fantasy nuts one iota. But who has been as regular as a Rolex, as safe as a Volvo, as blue a chip as IBM ever was? Maddux. Greg Maddux. The tail end of '98 and the first half of '99 were a bit rocky, however. Chinks appeared in his shining armor. But come June, all that doomsaying went away and he rattled off another 19-win campaign. Perhaps the most telling tribute to Greg Maddux is that *he has won at least 15 games every year since 1988.* You buy him, you take him to the bank. Or take him home to meet the folks. Take him out for sushi. Take him *everywhere*. In fact, don't leave home without Greg Maddux. You won't regret it.

Before you go hog wild drafting every pinstriper (or as they are known in some Yankees-hating circles, "candy stripers") in sight, hold the bullpen phone. Don't overlook the shoddier teams, where discount pitching gems abound. There are more mediocre teams than good teams, after all.

Sometimes they'll have that one ace they'll try to build around (like the Phillies' Curt Schilling), or sometimes they'll have aces in the making working out their kinks at the major league level (like the Padres' Matt Clement or the Mariners' Freddy Garcia).

Even the worst team on the planet will have a double-digit winner on the payroll. You get a few guys like that on the cheap and you'll laugh all the way to the awards ceremony.

Better to Have Struck Out Than to Never Have Struck at All

Strikeouts are to pitchers what homers are to hitters. They are the ultimate display of power over the batter. I win, you lose, grab some wood, bub.

As a fantasy category, however, they are not as valuable as the home run. They are the consummate volume stat. Not everyone hits home runs or steals bases. But just about every pitcher strikes out his share. Even the worst starter in the league will rack up triple-digit strikeouts by the end of the year (assuming he keeps his job). So if you end up with one of these batting practice arms, you can take comfort in the fact that at least he's doing something for you.

The real power pitchers get the glamour. Curt Schilling, Pedro Martinez, Randy Johnson. Studs all, and very expensive. You might be able to afford one of them, but not all of them. That's where the draft prep comes in. If it's a tossup between two comparable pitchers, go for the guy who has a history of striking out more guys (duh).

If you go by the blueprint that says it takes two closers to compete in the saves category, then ideally you would fill out the other eight pitching slots with starting pitchers. Strikeouts pile up nicely. But believe me, drafting eight decent starting pitchers isn't as easy as it sounds. You'll probably spend too much and lose out on offense. Either that, or you'll be saddled with dirt-cheap fifth starters from lousy teams. Which means that your daily profanity quota will be met over morning coffee before you reach the fourth box score.

But hey, your strikeout total will be the envy of the league!

Foul Tips

Bottom line, there just isn't all that much strategy involved in strikeouts. It's easy: The more innings your pitchers log, the more strikeouts will pile up.

Strategy enters into the equation when you see what your opponents do. If you're dominating the category, you might want to trade a pitcher for something you lack. But beware: Make sure that your ERA and WHIP totals won't be adversely affected. Remember, you're building a beer can pyramid. You yank the wrong can and the whole thing comes down.

Saving for Your Future

I left saves for last. Why? Saves stink. They'll eat a hole in your stomach. They'll rot your teeth. They'll scratch your CDs. I hate saves. Hate 'em like I hate telemarketers and politicians. Saves are the ATM fees of fantasy baseball.

But I will grant them one tiny concession: Saves can win you the whole stinking league.

No Stat Is Worth More

How so? As a volume category, saves is the one with the least volume. Pound for pound, no individual number stat is more valuable. Think about it. You have one, maybe two guys on each major league team accumulating a useful number of saves. That's it. There simply aren't that many saves to go around.

As a result, no other category can be impacted as quickly or as drastically. Ten saves in either direction could mean a five-point swing in the standings. That's huge. A good closer on a hot streak can turn your season around inside of a month.

Alas, you could easily spend an entire season managing your closer situation. It's that pivotal. And at the same time, it's that useless. What do I mean?

The closer is a madman. He needs daily short-term memory loss like most people need daily showers. One day he's riding a 10-game, 10-save scoreless streak, the next he's giving up four runs in a third of an inning and beating the tar out of a urinal with a fungo bat. Then he goes out the next night and starts the streak over again.

Back in Chapter 2, "Going Batty," I mentioned how fickle the leadoff hitter's job can be. The closer's job is two hundred thousand times worse. You have a bad stretch, lose a few close games, and—*bam*—you're fired. Next thing you know, you're mopping up blowouts faster than a frat pledge at the house's annual Salute to John Belushi Night.

Don't believe me? Flash back to 1998. Rod Beck, Kerry Ligtenberg, Gregg Olson, Randy Myers, Rick Aguilera, Mark Leiter, and Jeff Montgomery all had more than

Foul Tips

In fantasy baseball, no other category can be impacted as quickly or as drastically as saves. Ten saves in either direction could mean a five-point swing in the standings. Fight for every last one.

20 saves. Flash forward to 1999: Not one of them broke into double digits. They either got hurt or just plain stank.

A few closers have been consistent for more than one year: your Trevor Hoffmans and Jeff Shaws, your John Wettelands and Mariano Riveras. But hey, by the time you read this, one or all of them could be has-beens.

Who emerged as closers elite in '99? To name a few, John Rocker, Matt Mantei, and Armando Benitez (but only after John Franco got hurt).

So why do I hate closers so much? They cost so much. If you draft a Hoffman or Shaw, you're going to shell out $35 or more for what is essentially a one-tool player. Sure, you have your occasional Billy Wagner who adds 120 strikeouts to the cause. But the number of low-ERA, low-WHIP innings a closer will contribute is just plain *low*.

And let's say you do shell out the bucks for not one, but two "elite" closers. That's $60+. More than 25 percent of your overall budget for two guys for one category. Then what happens? One guy blows out an elbow and the other is so ineffective he makes Cliff Claven look like the Postmaster General. All that money down the tubes.

To Save, or Not to Save

Now that I've vented, you can do one of two things. Forget about saves entirely and try to win without them. It's difficult, but not impossible. I punted the whole category in '99. (We'll see how I did later.)

Your second option is shelling out the bucks and fighting for the points. It's your choice.

Overheard in the Dugout

In May '98, I was offered either John Smoltz or Mark Wohlers as part of a trade. Both were hurt. Smoltz's return was questionable before the All-Star Break. It was his elbow—a scary injury. Wohlers was coming off a strained ribcage muscle, so I opted for him. I needed saves and up until that injury, Wohlers and his 98 m.p.h. heater were as good as gold. Well, Wohlers imploded. Couldn't throw a strike. I cut him loose and he later blew out his elbow trying to make a comeback with the Reds. Meanwhile, John Smoltz not only came back earlier than expected, he was brilliant the rest of the way. *That's* why I hate saves.

If you choose to punt, there are a few things you can do that might save your saves from being a total loss. Like I said before, many closers lose their jobs. Which means someone takes their place. Do the homework and find out who those guys are. Chances are you can scarf them up cheap either at the end of your draft, as reserve picks, or later in the season as free agents. They're lottery tickets, but they pay off more than most.

Foul Tips

When shopping for closers, pay close attention to the last place teams. They always seem to come up with 30-save guys every year. Think about it. If a closer saves 50 percent of a team's total wins, even a team that loses 100 games still wins 62. Which means the closer saves 31 of them. And that closer just might be cheaper than you think.

Another cheap alternative is to wait for these fallen closers to hit bottom. Then try to get their frustrated, enraged, and very vengeful owners to dump them on you as a trade throw-in. You can park them on your reserve roster and maybe, just maybe, come August they'll make a comeback. The baseball season is a long and unforgiving road. It happens more than you think.

But let's say you want to fight for the points. You have just as much homework ahead of you. If you're serious about it, don't mess around. Go out there and draft the best stinking closers available. Shell out the cake. You can draft one good one and rack up some token points. But if you want to truly compete for the category, you'll need at least two, so be prepared.

Overheard in the Dugout

You can always go to the opposite extreme in any situation. In '99, one owner in our league actually drafted three elite closers for big bucks. Which isn't a bad move: Everyone needs closers, so the trade demand is always high. A closer can bring you just about anything you need. Alas, the owner, my friend, was unable to pull the trigger on a trade and was stuck with three closers all the way. Did he get greedy? Did he ask for too much in return? We'll never know. But these days he rests easy knowing that he won the saves category by 20—a league record.

And yes, sleepers abound in this category. Be vigilant. Every year one or two young hotshots break out. In '99 it was John Rocker of the Braves and Matt Mantei of the Marlins (later traded to the Diamondbacks, where he flourished). These are the guys you want. The guys on the verge. The owner in our league who took Rocker got the bargain of the draft. His auction price? One dollar. Our league's been choking on them apples all year long.

Saves. Ya gotta love 'em. I know I do.

Pitching Categories You May Not Have Thought Of

Like in batting, there are numerous interesting pitching stats that would make fun fantasy categories. Some could seriously affect player values, so if your league decides to try one or more of these stats, prepare accordingly.

➤ **Net wins.** Works just like net steals. Which means a pitcher who goes 15-2 (13 total wins) is potentially worth more than a pitcher who goes 20-9 (11 total wins). Unfortunately, this is very, very tough to predict. Just be sure luck is a lady that night.

➤ **Net saves.** Even more fickle than net wins. You think normal, everyday saves are fun? Put away all sharp objects for six months and take a whack at this category.

➤ **Complete games.** This category just makes the stud aces that much more expensive. Who needs that?

➤ **Shutouts.** Ditto. Actually, did anyone pitch a shutout last year?

➤ **Strikeouts per nine innings.** Here's where the big, hard-throwing rookies and relievers can help you. It's a performance category that doesn't depend on the number of innings pitched. There are a lot of pitchers out there with 5.00+ ERAs who strike out a ton. This changes their values utterly.

➤ **Holds.** A pet category of mine. Why? I just can't resist staging a draft where set-up guys like Mike Remlinger and Anthony Telford go for $20. I've been lobbying our league to adopt this stat, but no dice so far. For one, you'll be hard-pressed to find stat services that recognize it. *USA Today* does, but only in printed box scores, not in their final stat tallies. If you manage to swing it, however, your draft values will take on a whole new face. Be careful.

➤ **Batting average against.** Another category that rewards the stud starters—but also bumps up the performance factor on dominant relievers, which makes it interesting.

➤ **Hit batsmen.** For you sadists out there. A tip of the face-masked batting helmet to Don Drysdale. In '99, Paul Byrd was your man. Unfortunately, draft values can be affected by time spent serving suspensions.

And while we're at it …

➤ **Games suspended.** This stat works equally well for batters and pitchers. Ya gotta love stats that reward poor sportsmanship. The lesser cousin of this would be *total fines.* This, of course, would make Albert Belle the first six-tool player in fantasy baseball history.

Any one of these categories can make your pitching experience better, worse, sane, or strange. As always, there are no guarantees, but anything that makes life more fun is worth taking a gander at. No?

Recommended viewing: *Baseball Bugs,* one of the all-time Bugs Bunny classics (but aren't they all classics?) that showed baseball fans of all ages how to paste a pathetic palooka and hit a screaming line drive. Plus, where would slow-pitch softball be today without Gashouse Gorillas populating leagues from coast to coast? Watch it with your gloved ones today.

The Least You Need to Know

➤ Playoff-caliber teams produce more wins to be divided among their pitching staff.

➤ Good middle relievers can be a cheap and helpful alternative when starting pitchers are scarce.

➤ You can manipulate your ERA and WHIP numbers with low-inning pitchers, but beware the effect it may have on the volume categories.

➤ Strikeouts are easy; the more innings your guys rack up, the more strikeouts you'll accumulate.

➤ Saves are the most valuable of any stat. Fight for every one you can get.

➤ Or save yourself the stress and forget the whole stinking saves category.

Part 2

A League of Your Own

So ... now you have a basic overview of fantasy baseball. You've heard a few rules, a few strategies, and a few useful tidbits. Now it's time to put pen to paper and butt to chair and form a league. Formally.

The chapters in this part will help you do just that—everything from assembling a group, to scheduling your first meeting, to naming your teams. Here is the most creative aspect of fantasy baseball. Here is where your individuality—and weirdness, blandness, perversion, what have you—boils to the surface and gives your team its identity. The same holds true for your league.

What kind of group will you have? Deadly serious? Bloodthirsty? Loose? Goofy? Apathetic? It'll all start coming out now, which is why the owner recruitment process is almost as important as drafting your team. So let's get it on. Daylight's wastin', chief.

Chapter 4

Lining Up the Unusual Suspects

> ## In This Chapter
>
> ➤ Personalities are like golf shorts—they usually clash
>
> ➤ Getting everyone together
>
> ➤ How to name your team (and create a monster)
>
> ➤ League officers have a tough job
>
> ➤ Elect the right person to the right job

So you want to form a fantasy baseball league. You've got the drive. You've got the knowledge. But you've only got five people. Nerts. You were hoping for a 10- to 12-team crew. National League, only. Deep. Intense. Vicious. But you're seven guys short. What to do?

Well, the Internet can help. Web sites exist with message boards and chat rooms where a cry for membership can be posted. But that's a lot like posting a personal ad. You don't know what kind of psycho will answer. Men without morals. Men without personalities. Or worse, men without brains. And if they're clear across the country? What good is that on Draft Day?

Happy People or Clash of the Titans?

The ideal situation is finding a dozen guys who know each other at least well enough to have a nonviolent cup of coffee together. When the wheeling and dealing starts, you don't want to be in a position where you won't approach an owner because he's a jerk, schmuck, moron, etc. Lines of communication should be open at all times, even if you're the worst of friends.

Foul Tips

One key to building a good league is finding owners who will stay involved for the entire season, no matter how bad their teams are.

Trash Talk

A **draft mole** shows up for Draft Day, has a blast, assembles a good team, and then burrows into the ground, not to be heard from again until next spring. Other names exist for this kind of person, but decorum prohibits listing them here.

If you can't find a dozen players? That's okay. You can have a small league or a large league. Just make sure everyone you recruit has the makings of a good owner. What makes a good owner? Glad I asked.

A good fantasy owner …

➤ **Is a reasonable human being.** That means he doesn't start bar brawls over Derek Jeter's trade value. He doesn't scream to make his point. He doesn't storm out of the room when things don't go his way. He doesn't carry on like he's the drama queen of *As the World Turns*.

➤ **Is not a *draft mole*.** That means he'll show up at meetings. He'll stay involved with the league for the entire season. He'll respond to any and all trade proposals even if he hates to trade. He'll honor his commitment to the league on every level.

➤ **Is a reasonable sportsman.** By "reasonable," I mean he isn't a bald-faced cheater. Fantasy baseball by its very nature involves a certain amount of lying, dodging, squeezing, and all-around used-car salesmanship. A good litmus test is to ask yourself, "Can I look everyone in the eye come October?"

Ideal owners are smart, passionate, and as devoted to the game as they are to their families. Every league will have a few. They are generally the founders, the officers, and the people willing to put in the time. It's no coincidence that these owners are usually the ones finishing in the money.

Just once I'd like to be in a league with 12 to 14 ideal owners. Guys who'll rip your throat out on Draft Day, but be man enough to buy you a beer next time they see you. A true competition from April to October. Sure, I'm dreaming of utopia, but there must be leagues out there like that. If you wind up in one, cherish it. They are rare.

That's part of the reasoning behind this section and Part 7, "For Your Commish Only." There will always be black sheep and troublemakers in any league. Hopefully you'll be able to weed them out beforehand. But if not, use the advice herein. It'll save some stress and strife—and keep your league running smoothly

Once you have your group established, it's time to make a date. Hopefully you've left yourself enough time to prep for Draft Day, because your group has a lot of ground to cover before it can call itself a league.

The first thing you have to have is a meeting.

Your First League Meeting

Call it what you will: the Owners' Caucus, the Winter Meetings, the Fabulous Freakin' Follies, whatever. But before you have a draft, you have to establish your league as a functional entity.

You have a minimum of four goals here:

1. Officially bless your league with a name. Likewise, all teams must have names, as well.

2. Elect league officers.

3. Create a rulebook.

4. Choose a stat service.

Strike Three

No one likes bullies and drama queens. Avoid potential owners with insecurity issues, beer muscles, and 'roid rage. Especially if you plan to have alcoholic beverages at the draft.

Foul Tips

The more you know about a potential owner, the better. There's nothing more frustrating than allowing a person to join your league blind, only to discover a month later that he's a jerk, moron, putz, psychopath, or worse.

These are the biggies. If you accomplish them, you're set to have a draft.

I won't lie to you. Some of this stuff will seem like administrative hogwash, a Big Red Tape Machine. Well, it can be. But truly, this is where you should let your creative juices run wild.

First of all, make a day of it—your league will seem more like an official group and you'll have more time to get to know the strangers. Weekends are best for meetings since it will take a few hours (minimum) to do a league up right. I recommend commandeering someone's house. You can try other places, like a bar. But the distractions will be mammoth. You just can't beat an empty house—that way all the barking and bellyaching can be done without offending spouses and corrupting children.

Have refreshments on hand. To be specific: tobacco products, processed meat in some kind of skin casing, melted cheese in a bowl, MSG dips, and the harmful beverages of your choice.

The point is, make the occasion as festive as possible. After all, the whole reason to start a league in the first place is to have fun (and win valuable prizes!).

Your next step is to create a written agenda so the meeting doesn't flounder. You'll always know where you are and how much more ground you have to cover. The agenda can be as simple as the four-point plan you just read, or it can be expanded, broken down, retro-fitted, you name it. It's *your* league.

Foul Tips

For your first meeting, make sure everyone understands that it's going to take a while. Above all, make yourselves comfortable. This is a good warm-up for Draft Day, which will be a marathon.

Overheard in the Dugout

My league always has a poker game after any meeting. This keeps the agenda moving and gives impatient owners something to live for. We must be real poker hounds, because you'll find that Draft Day has more to do with poker than with baseball. Other post-meeting incentives can include a big game on TV, a movie marathon, or a dart/pool/horseshoe tourney. Or even better, a full-blown party (with girls!).

Once you have an agenda and everyone is present and accounted for, don't waste any time. For now we'll go with my four-point plan. If everyone has a cold drink and some processed food product, it's time to begin …

What's in a Name? (Except Your Identity)

What's your name, big boy? Good question. I imagine there has to be a fantasy team out there with an owner named Bob called Bob's Big Boys. It's inevitable. But that's the perfectly putrid, poetic kind of name that is the hallmark of fantasy baseball leagues everywhere. As I said, let your creative juices flow. This is where your team becomes an extension of your identity. Give it some thought. Bad puns, bad metaphors, bad taste: Nothing is out of bounds.

Over the years, our league has had such catchy names as the Shepherds of Fury, the Black Crackers, the Stogies, the Diapers, the Gods, and the Red Nexx. We've also had more traditional fare such as the Phantoms, Lions, BigDogs, Bulldogs, Seminoles, Reds, and Bullets.

My team is called the Fedora Brigade, or sometimes the New York Hats (Fedora. Hat. Get it?). Why? Well, the Brigade moniker has been with me since high school. I used to write these ridiculously violent short stories starring a quasi superhero team called, you guessed it, the Fedora Brigade. Team members included Belch the Unsavory, Rufus Manhattan, and an ornery guy called the Gray Slayer. All wore fedoras. No villain was too dead, no machete too small. Needless to say, they weren't the second coming of the Super Friends. Anyway, my point is, the name means something to me personally. Plus, the Brigade—like the Crackers and the Shepherds of Fury—is now a genuine part of our league's lexicon.

That's how it's supposed to work. A natural extension of fantasy baseball is role-playing. I'm just the owner, Mr. Mike Zimmerman, Zim to his colleagues. But if you want to trade? Talk to my general manager, the Gray Slayer.

Sure, this may sound a little weird, but it's not. It's all a big joke, down to the fake press releases I send out to the league whenever I make a trade. Like so:

Strike Three

Keep an agenda. If you don't, any yahoo will talk about anything that comes to mind. You'll suddenly find yourself surrounded by a barnyard worth of farm animal metaphors.

Foul Tips

Think long and hard about naming your team. The name you choose should be an expression of who you are. Your league will become a big part of your life. Your team name will become part of everyday language. So don't skimp on the name. Your experience will be far richer. And funnier.

> *Dateline New York City.* The Fedora Brigade has pulled the trigger on another deal, this time sending perennial underachiever Ken Griffey Jr. to the Shepherds of Fury for veteran fireballer Doug Jones. When confronted about the stupidity of the steal, er, deal, Brigade GM the Gray Slayer responded tartly, "It's easy for you media pigs to sit in judgment, but you're not out there everyday, making it happen. This deal will turn out to be the one that puts us over the edge. By Trump's teeth, I swear it."

The Slayer then ended the press conference and exited the building in the company of several young starlets. He was later spotted that night at the King's Ex nightclub, gnawing on a velvet rope in the VIP section.

Reached for comment aboard his yacht, the Happy Barge—currently anchored off the coast of Sri Lanka—Brigade owner, Mike Zimmerman, remained coy about the whole situation: "Lacy! Be a dear and go ashore for more olives!"

Hey, don't blame me. That's why they call it fantasy baseball.

Who's Responsible for This Mess?

Once the official names have been named, move on to the next big step: electing league officers. Your league has to run, after all. And like I said in Chapter 1, "Get Into the Game," it has to run well. Your potential leaders should be serious about the job, because while it sounds special, it usually means getting stuck with the grunt work. Here are the usual offices and their responsibilities.

Foul Tips

Our league created the Trade Commish position to put a leash on unfair trading. The jury is still out on its effectiveness. We still had some questionable trades in '99, but the owners involved backed up their moves with halfway credible explanations. Your league will need some kind of trade approval process and someone to step in on rule disputes when the Commish is part of the problem or absent.

Commissioner (a.k.a. Whipping Boy)

Note the root word, *mission*. Call it what you want—mission impossible, mission from God, moron mission. Why do I blaspheme the highest office in the land? Because I was once a commissioner. The Commish is the Man when it comes to interpreting rules, resolving disputes, running meetings, and approving weekly transactions before they are sent to the Secretary. There is an upside to all this busywork, but I'll discuss the office more in Part 7.

Assistant Commissioner (a.k.a. the Ass.com)

Acts as Commish when Commish is directly involved in a dispute or simply unavailable. In our league, the Ass.com also acts as Trade Commish, assessing and approving all trades. His main function here is to make sure that all trades are "reasonably" fair and balanced. As you'll read later in the trading section, this is more important than you can possibly imagine.

Treasurer (a.k.a. the Bean Counter)

Sometimes your pot won't amount to a hill of beans, but it's your hill, and they're your beans. So make sure you can trust the guy who's counting them. The Treasurer is in charge of all financial matters, including kitty management (embezzlement), fund collection (extortion), and salary cap supervision (devoted reader of *The Complete Idiot's Guide to Money Laundering*). League funds should always be stowed away someplace safe. I suggest one of my sterling Zimmerman high-risk, big-load, growth-and-income mutual funds. For more information, call 1-900-GIVE2ME.

Secretary (a.k.a. Executive Assistant ... or Stat Boy)

Stat Boy receives collated transactions after they are approved by the Commish. He then enters the data into whatever bottomless pit of a stat service you employ.

I can't emphasize enough how important these functions are. They're the lifeblood of your league. Without good people running the joint, you'll be shut down in no time. Which leads me to the next important goal of your first meeting ...

Foul Tips

A trustworthy and diligent Bean Counter will send out weekly financial updates including who is over the salary cap and who owes how much to the league. Deadbeat owners should be fined and humiliated accordingly.

Staging Nonviolent Elections

Remember what I said in Chapter 1 about guys and their egos? Well, by this stage of the meeting, you should know who has something useful to say and who talks just to hear himself slur. The problem with a group of guys (with apologies to the precious few—if any—women who play fantasy baseball) is the whole "pack" mentality. The alpha males, God bless 'em, always want to take over the schoolyard.

Thankfully, democracy still reigns in our time. Keep things simple: If you have a dispute, vote on it. Even the most stubborn knucklehead will find it hard to reject the majority's rule.

Strike Three

Each office is crucial to your league's survival. Make sure you elect responsible people to these positions. If you don't, you may end up with no money, no stats, and no rules.

Our league maintains the ol' double-secret ballot style, tossing folded scraps of paper into a sweaty Phillies cap. I personally prefer a stand-up election where constituents raise their hands to be counted—and later have to live with their public decisions. But alas, guys are cowards at heart—at least in my league—so we go the anonymous route.

One disadvantage with public balloting is the psychological effect it has on guys who can't make up their minds. They'll see a majority of hands go up to vote one way, and they'll say "the hell with it" and vote with the crowd. However, if you stick with a secret ballot, these sheep have to think for themselves and toss their written decision into a hat. No fuss, no waffling.

Don't get caught in the classic trap: Someone will insist the league vote on choosing a voting style.

It's enough to make you scream, but I guarantee you there will be one by-the-book owner who will try to maintain formal rules and decorum throughout the voting process. I vote you stuff a sweaty sock in his mouth and make him blink once for yes, twice for no. Keep the voting process fast and loose—for everyone's sanity.

Once you have congratulated the winners, sworn them in, cursed them out, whatever, you can proceed to the most crucial part of your first meeting: creating a league rulebook.

You think voting for officers was hard? Well, the voting has only just begun.

Recommended viewing: The *Major League* trilogy. The first one is the best, of course, but any movie with play-by-play commentary by Bob Uecker must be a modern sports-film classic.

Foul Tips

Keep elections simple. Choosing officers should take the least amount of time at your first meeting. Either someone wants the job, or he doesn't.

The Least You Need to Know

➤ Recruit owners who will stay involved in the league for the entire season, no matter how bad their teams are.

➤ Avoid potential owners with personality disorders.

➤ Go hog-wild naming your team. Your team is an expression of who you are.

➤ Good league officers are crucial to your league's survival. Elect dependable people to those positions.

Rules: Democracy or Death? (Death's Easier)

Your first league meeting should now be closing in on what can be the easiest part, or the hardest part: Making the rules by which you will live.

It depends on your crowd. Are they fussy? If so, you could end up debating teeny tiny points of contention for hours. The question you need to ask yourself (and everyone else) is, "Is it worth it?" Yes and no (how's that for a definitive stance?).

Let's line up some clichés: Absolutely, positively, bar none, without a doubt, no bones about it, get it straight as an arrow—creating a rulebook is the most important part of forming a league!

Why You Need a Rulebook

A good *rulebook* gives your league structure, definition, and security. On an average day, it levels the playing field. On a good day, it prevents cheating. And guys *will* cheat if given the chance. I don't care how honorable you think everyone in your league is. Victory is too sweet for guys to be worried about honor. Someone will turn to the dark side. Always. Forever.

It's like NASCAR. The rules force every driver to adhere to a strict and measured design when building their race cars. That way—theoretically—everyone is driving the same car. But if that were literally true, you'd have 30 cars flying down the track at precisely the same speed. The good drivers find the angles. They slip between the lines of physics, the limitations of their cars, and the edges of the rules to eke out that extra half-mile an hour. And it's all legal. That blurring of the lines makes champions.

It's the same in fantasy baseball. Before your first draft, you should have a solid set of rules in place. But it's what you do on the ragged edge of those rules that will give you an advantage.

Trash Talk

A good fantasy **rulebook** functions just like the real baseball rulebook. It sets parameters and prevents cheating. In theory. That's why you need a good Commish to enforce these rules.

Fantasy owners must be creative. Plain and simple, if there isn't a rule against it, then it's legal. Which means that some owner will do it.

Remember what I said last chapter about employing a certain amount of used-car salesmanship? Words as true as glue. Always accentuate the positive, especially when selling a lemon.

Am I telling you to break the rules? Not at all. But you should bend them. If you don't, I guarantee you that someone else in your league will. He'll benefit nicely by exploiting some angle you didn't think of. It'll piss you off. It'll make you want to screech "infidel!"

Strike Three

Beware: Creative owners will bend the rules for an advantage. You have to decide if you want to play it straight or bend your own rules, because no one likes a crybaby.

But think long and hard about what's bothering you. First off, was a rule actually broken? Answer honestly. If not, are you mad because a rule has been bent? Or because you didn't think of it first?

The bottom line is, if something's going to present a problem, it's best to have a rule against it. Peace, love, and harmony will reign supreme and everyone will have a fair shot at the kitty. Until someone finds another loophole ....

Overheard in the Dugout

As a former commissioner, I have many stories of guys bending the rules. One of my favorites—because I, too, used it to my advantage—was the practice of drafting injured players cheap, putting them on the active roster, and then picking up free-agent replacements at the "injury discount" rate before opening day—a discount that helps immensely against the salary cap. This ticked off a lot of guys, but it was a perfectly legal way of stockpiling both free agents and good injured players who would later return to duty.

Where to Begin?

There's a sample rulebook conveniently located in Appendix A of this book. It's basically the same one our league uses, although I've smoothed out some rough edges where I thought necessary (to create my own utopian vision—just like George Steinbrenner does). I've also included many alternatives to the stated rules so you can see how nebulous and subjective rule-making can be.

You can certainly adopt this rulebook as is if you like. It'll save you time and should serve you well. But I seriously recommend reviewing it—this goes for any rulebook you pick up from alternative sources—and customizing it to fit your needs.

These things—rulebooks, charters, constitutions, what have you—are not cast in stone until your league ratifies them. You're forming *your* league. So you should make your own rules.

However, a few words of caution: Don't go overboard. Any rulebook you adopt—from this book or another source—has no doubt been perfected through years of debate, strife, and poor anger management. It's been tried, tested, true, totally. So don't completely dismantle it.

Foul Tips

Good rulebooks can be found in many places (books, Web sites, and so on) and adopted as is. Or you can write your own rules—it's *your* league. Either way, take the time to be sure whatever rulebook you adopt is right for your group.

If You Decide to Tweak Established Rulebooks ...

As the owner of an overweight Labrador retriever, I'm constantly amazed how she can sit there watching me eat liverwurst, a rope of drool running from her jowls to the carpet. She never takes her beady little eyes off my hands. What anticipation. What desire. You'd think there was no better tasting processed meat product in the world (is there?). But what happens when I toss a scrap to the mutt? She inhales it, not even chewing it—let alone tasting it.

Foul Tips

When struggling to approve rules, have a formal debate. Give interested owners two minutes to make their cases—no more. Then vote on it.

Strike Three

Debating is an art form. A lawyer can know every law from here to paternity, but if he's short on charm he won't be a good trial lawyer. If you want your proposals to pass, you have to be one charming dude (either that, or hope no one cares enough about the issue to vote against you).

Which illustrates my next point: Take your time, chew your rules, and figure out if you like their taste. If you blow through the approval process—voting at the speed of light—what's the point?

Maybe you think this conflicts with what I said about keeping the voting fast and loose. Nope. Use common sense. If everyone is arguing about which rule should go where, you'll bang nails into the floor with your forehead all day long. So organize it. Debate.

Is There a Lawyer in the House?

At this point, you've elected a Commissioner. Make him earn his first merit badge by regulating the discussion. That's part of the job.

But be warned: If you decide to have a discussion, you'll end up with a bunch of barking baboons, each trying to be louder than the other. Because, as the formal mentality of the American male dictates, if you're louder, you must be right.

Alpha males will try to berate and intimidate while the heart of the argument—what's best for the league—will be forgotten. The reason for a debate is to listen to the argument, not the person.

Bottom line? Make it formal. The Commish should decree that each interested owner can plea a two-minute case before the group. No one speaks, no one groans, no one throws half-empty beer cans. When that person is done, he's *done*. He can make no further argument—so the argument he makes better be his best.

Now is each owner's chance to be a lawyer arguing before the jury. If you keep up with your legal thrillers, you'd know that a trial lawyer is just a salesman. If he can sell his lemon of a client to the jury, he'll most likely win. So open up a can of charm and use that old used-car salesmanship I spoke of.

Overheard in the Dugout

At our league's last winter meeting, one owner—a guy as dedicated to the league as anyone—presented something like 10 proposals for rule changes. Each and every one was voted down. By the eighth proposal, he was just shaking his head, muttering to himself. The point is, you can't win them all—so don't fight it. You're not the only voice in the room, and majority rules. (By the way, that owner also lost his shirt in poker after the meeting, teehee.)

They Signed Ya, Bill, Now Yer a Law

When everyone is done presenting his point of view, vote on it. Majority rules and the results are binding. Which means that once an issue has been put to the polls, it's a matter of record. Which also means the losing parties should shut up about it.

Be prepared. Guys who don't get their way will gretz and groan, but that's more because they lost, less because they really think their proposal was better. Guys hate to lose, remember? So as soon as a vote is official, move on quickly.

Assuming there are no fisticuffs, your rulebook will gradually take shape. When you're finished—when all proposals have been heard, when the last of the Dershowitzes and Baileys have said their piece—your Commish can declare proudly, "By the power invested in me by the League of Whatever, I hereby ratify this rulebook/constitution/charter/manifesto and all articles within."

At which point a collective sigh of relief will pollute the room. It's now up to the Secretary (or whoever volunteers) to type up a formal copy and distribute it to one and all before the draft.

Be happy. You did it. You now have rules. You now have order. You now have civilization. Know what that means?

You now have a *league.*

Don't Change, Baby ... at Least Not 'Til October

Let's pretend.

It's late July. A National League–only fantasy league is running hot. The race is tight, reserve rosters are full, useful free agents are scarce, and salary caps are maxed out. Along comes an owner—someone near the top of the standings—who pulls something questionable. Let's say he used one injured player to acquire two free agents at the injury discount (a rule option we'll discuss later).

How did he do this? Well, first his shortstop went down with a pulled groin. Out for a month. So the owner, we'll call him Floyd (of the Orwigsburg Pink Floyds), acquires a discounted free agent shortstop to replace him on the roster. Floyd then reserves the injured player. Fine and dandy.

Next week, Floyd discreetly activates the injured shortstop in place of an ineffective middle infielder. He says he is doing this because he doesn't want his batting average hurt anymore by the lousy infielder. Still fine and dandy.

But something has developed that is about to throw a wrench into the works. It's late July. The major league trading deadline looms like an extra Christmas. And the Mariners have just traded shortstop Alex Rodriguez to the Mets (a long-rumored possibility that may be a reality by the time you read this). It's the mother of all crossover trades.

Foul Tips

If you have an even number of owners, "majority rules" might not cut it. You'll end up with some ties. Either develop a reliable tie-breaker system or bump up the winning count to two-thirds rules or three-fourths rules. Because ties suck.

Guess what: Floyd has dibs. His eyes lit up like twin Cartmans in a Cheezy-Poof factory. But Floyd has a problem. He's close to the salary cap. He eagerly puts in his transaction: Reserve the injured shortstop, and acquire free agent A-Rod at the injury discount. Floyd now has superstud Rodriguez and a second shortstop at the discount, plus the original shortstop who will be back in two weeks from his injury. And he's snugly under the salary cap.

Everyone in the league freaks. How can an owner use one injured player to acquire two free agents at the injury discount? Not fair! Illegal! However, when the Commish checks out the rules, they don't say anything about this predicament. Which means, if you remember my previous point, it's totally legal.

So where is all this going you might ask. I'll tell you. The Commish has no choice but to let the transaction stand, even though it gives Floyd a big leg up for the second half of the season.

But the Commish is feeling impotent. Since no man likes to feel impotent, the Commish uses his executive powers to call a vote to immediately change the rule to prevent any more bogus moves. Logical, right? Maybe. But it could also be a big mistake.

Our league has one standing unwritten rule (meaning it's not in the rulebook): Don't change in mid-season. Don't change rules. Don't change policies. Don't change anything at all.

This may sound a bit daft, but think about it. Every strategy you concoct, every draft salary you compute, every keeper you contemplate have all been created based upon the rules *as they existed after the winter meeting.*

If you change a bunch of rules in mid-season, your strategies could be seriously affected. For instance, when you're drafting your team, especially if you draft minor leaguers, you're also planning beyond the coming season. All that could be affected.

However, and this is a big however, a theme is a theme. And mine is, it's *your* league. I make recommendations, only. If changing a rule in the middle of a pennant race is what your league wants, then do it. Just beware of possible fallout down the line.

Sometimes changing a rule in mid-season is the only way to solve a problem—especially if some owners are rampantly taking advantage of loopholes. In fact, it just may be "in the best interests of baseball" for your Commish to act.

Use your head. If you have any common sense, you'll know right from wrong (but beware the dark side). Which brings me to my next point …

Foul Tips

I don't recommend changing rules during the regular season. It can ruin strategies that owners had planned months in advance. On the other hand, don't let me tell you what to do. If a rule is harming your league, change it. If the owners want to add something that will enrich the league, do it. A happy league is a strong league.

Overheard in the Dugout

Late in the '98 season, I had a brainstorm: winter trading. Our league didn't allow it, but I wanted to give it a whirl. I brought it up and it even went to a vote. But before we could cast ballots, one farsighted owner reminded us about the "no mid-season" rule. See, many guys already had their keeper plans set. Something as major as winter trading—had we established it in the pre-season like we should have—would have altered some owners' previous draft strategies, let alone their current keeper strategies. Not changing rules in mid-season has proven correct and fair—for *our* league.

The Rulebook as a Work in Progress

If there's one rule, it's that no rulebook is perfect.

I defy you to have a fantasy season without a few bumps in the road to tranquility. Like I said, some owners will get creative, bend rules, and basically challenge the authority of the league as a whole.

If you've got the disease, there is a cure: Change the rules. Sounds simple, right? Well … sometimes.

Strike Three

If you allow a single owner the power to call a league-wide vote on rule changes at any time during the season, you'll be having a couple of votes a week. To avoid this, make it necessary for a certain number of owners to call a vote. This is a quorum.

If you decide to forego the no mid-season change stuff I mentioned before, then you need some mechanism in place governing rule changes. Can one angry owner force a league-wide vote on a rule? That's up to you—but you could have a free-for-all on your hands. You can do it like Congress and make a quorum necessary. (For those of you who don't know how the U.S. government works—you know who you are—a quorum is a certain percentage of a group needed to have a vote.) You can make your quorum three owners, half your league, three-fourths, whatever. It's up to you. Have your vote. Change your rule. No problem.

However, if you decide on the no mid-season route, you will have to do two things. Bite the bullet and endure the loopholing for the balance of the season. (If you have any sense of honor, you can refuse to participate.) Or you can join the party so the playing field is level once again.

Add that particular loophole to your list of rule proposals to be addressed at the upcoming winter meeting. All your rule changing will be done there, so start your list early and add to it often. It's vital.

The rulebook is a constant work in progress. The harder you work on it, the smoother everything will be—but it will never *ever* be perfect. Don't fret. Who wants perfection, anyway? Pleasantville might be a nice place, but without a Reese Witherspoon to add some spice, it'd be boring. So make your decision: Are you a bland citizen of Pleasantville, or are you a Reese?

I bet you're a Reese. I mean, aren't we all … just a little bit?

Going to Bat for Stats

At last—the last! Your meeting is almost over. You have team names, officers, and a rulebook. Now all you need is someone to take care of the paperwork for you. That is, someone to manage your league's stats.

Many stat services exist on the Web. There is software, too. Some cost more than others. Some are free. All have advantages and disadvantages. In fact, I'm going to go out on a limb and say I'm not going out on a limb. I can't comfortably recommend a particular stat service for your league. Invariably, it will seem like a commercial for the service, while other perfectly serviceable services would be ignored.

Here's another potential problem with recommending services by name: What if you take my advice and don't like the service? If you'd have done your own homework, you might have found a stat keeper more suited to your league's needs. How could I live with myself?

So here's what I will tell you: Do some research. Go to a newsstand and peruse the sports 'zines for ads. Read fantasy columnists on the Web and in print media. Hit some message boards and chat rooms on the Web. Ask questions. The best critics of fantasy stat services are the people who play the game. Listen to them.

There are some Web sites listed in the back of this book in Appendix B, "Useful Web Sites." Take the time to check them out. Fantasy baseball owners are an opinionated lot. You'll always get a nice array of no-bull answers.

Foul Tips

Take the time to research potential stat services. They are the backbone of your league. Good sources of info are the Internet, fantasy baseball chat rooms, and ads in sports magazines.

Your stat service is the backbone of your league. Without it, you have none. So do some homework. Be prepared to shell out some green. Be sure to get exactly what you want. Because like I've been saying all long (see my blue face?): It's your league. It will live or die by your effort.

Overheard in the Dugout

Back in '98, our league was in the market for a new stat service. We wanted to try a free service, but weren't convinced how good it would be (because usually you get what you pay for). So we compromised: We used both. We ponied up $8 a head for the pay service while simultaneously registering for the free service. If either one stank, we were covered. The point is, if you can't decide on one stat service, try two. It doesn't cost all that much.

The Least You Need to Know

➤ Don't skimp on setting up the league's rulebook. Time invested in it now will prevent bloodshed down the road.

➤ To save time and screaming, use a formal debate system to argue rules—once each owner has had a turn, vote—and then move on.

➤ Bending the rules is not illegal. Be prepared to deal with the benders, or choose to become one yourself.

➤ Changing rules in mid-season can disrupt teams' legitimate strategies—if you change something midstream, be careful.

➤ Take the time to search out a good stat service—it's the backbone of your league.

Part 3

"Do You Feel a Draft?"

The fun officially begins now. Your league should be up and running—as should be your enthusiasm. It's time to take the next step: preparing for your draft.

If you went to college, think finals. You have to cram the immediate value of nearly a thousand professional baseball players into your shallow little brain—and be able to recall said values instantaneously. Not only that, you have to know the life and loves of your opponents who will be leering at you from across the draft table, a look of savagery in their eyes not seen since the days of the wooly mammoth.

So be careful. Be prepared. But above all, be ready to curse when your initial draft strategy is blown right out of the water. Because it always is.

Chapter 6

Draft Day Prep, Part 1: Fantasy

> ## In This Chapter
>
> ➤ How to compute your own player values
>
> ➤ Using your opponents' values against them
>
> ➤ Where to find intelligence (cheap)
>
> ➤ Some helpful valuation methods

By this time, you probably have a stack of magazines and Web printouts giving you the cold stare of a supermodel: "You don't have a chance with me, so don't bother." Oh, really? Sure, you're just a regular schmoe. But you have a lot to offer. What if you really tried to ask out a supermodel? Naturally, you couldn't just walk up to her on the street and offer to buy her a drink. She'd laugh at your puny attempt at machismo. Then she'd call a cop.

You have to worm your way into her life, eating away at the hard shell protecting her from scumbags and telemarketers. You'd have to get to know her first. Then she'd see that you are indeed a scumbag, but an irresistible one. You might just get that drink with her.

It's the same thing with that endless stack of baseball information that has to somehow worm its way into your brain. You have to start slow. Get to know it drip by drip. Pretty soon you'll be on friendly terms with it. And then, before you know it, you'll be so enamored of each other that you'll be inseparable. That's the theory, at least.

Anyway, this chapter will help you with the first part of your draft prep: the fantasy aspect. Don't think about reality yet. It's too soon. You don't have the tools. You have to start slow, and at the beginning. And the beginning of any draft prep is establishing player values. Do you know how to do that? Didn't think so. Better read this, then.

Do It Yourself and Trust Yourself

To me, one of the biggest problems in fantasy baseball is the temptation to rely on outside sources for player values.

Foul Tips

Using player values from outside experts is a useful tool. But eventually you will have to come up with your own value system and be able to trust yourself with it.

Don't get me wrong: Outside sources are invaluable. But at some point—after reading 20 value lists compiled by 20 experts—you have to say, "I get it, but I need to do this myself." Sort of a moment of clarity for soon-to-be fantasy junkies.

The experts can help you only so much. They can give you an overview. They can give you opinions. But the bottom line is, on Draft Day, your league's value of a certain player will be perverted by so many variables it's ridiculous.

Here are just a few:

➤ **League size.** Experts' values are usually based on a 14- to 15-team league using a $260 to $280 draft budget. If you don't have the exact same number of teams in your league, your values will be different.

➤ **Fandom.** Experts never factor in human tendencies such as fandom, overspending, and bidups. Their computed values will top out at $38 to $40 for elite players. But there will always be a $45 player in any draft.

➤ **Time.** In the time since the experts' player values were printed (especially in books, which have a longer lead time), players can be traded, injured, or benched, radically changing their value.

Strike Three

The bottom line is, a negative-value player will probably hurt you (duh). But in a super-deep league, you still have to fill your roster. A .250-hittin', 30 RBI-drivin' third baseman will end up on someone's roster. And you know what he's worth? A buck. Because that's the absolute minimum bid.

Some experts use formulas that are so complex that low-end players will actually have a *negative* dollar value. I hate this. It doesn't help anyone. After all, you have to pay something for every player.

So take the expert values with a grain of salt (lime and tequila sold separately). They may be the experts—and make their living writing about sports—but they won't be sitting across the table from you on Draft Day.

As for me listing player values in this book? That would be a pointless gesture. I have my own value system, for one, and the lead time for printing this book is so long that any values listed would be uselessly out of date.

What's a guy to do? Start with the experts. But like I said, use them as signposts, not burning bushes. Your ultimate destination should be a player value list that is uniquely your own. After all, only *you* really know what you'll pay for Mike Piazza.

So how do you arrive at your own unique values? Glad I asked.

Foul Tips

You won't find a list of player dollar values in this book. Why? It's not my job to tell you how much to pay for Kevin Brown or Gary Sheffield. It's *your* job to figure it out on your own.

How Much Is That A-Rod in the Window?

Really, truly, what's the actual value of Alex Rodriguez? Well, he has value in several ways—not all of them relevant to your dollar list.

Hmmm, can it be true? Can a player have "the intangibles" in a stat-based fantasy game? Yes, to an extent. Here's how.

The Many Faces of Value

First you have A-Rod's perceived value on everyone's draft sheet. To a man, those numbers will probably be within five bucks of each other.

Then you have A-Rod's actual value—what someone actually pays for him at auction.

And finally you have A-Rod's *bid-up value*—that is, what he's worth to the rest of the league in terms of the dollars they can get a gullible owner to overpay. Each dollar that A-Rod is bid up is one less dollar the winning owner has to spend later.

Trash Talk

Bid-up value is how many dollars above a player's perceived value the league can get one owner to pay. Five-tool fantasy studs and over-hyped rookies are the easiest players to bid up—and someone will always pay.

More on (Moron) Value

Here's the scenario: Bubba goes to the draft convinced that his team's success depends on nabbing A-Rod at any cost. Jocko goes in thinking his team's success depends on not nabbing A-Rod at any cost.

Right there you have two distinct values for A-Rod. The dollar value for Bubba and the bid-up value for Jocko. Imagine what will happen to Bubba when Jocko realizes how badly Bubba wants A-Rod. Especially when the bids hit $40. Bubba will probably go to $45, he wants A-Rod so bad. He might even go to $50.

Jocko is shrewd. He smells blood in the water. He knows that his bids of $45, $47, and $49 will be topped by the now nervous, borderline panicked Bubba.

Bubba will eventually win the auction for A-Rod, and he will have bought one of the most valuable names in the game. But at what price? Did he really want to spend $50 out of $260 on one player—even if it's A-Rod? Probably not. And neither should you.

Players like A-Rod, Griffey, Bagwell, McGwire, Sosa, Maddux, and the like have tremendous bid-up value. I mean, what are they *really* worth? No one knows. It's almost impossible to put a value on what 65 dingers or 200+ innings of sub-1.000 WHIP can bring to your squad. Is Sammy Sosa worth $45 bucks? He is to someone.

How will you know who that is? There's only one way to find out.

Know Thy Fellow Owners

Before they were omniscient sleeper keepers, before they were Steinbrenner-esque spenders on free agents, before they snatched the league championship with an 11th-hour move, every fantasy owner was just a baseball fan. That could be their greatest weakness—a weakness that could directly affect player values. To paraphrase George Thorogood by way of Ellis McDaniel: "Who do they love?"

Guys love to own players from their favorite teams, especially the superstars. They see a big five-tool stud prowling their home field and they can't resist. They feel like a kid again. It also makes cheering for your favorite team that much sweeter.

Beware: The seasoned fantasy owner will know how to bypass team loyalties for the sake of a good roster (though you should still watch them carefully—they might try to sneak a favorite player by you by *pretending* not to care). But the fledgling owner? *Prey.*

Remember my $67 Von Hayes story? It always happens. What you need to do is find out which owners like which teams. Try to go even deeper—does Dude Freddy have a hankering for Roger Clemens, even though he's a Marlins fan? How about your pal, Arnie? You saw him wearing a Sosa jersey over the winter, and you guys live in Dodgertown.

Pay attention. This knowledge could mean a difference of only a few dollars. But that's usually the difference between a good draft and a great draft.

Overheard in the Dugout

Our league has some guys who just love the Phillies. (Despite my love for the team, I'm not a fantasy Phillie fan—the only Phil I've owned in the last two years was Wayne Gomes.) There's a Reds fan, too. No matter how wily these guys become at bidding, they always end up with Phils or Reds on their respective squads. Coincidence? I think not. Phillies and Reds are always a little inflated in our league. It'll happen in your league, too. You just have to figure out which teams ring the bell.

Falling in Love with the Wrong Guy

As any Darth Maul knows, the sword cuts both ways. If you have an unexplainable attachment for a certain player, follow old Obi-Wan's advice: "Bury your feelings deep down, Luke. They do you credit, but they could be made to serve the Emperor (in this case, your fellow owners)."

Pretend you're at a car dealer trying to land that sweet SUV. But the dealer has seen the look in your eyes and he knows you want that truck. He thinks you're a sucker—wrapper, stick, and all—and won't budge on his price. Get mad. After all, someone is trying to screw you out of something that you badly want. So what do you do? You walk out.

Strike Three

Say you've been a Cal Ripken fan since '84. If this is your first fantasy draft, any owner who knows you will know your loyalties. They'll be watching you like cats watching a lame bird. Play it cool when Cal's name is called. In time, the bids will hit the ceiling of Ripken's value. Your buds will be staring at you, waiting for the bidup. Don't give them the satisfaction.

Sure, it hurts. And it'll hurt to let go of your child-hood hero. But you have to. You can't afford to overpay for a player just because you admire him. The other owners will rake you.

The best strategy? Find the most aggressive bidup owner and play his gambit against him. Bid the player up an extra buck or two. Fake frustration at the rising price. If the other owners don't go for it, the worst you get is your idol at a couple bucks above value.

But if a bullish owner bites? Wait until the player's price is uncomfortably high. The aggressive owner will tease you by bumping the price one more buck. What do you do? Don't say a thing. Watch that aggressive owner's face as the player goes once, goes twice, and is sold to him for $5 more than his value. If that doesn't soothe the hurt of seeing your hero on someone else's roster, nothing will.

Where to Find Intelligence (Cheap)

As I've said before, this is a game about intelligence: smarts, common sense, and information. You've heard a lot about the smarts and common sense. Now we should talk about information.

No war has ever been won without intelligence. Patton needed to know exactly where Monty was as much as he needed to know where the Germans were. And so do you. The only way to establish accurate player values is to know what's going on day to day in each team's camp (that goes for both major league teams and your opponents' teams).

Thankfully, there are numerous outlets for up-to-the-pitch news on just about every team. The Information Age has exploded and nowhere is that more evident than in the universe of sports reportage. Here's a sampling of the best:

➤ **TV.** ESPN's *Baseball Tonight,* CNN, and Fox SportsNet, for example. Also, ESPN 2 runs a never-ending ticker at the bottom of the screen for scores and updates. If you don't have cable, invest in a satellite dish. You're probably not watching enough TV anyway.

➤ **Internet.** spn.com, cnnsi.com, and rotonews.com. Three great sources for up-to-the-minute box scores, stats, and roster news. There are others out there, as well—all equally valuable—but these are the giants.

Foul Tips

When searching for information on a certain player, no source is better than local papers. They know the players best and will devote the most space to their home team.

➤ **Print.** *USA Today, Baseball Weekly, The Sporting News,* and *Sports Illustrated. USA Today* is my favorite because of their thorough national coverage. I live in the New York metro area, and if it weren't for *USA Today* I wouldn't know that there were teams other than the Mets and Yankees in the world. The other three are fantastic weeklies that give you updated stats as well as in-depth analysis. Plus, as a fan who appreciates such things, I find no better sportswriting than in *SI.*

But the best source of info about specific players?

➤ Local papers. There is no substitute. Who could possibly know the scuttlebutt—injuries, rumors, benchings—better than the media who are in the clubhouse every night with the players? They're homeys and they have more column space to fill. Plus, many of these reporters have been going at it for years, forging ongoing relationships with players that could reveal even more info.

Don't worry—you don't have to buy every major city's newspaper every morning. If you're looking for information on a specific player, log on to the local rag's Web site and check it out. You'll find the address of every major league team's respective newspaper in Appendix B, "Useful Web Sites," in the back of this book (how convenient!).

For information, that's as good as it gets. Naturally, there are hundreds of sources out there for fantasy intelligence: books, 'zines, and Web sites. I have my favorites. You need to find yours. Just don't skimp on the homework. Your draft depends on it.

After all, no one really wants to be considered a complete idiot. Do they?

The List Is Life

In case I haven't made myself clear: The success of your draft will hinge on your list.

In the weeks leading up to the big day, use the experts' value lists to forge your own preliminary draft sheet. Catalog players by position, from highest to lowest (and don't forget minor leaguers if you're planning supplemental drafts). If you can, do it on a computer. As the spring progresses, you'll be cutting and pasting like an over-caffeinated kindergarten class.

This first list is your foundation. From there, it's all about maintenance—reacting to what happens on the trade front and during spring training. This is the stuff of reality baseball, not fantasy. We'll talk about that in the next chapter.

For now, concentrate on your preliminary list. There are a couple more things I can tell you to help with this.

There Are No Magic Formulas

I'm glad there are no magic formulas for player values. Why? Then everyone would use them and the draft would be as boring as a tic-tac-toe tournament at Fredo's House of Lobotomies.

Each owner's unique perception of value is what keeps things spicy. It creates both reckless spending and insane bargains. It creates suspense.

Strike Three

Keep your draft lists on a computer if possible. This keeps your copy clean and easy to update. Not to be too anal, but sloppy record-keeping leads to lost information. Beware.

Foul Tips

Value is subjective. You can put anything you want on paper, but no one knows what a certain owner will pay for a certain player until Draft Day. If you set up your draft sheet intelligently—and don't lose control while bidding—you probably won't overpay for any one player (the death sentence of any draft strategy).

Trash Talk

The 10 dollar theory says that, as the draft progresses, a player's actual price will most likely fluctuate five dollars up or down from your price list. If this happens consistently, you've done a good job establishing values.

You can try to create formulas. How much should you pay per save, per home run for instance? How much is 550 at-bats of .325 average worth? Should you pay $.50 per stolen base?

Like I said, no one knows. And any formula you develop will be based on math and science. Which, as anyone who saw the movie *Contact* knows, cannot possibly take into consideration human nature: emotion, fandom, recklessness, and lack of preparation. You might be able to predict Mark Grace's batting average within 10 points, but you can't predict exactly how high a devoted Cubs fan will go for him.

To me, that's what this game is all about. Not stats. Not formulas. Human nature.

When I create my player value sheets, I naturally try to nail the most accurate price I can using all the information available. At the same time, however, I understand *the 10 dollar theory* (my own)—that a player's price could fluctuate five bucks in either direction depending on the mood of the draft. This neighborhood value serves me well. When the bid hits that $10 window, my hackles are up. That $10 window is the kill zone.

As the draft progresses, if you see that most players are going for prices within your $10 zone, you probably did a good job creating your own values. If your values were way off, however, you might want to rethink your system. (On the other hand, your values might be okay while the rest of the league is screwed up—but that's doubtful.)

The bottom line is, the only player values that matter will be your own. You can try to predict bid-up value of the stud players, but again, you won't really know what they are until the heat of the auction—when human nature takes over.

The best thing to do is arrive at a *ceiling price* for every player—especially the ones you're jonesing for—and absolutely *do not go higher.* Just walk away.

Indeed, walking away from a player you want may be the hardest thing to do in fantasy baseball. It is the undoing of many a draft strategy. But it is also the sign of a strong owner—an owner who wants to win more than he wants to own his favorite player. Which owner do you want to be?

So make your lists. They can be as complicated as you want. You can include perceived values, $10 windows, ceiling prices, anything. It's up to you. But on your road to knowing all and telling all, X-file away one simple piece of advice: Trust no one.

Your list is your life in fantasy baseball. Spies are everywhere. Which leaves us with only two words: Make fakes.

Next!

Recommended viewing: *Bang the Drum Slowly.* Robert DeNiro. Baseball. Need I say more?

Trash Talk

Ceiling price is the absolute limit to what you will pay for a given player. When the bidding hits the ceiling, walk away.

The Least You Need to Know

➤ Use the experts' player values as a guide, not gospel. Do your own research and trust your own judgment.

➤ Know your fellow owners' favorite players—they will always overvalue them.

➤ Up-to-date information on players is essential—find the best sources and use them religiously.

➤ When seeking hard-to-find details on a specific player, check out his team's local paper on the Internet.

➤ Ultimately, this game is about human nature, not stats. Use everything you know about your competitors when establishing player values.

HE'S RETIRED, HE'S BEEN INJURED...

Chapter 7

Draft Day Prep, Part 2: Reality

In This Chapter

➤ What to do when pitchers and catchers report

➤ Evaluating off-season moves

➤ Following transactions as they happen

➤ The ins and outs of spring training

The air is different in spring. Gone is the frosty bite of winter, replaced with a deep, rich, rotting smell. The ground thaws, spewing up all the dead grass and bugs from last fall. It's a beautiful time of year, filled with promise, hope, anger, disgust, and frustration. Why? Because the fantasy baseball season is heating up like the cheeks of an offended church lady.

By now you should have solid player value lists for every position. But these will fluctuate faster than a batting average. As spring training progresses, trades, injuries, and benchings will make instant goats of heroes and vice versa. In this era of America's game, nothing is sacred. In every off-season, it is now routine for some of the best players in the game to change address by trade or free agency. Expect anything, and be prepared to respond to it the day it happens. Fast response to change is the only way you stay on top of your league.

Let's get started on phase two of draft prep: reality baseball. As I said last chapter, your player values—as you alone made them—are just preliminary. Now you'll learn how to tweak, torture, and terminate them as the real world dictates.

Hmmm. How to do that? There's only one way to find out. But let's try this instead ...

Recharging the Batteries

Valentine's Day may put love in the air (buy Lysol), but the real function of February is to get pitchers and catchers back in camp. Nothing is more important than putting a team's starting battery back on the field to test out those off-season training programs, those surgically repaired knees and elbows, and those dormant lungs.

Your job is to follow the progress of each team carefully. Spring training is a strange time, and if you're not careful, you can be misled by what you see, hear, and smell. Yes, smell. Sportswriters will talk about the cut grass, the glove leather, the concession popcorn.

Makes you feel good. Almost spring-like. A fresh-faced goober fluffing the pillow of your inner child. Give this sentimental (emphasis on *mental*) stuff its appointed 15 minutes and move on. Because the smell you should be looking for is a rat. Or a fishy rotten-in-Denmark thing. Because that's the smell that tells you a player/manager/general manager is full of it.

You will hear all sorts of claims from these guys. Some will be important. Some will mean bubkus. But all will have a bearing on player values. So let's talk about the biggies, the informational mileposts you'll encounter during the average spring training. Because interpreting this stuff is as important as any draft prep you will do.

Are you ready for your next evolution? Hoo-yah, master chief.

Foul Tips

Spring is the time to refine your player value lists, reacting to injuries, waivers, trades, and benchings as they happen.

Strike Three

Be vigilant. Use all the information sources at your command (see the last chapter). Missing a week's transactions is like missing a week of school. You'll have to make it up while your enemies skip ahead a grade.

Best Supporting Transactor

By the time March rolls around, most of the free agents will have settled their contracts and itineraries. Who's going where? And what about the trading season when owners sit around a hot stove evaluating players—the real-life winter meetings that send so many players packing to so many places?

One beautiful—and sometimes infuriating—fact of baseball is that transactions never stop. Billionaire owners and their general managers truly are nothing more than old kids trading baseball cards. Instead of players' photos on one side and stats on the other, they trade contracts with players' signatures on the bottom and their road-trip perks inside.

Kind of sick when you think about it. As usual, the people who make out the best in all of this are the people who create nothing: the lawyers, agents, and bankers. After all, should you really blame a player for wanting a $100 million contract when other guys are getting them? (Absolutely!) "What do mega-contracts have to do with fantasy baseball?" the impatient reader may ask. Plenty, I answer.

Contracts rule the game. They can determine who plays. They can determine who is traded. They can determine what the next free agent in line will receive. And, naturally, they can affect player values.

A good example from '99 is second baseman Delino DeShields of the Orioles. A solid fantasy middle infielder with good speed. The Birds signed free agent DeShields in the '98 off-season to a fat three-year contract, expecting him to anchor their middle infield all the way to the playoffs.

Now, I don't know DeShields personally. Nor do I know what happens behind closed clubhouse doors. All I know is what I get from my media sources, which is this:

> First, DeShields underperformed and got hurt.
>
> Then, the Orioles flew south as a team by mid-season, their mega-payroll an albatross around their craning necks like a bad bird analogy.
>
> Next, they have a promising youngster, Jerry Hairston, ready to take over at second base.
>
> Finally, their efforts to trade DeShields during the season failed—according to conventional wisdom—because no team wanted to take on his multi-year contract.

Trash Talk

A player's **contract** can directly affect his performance, playing time, and marketability—all of which determine fantasy value.

If you're the Orioles, what do you do? Sit DeShields while you're paying him big bucks? Or do you hand his job to a rookie who may take a year or more to blossom? Either way, DeShields' contract has directly affected his playing time and fantasy value.

Watch off-season moves like these carefully. I wouldn't be surprised if you see a trend toward shorter contracts. Then again, I wouldn't be surprised if a middle reliever was signed to an eight-year deal. You just never know with these owners.

Another facet of the mega-contract is the pressure it puts on the player. Back in '97, Sammy Sosa was a dependable run producer, but not spectacular. He was good for a 30-homer, 100-RBI, 700-strikeout season. Still, the Cubs rewarded him with a big-time contract approaching $9 million a year.

Fans howled. Sports radio switchboards lit up. Governments toppled. Sosa went on to have a typical/substandard season in '97. Again, I don't know Sosa personally, but

everything I read said that he was immature and was feeling the pressure of performing up to his contract. He fizzled.

Look what happened a year later. Sosa found himself—in every way a pro athlete can. But, man ... that fat contract had its way with him in '97. It's just plain hard to predict how a big multi-year deal will affect a guy.

And don't get me started on players who are in the last year of their contracts .... Okay, I started myself. These players almost always come up with a big year to justify their next big contract. In fact, many career years come the season before a player is first eligible for free agency.

Should you find out who these players are before your draft? Gee. Hmmm. You do the math.

> **Foul Tips**
>
> Players don't like to admit it, but when they're in the last year of a contract, they usually perform at a higher level to justify the next big deal. Keep your eye on these players come Draft Day.

Learn a Good Trade

As with free agents, you should carefully watch the trading front. The winter always produces some interesting deals, but the trade market heats up in spring training as teams fine-tune their needs.

You're a baseball fan, so naturally you know the feeling you get when your home team makes a deal—*any* deal. Excitement. Trepidation. Sometimes anger if they dealt a player you liked, or if the deal seemed shortsighted.

Now you have the whole league to worry about. If you play in an NL-only or AL-only league, you'll feel that excitement and fury, but at 10 times the pitch. Excitement when good players come over to your league, fury when they leave (especially if they're one of your keepers).

> **Strike Three**
>
> A trade can affect a player's value more than any other transaction, short of waiving him. It also has a residual effect on other players who may increase or decrease their playing time as a result.

Keep the following points in mind:

1. **Be prepared.** A trade affects a player's value more than any other real-life transaction, short of waiving him. When a deal turns over, you should ask yourself some key questions about how it affects fantasy value.

2. **Why was the player traded?** What will his role be on his new team (starter, platoon, bench fodder)? Just because a guy started on one team doesn't mean he'll start on another. On the other hand, a part-timer could end up a starter on his new team.

3. **How does the trade affect other players?** For instance, if a starting second baseman is dealt for a starting pitcher, someone will have to step into the second baseman job on the one team, while the other team will have to find a reliable pitcher. These replacement players will shoot up in value.

4. **Is the traded player happy about it?** Human nature rears its ugly head once again. If a player's not happy, he might pout. On the other hand, if he's happy (like going from a loser to a contender), he might flourish.

Like anything in sports, no situation is totally predictable. But at least you can make educated guesses. Keep reading, keep digging—the more you know about a player, the more you'll know what's going to happen to his value if he's dealt. As always, information is king.

Alas, trades and free agent signings are just the beginning. Spring training offers its own pitfalls and value killers, especially when pre-season games begin.

So, unlike umpires, let's move this game along …

Stats Don't Count in Spring … Do They?

It happens every year. The same buzz. The same debate. The same inconclusive answers. A rookie tears through the month of March, ripping homers like mad, stealing bases, hitting .520. At the same time, an established veteran starter on the same team, at the same position, flounders at .180.

Fans and media types screech that the rookie has earned the job. The vet is lazy and unprepared. He *should* lose his job. Yet by Opening Day, the vet is back at his old position full-time while the rookie is back at Double-A.

Wait a minute. Do the fans and reporters know something that the manager and coaches don't know? Not bloody likely.

No, spring training stats do *not* count. But yes, they *are* relevant.

First off, get something straight: No star player is going to lose his job in spring training, even if the rookie chasing him hits like the second coming of Teddy Baseball.

Don't pay so much attention to the established veterans with secure jobs. They have seen their share of springs. They know what work needs to be done to prepare themselves for the season. They won't care if they hit .200—and neither will the manager.

Strike Three

Stats are not always the defining factor in a player's spring, especially when talking about veterans. Playing time and a manager's quirks can tell you more about potential value.

Spring training is where roster questions are answered. Where jobs are won. Where the twenty-fifth roster slot is filled. If a team has a hole at shortstop, the manager will take two players and say, "the best man wins the job." Or sometimes every shortstop in the organization will get a shot.

Spring training is also the place where prospects get a good look from management. Young batters face the likes of Roger Clemens, Greg Maddux, Randy Johnson, and Pedro Martinez—pitchers with ungodly stuff not seen in Double-A. Likewise for rookie hurlers facing hitters like Mark McGwire, Sammy Sosa, and the rest.

This is the main reason that you should ignore extreme stats in spring training. Just because a young player has a great spring does not mean he will make the major league squad. There are so many minor league players in camp, rookies and veterans alike simply aren't facing a full-blown major league roster.

However, stats can telegraph other useful information, such as playing time. Who's getting all the at-bats at third base for the Cubs this spring? This might give you a clue to who will end up starting in April.

Hey, Trevor Hoffman hasn't had a save all spring—who's finishing games for the Padres? That guy might be the go-to closer should Hoffman get hurt. See what I mean? No one will displace Trevor Hoffman as closer just because of a great spring. But that pitcher finishing games in spring training could win a slot on the staff and be a factor later in the year.

Overheard in the Dugout

A great spring training story from '99 was pitcher Scott Williamson. The knock on him was that he was too young and too short. But he came into the Reds camp throwing 95 m.p.h. heat. He impressed management so much that he won a slot on the staff. He went on to be one of the most dominant relievers in the game, winning 12 and saving 19, and of course, grabbing the Rookie of the Year Award. Any fantasy owner paying attention to spring activity would have known all about this prime sleeper candidate. So keep your eyes open, kids, and stay in school.

Spring training is great for this kind of stuff. And playing time will tell you a lot about how a manager feels about his prospects and bench players. The guys who later become sleepers. The guys who can win you a fantasy championship.

Talking Double

Spring training also gives rise to the almighty daily press conference. Spewed forth will be whoopee superlatives, veiled threats, and vague injury updates. Who says managers aren't poets and politicians?

This is the stuff you read in the paper, the quotes that unfortunately you will be depending on for vital insights into the fates of players. Just remember that this is spring training—emphasis on *training*.

Guys are playing themselves into shape, and that goes for managers, too. Which means that when they talk about competition for a starting job or a slot on the pitching staff, they will be evasive until the day they actually make a decision. Until then, you have to read between the lines.

Here are some classic managerial *bon mots* and their literal interpretations:

➤ "He's pacing himself; it's a long season."

Don't worry, he'll play every day and put up good numbers just like he always does.

➤ "The kid has great stuff, but we've been working on his command and poise."

No way this wild hothead makes the staff this year.

➤ "The kid doesn't overpower you, but the command and poise are right there."

Book him a ticket north.

➤ "He has all the tools. Now all he has to do is put the pieces together."

Back to the minors for another year.

➤ "This guy will be a major leaguer for a long time."

He's not ready today … but he'll get the call later this season.

➤ "We need him to step up and be the player we all know he can be."

The starting job is his to lose … and he's losing it.

➤ "I'll know who's starting when I fill out the lineup card."

The competition is a dead heat. Stay tuned.

➤ "So-and-so is our guy. He's proven himself in every way."

Until he slumps, then he's gone.

How about injuries? Sure, if a player goes on the disabled list, he's hurt. But if not? These undefined injuries have a language all their own:

➤ "He's day to day."

He can play, he just doesn't want to.

➤ "He'll sit for a few days."

He'd play if the games counted.

➤ "We don't know if he'll go on the DL."

Could actually be hurt. Use caution.

➤ "He's experiencing normal spring soreness."

He's out of shape.

➤ "We've been working on his conditioning."

He's really out of shape.

➤ "He'll play his way into shape."

He toured Ben & Jerry's in the off-season. The whole off-season.

➤ "He's in the best shape of his career."

We can't believe he actually worked out over the winter—but we're happy about it.

And the list goes on and on. Just remember that a managerial endorsement doesn't go as far in spring training as it does in the regular season, when the games count.

In fact, spring training is a bit like Little League. The coaches are trying to get everyone into the game to see what they can do. You should do the same, with an emphasis on rookies. A strong spring could mean a mid-season call-up. Your vigilance should intensify as Opening Day approaches. The cuts will increase. The rosters will gel. Playing time and doublespeak will tell you more than ever.

The rest of your preparation depends on when you have scheduled your draft, which we'll discuss in the next chapter. For now, be content that you finally have all the tools necessary to prep for a draft. (The sound of raucous celebrating can be heard from the dungeon.)

There's just one last thing to say …

The Teacher Speech

Here's the kicker: I can't make you do the work. But the pragmatist in me always asks, "If you won't make the preparations necessary to win, why play?"

If you find yourself slacking, ask that same question. And be honest with yourself. I'm not saying you should go into this like a Navy SEAL and devote your life to it. But there is a good amount of effort required to be successful. Are you up to it?

Of course, you'll be burying yourself in paper. Outsiders won't understand. Employers will puzzle at your closed office door at lunch. Spouses will wonder why on earth their Yankees fan partner has to watch the White Sox-Twins game on ESPN.

Don't bother explaining. They won't get it.

If you love the game and are into the fantasy realm for the long haul, none of this will seem like work. In fact, it'll seem like you're paying yourself to watch baseball (if you're playing for money, that is). Who wouldn't want that?

Overheard in the Dugout

One guy at our '99 draft was clearly out of his element. He didn't know what he was doing, and it showed. Most of it was a lack of research and a general lack of preparation for the demands of the auction. He dropped out of the league after a couple months. So do the work, people. If not, you'll be in it up to here when it counts.

But if you decide to procrastinate, or skimp, or follow major league soccer instead, don't be surprised if your draft goes south quicker than the AARP in winter.

Do the work. It's worth it. You'll know what I mean when you hit the late rounds of your draft and snap up two or three players that no one else knows about. Or how about in July when the sleepers emerge, and the real payoff comes in the form of a cherished spot atop a league that you helped create?

Recommended viewing: *A League of Their Own.* Great baseball flick on the women's leagues during WW II. Tom Hanks sums up the game in a few brilliant words: "It's supposed to be hard. If it wasn't hard everyone would do it. The hard is what makes it great."

The Least You Need to Know

➤ Stats aren't the most important part of spring training.

➤ Playing time will tell you more about who might make the big club.

➤ Don't worry about slumping veterans in spring training—they'll be themselves when the games count.

➤ Read between the lines when a manager talks to the press—he's being evasive on purpose.

➤ Don't slack on draft prep now. You'll see the payoff later in the season when your team flourishes.

Chapter 8

The Day the Earth Stands Still: Your Draft

In This Chapter

➤ First you need the time, then the place

➤ Auction style or draft-pick style?

➤ Let the bidding begin!

➤ "Poker Face" is not an insult

➤ Alcohol and the art of fatigue

You won't sleep the night before Draft Day, but try. You'll need it, because Draft Day is a marathon. Like any marathon, it has moments of pure joy and utter heartbreak. You'll laugh 'til you cry. You'll sweat. You'll beg for potty breaks that won't come. All the while, you'll be shuffling papers and papers and papers that will be crumpled and smeared with so much ink you'll think a giant squid mugged you.

When it's over, you'll have a full roster. If you're successful, a good percentage of that roster will be players you wanted to get—and did get—at good prices.

But there's more. You'll have a handle on everyone else at the table. Even though you're competing, a certain amount of bonding will emerge. You'll all have gone through the ordeal together. And finally, once and for all, you'll understand what an amazing experience it is being in a fantasy baseball league.

When and Where

The first question is, when to have the draft? The next question is, where?

Hopefully the second question is already answered. Is the winter meeting site available? If not, find some other gullible, er, reliable schmuck to play host. Once again, a copious array of processed meat and cheese food is preferable. If it occurs in nature, you probably don't want it at your draft. Sometimes, food must be touched by many hands and machines before you eat it. It is the way of things.

Then there's the matter of beverages. Alcohol will no doubt be part of the proceedings, which is fine. But I will speak in more detail about the blessed fruit of the barrel a little later.

That leaves question one: When? The closer to Opening Day, the better. You'll know more about each major league team. Most of the sucker rookies will have cleared out of camp and the roster picture will be clearer.

Foul Tips

The closer to Opening Day you can have your draft, the better. You'll have more definite information available.

There Is No "Perfect Time"

The ideal timetable does not always exist, however. Don't be afraid to stage your draft earlier. You'll just have to update player values as best you can with the information at your disposal.

But what if you're late? What if you spotted this book on the shelf April 1st and have a group that's gung-ho to draft on April 15th (assuming you have your taxes done)? I say go for it.

Two weeks' worth of games will be in the can. That's okay. You'll also know who's playing where, and who's off to a hot start. That's okay, too. However, I recommend that you don't count any of those stats toward your league. Make stats official when your rosters are official.

Why? It's just a way to keep everyone honest. There will always be one owner who will try to stockpile players off to hot starts to be able to open the season in first place. As for you, you'll be tempted to pay more for a player off to a hot start, which you shouldn't do. All in all, the more level the playing field for the league, the better.

Foul Tips

If your league forms late, you can *still* have a draft. Just don't overpay for early season stats. Even if you draft in mid–April, you still have nearly six months of baseball ahead.

Tardiness Won't Kill You

The lateness issue brings up another question: Is it ever too late to have a draft? Technically, no. Online leagues exist that have mid-season drafts and second-half competition. There's nothing wrong with that. Also, most stat services allow you to tally numbers on a weekly basis, so you can almost start a league anytime.

The main drawback of being late is the effect on player values. Sleepers will have already awakened. Stars will have already gotten hurt or slumped. And what you bid on a player in June is not what you would have bid on him in March.

But this is fantasy baseball, kids. You can do whatever you want. Just be mindful of the differences and you should be okay.

Strike Three

It's never too late to have a draft. But the prep work will be different—don't use pre-season player values.

Overheard in the Dugout

Our league stages its draft in the first week of March. I don't necessarily recommend this timetable, however. It's unusual. Spring training has barely begun. So much can happen to your roster before Opening Day. But that's the way we like it. We're masochists.

A Marathon You Can't Train For

The human factor will once again rear it's ugly (look in the mirror) head on Draft Day. Put simply, it's a long day.

Our league's '99 draft lasted a good eight hours. That's a 12-team, NL-only auction draft, five-player reserve draft, and eight-player minor league draft. That's 432 players total. We moved it along pretty well, too. So if this is your first draft, be prepared for the long haul.

Naturally, the fewer teams you have, the shorter your day will be. But if you have more than 10 teams, be prepared to settle in for the long haul. Personally, eight hours is a nice length. By the end of the day, I wish it would last longer. You have only one

Draft Day a year (unless you're in more than one league) and if you're into the game like I am, you wish it would last longer.

Savor every moment. It's intense. Stay involved. Watch your fellow owners. Feed off their hunger. Let them feed off yours. Keep your blood sugar elevated with food and drink. As for your bladder, void except where prohibited. (Everyone else will have to go, too—use that to your advantage.)

Foul Tips

If necessary, you can spread out your draft over two days. Make a weekend of it. However, this can put a damper on momentum and make it more difficult to get everyone together in one place.

And if you can't have the house for a long day, spread your draft out over two days. It's possible, but try to make the days back to back on a weekend. If you do something like consecutive Saturdays, you'll no doubt run into problems. Something could happen on the spring training front to skew player values. Or, even more common, one guy won't be able to make it.

Trust me, there's nothing more frustrating than having a half-drafted league with one guy missing. And it *will* happen. It's March, after all. Gutters have to be cleaned. Lawns have to be thatched. Real life has to be lived.

So get it done in one day. Your family needs you.

What's Your Style?

Now your league needs to decide what style of draft you're going to have. There are two choices: *auction-style draft,* which we've been taking about all along, and *draft-pick-style draft,* which is simpler and quicker.

Trash Talk

In an **auction-style draft,** owners bid on players in $1 increments. Players go to the highest bidder. In a **draft-pick-style draft,** owners select players one by one in turn until rosters are full. This is a simpler and quicker draft style.

Buying the Farm (at Auction)

Auction-style draft you know about. It's the whole reason for establishing player values in dollars. I'm a fan of auction-style draft. It makes Draft Day one of the most important parts of your season. You build the foundation of your team by competing against your fellow owners for players.

It's a rush. It's a game in itself. To me, it's one of the most gratifying (and frustrating) aspects of fantasy baseball. Highly, highly, highly recommended.

But we should talk about draft-pick style since there are a number of leagues out there that do it.

Picking the Litter

Draft-pick-style draft doesn't strengthen team competition in the way that auction-style does. You establish a pecking order and you go down the line, selecting players one by one until everyone's roster is full. Clean and simple. Like any alternative style, there are advantages and disadvantages. Here are a few—and they could be either one depending on your point of view:

➤ **No dollar values for players.** Your draft prep will be much quicker.

➤ **No bidding wars.** Your draft will fly.

➤ **Simpler rules.** Gone are salary caps, free-agent salaries, and anything else financial in nature. Your treasurer will have limited duties if you play for money. If you don't, you won't need a treasurer.

This is not to say that you don't have to prepare for the draft if you choose to go with draft-pick style. You do. But when it's your turn to pick, your job is to nab the very best player available. Who will that be? Tough call, depending on what you need. But if you've already picked Mark McGwire and Albert Belle, I'd snag pitching or some speed before it's gone.

Monitoring the Trendsetters

Another useful strategy—and this goes for auction style as well—is to go against the league trend. If five straight owners select a power hitter, you should pick speed. Or if seven straight owners pick pitching, snag a power guy. Why? Well, everyone will be looking at the power numbers to see what's left, thinking, "Oh my God, am I gonna get shut out of the category?"

Meanwhile, you're picking prime players from other categories. You might catch owners looking the other way and get someone great—who you can later trade for the power you missed out on earlier.

That's the gist of draft-pick style. From here on in we'll talk about auction style, but even if you opt for the former, you should still read on. There are many strategies that apply to both styles—and everyone needs a helper now and then.

Onward.

Let the Bidding Begin!

It's time. The food's out, the keg's tapped, and the boys are ready to rumble. All you have to do now is throw out the first name. Who gets that honor is up to you. You can have the Commish do it, or the host, or the dog, if it can speak.

When that name is called, be prepared for a gusher of bids. Everybody will throw one. Don't be shy. If he's a player you want, fight for him. Just don't overbid.

The opening rounds of an auction are the most dangerous. Everyone has a ton of money to spend. The names being tossed out are the biggest in the game. Even if your strategy doesn't call for them, you'll wonder how you'll ever live without Maddux, McGwire, Sosa, and the others.

You'll live just fine—trust me. Stick to your plan. The best you can expect in the opening rounds is a "fair" price for the superstars. No one will let a stud go for less than his perceived value. There's too much money at the table for that. Judge just how fair those prices are and don't go nuts. You have a long way to go.

How to Spend the Money

You've got $260 (or some denomination of that number) burning a hole in your budget. Like any pile of money, it won't take long to spend. So your plan has to be firm—but not cast in stone. You'll need the flexibility to jump on an underbid player, but you also need to have a few bucks left so you're not shut out of the late rounds. Remember, you must keep at least $1 for every open slot on your roster. You can't bid less than $1.

How do you decide on a budget? There are many ways. You can try formulas, but they tend to box you in. You should definitely remember that while hitting and pitching are evenly divided into scoring categories, they should not be sliced 50/50 in your budget.

Think about it: You have three more batters on your roster than you do pitchers. The actual breakdown of a $260 budget is $11.30 per player (260 divided by 23). That's $113 for 10 pitchers. Which leaves you $147 to spend on batters. Not quite 50/50, is it?

> **Strike Three**
>
> Remember, it's a marathon. You can't win a race in the first mile, so don't spend three fourths of your money in the opening rounds. Be cool.

> **Foul Tips**
>
> Think of every player as an investment. How much of a risk are you willing to take?

I'm not going to sit here like an oracle and tell you you're stupid for spending more than $113 on pitching. You can do whatever you want, but there are historic trends that you should consider before blowing the wad on hurlers.

Veteran hitters are more likely to post their usual career numbers in any given season than are veteran pitchers. Pitchers can go south at any time. I could give you a list of names as long as my arm. Hitters, however, can have a bad first half and still put up good numbers. This is a hitting era, not a pitching era. The bottom line is that hitters are historically more dependable than pitchers. Spending money on a player is an investment. What's your risk threshold?

Overheard in the Dugout

I'm a notorious pitcher lover. I pride myself on assembling stellar pitching staffs for decent prices. Which means I will spend a little more on pitching on Draft Day to nail down the hurlers I think will blossom that year. Not many owners do that. You need to figure out what makes you comfortable. For only you know what you'll pay for a player.

Once you arrive at a credible budget, remember one last thing: flexibility. A big part of an auction draft is improvising, adapting, and overcoming. If a good pitcher at a good price is staring you in the face, by God, grab him. Your goal is not to stay within a strict pitching/hitting budget. It's to assemble a kick-ass team.

The Art of Poker

Do you know what a *tell* is? It's a poker term. It means something a player does to tip his hand. Supposedly every poker player shows his intentions, no matter how subtle.

It's the same thing in an auction draft. You can't tip your hand. You can't let the other owners know how bad you're jonesing for a certain player. A big mistake is thinking your auction draft has something to do with baseball. It doesn't. Ballplayers are just cards. A bid is a bet.

Etch Your Face in Stone

How you react—your face, your voice, or your body—will tell a shrewd owner what you're thinking. Which is the kiss of death.

➤ **Keep your tone even. No shrieks, squeals, groans, or wails.**

➤ **Don't get excited.** Stare your opponent down: He might give something away.

➤ **Don't tip your own hand too early.** A sharp owner will know when you're serious about a player, because he'll be serious, too.

Trash Talk

A **tell** is an unconscious action that gives away what cards a poker player is holding. Or what a fantasy owner is planning to do.

Eventually, the bidding will come down to two owners. That's when it gets intense. Who's willing to go up another buck? Will he, or won't he? Maybe you'll get him to bite. Maybe you'll get stuck with the player. You need to be willing to withstand either result.

A suicidal move would be to get involved in a bidup war when you can't afford it. Remember, there are other owners at the table who will execute their own bidup moves on other owners. Don't think it's your responsibility to make sure every owner overpays for every player. You'll get a reputation for bidups and eventually they'll backfire.

Overheard in the Dugout

Some guys hold their cards better than others. One guy in our '99 draft had one of the worst poker faces I've ever seen. Someone would bid him up a buck. He'd curse and slam the table ... then raise his bid. Of course we bid him up another buck. And he'd curse again. No one at the table acknowledged his actions—all of us knew we had this guy over a barrel. Needless to say, he didn't do well.

Be Fonzie

Some of the most compelling, suspenseful, and tense bidding wars of the day may not include you. Enjoy them and learn from them.

➤ **Always pay attention to what's happening.** Respond to it. Provoke responses. Make owners wonder what the heck you're thinking. "Why's he bidding on that guy? Is he serious? Does he really want so-and-Sosa on his squad?"

➤ **Don't be tentative.** Don't hesitate. Every bid you make should at least *seem* like it was the cool thing to do. If you make a mistake—and you will—don't acknowledge it. Let the others know that you don't know what they know.

➤ **Whatever personality you decide to split into, keep it consistent.** If you're Hawkeye Pierce, continue to crack wise throughout any bidding war. If you suddenly clam up, everyone will know you're serious about a certain player. In fact, use it as a ploy to make them think you're serious.

Some of this goes to the role-playing aspect of fantasy baseball. Don't be foolish: Your friends will know if you're putting them on. But they'll understand a game face. It's all subterfuge.

Overheard in the Dugout

I like to bid on every single player at least once. It keeps me alert and quickly drives up the price to a respectable level. But I'm not reckless. You'll know when owners are getting serious about the bidding. If you're not, that's when it's time to let them do their work. If you don't, you could end up with a player you don't want.

If all this nonsense makes you uncomfortable, or if playing poker just isn't your bag, baby, don't worry. Just be yourself. You'll be reading guys' faces without even knowing it. And if you act like your normal self? Guys won't be reading your face because there won't be anything unusual to read.

Bid smart and watch your little garden grow.

Keeping the Pace

As your marathon progresses, take frequent breaks—at least every hour. Use the time to establish how much money everyone has left. Every owner worth his salt should be keeping track himself, but you need to make sure that everyone's math is right. If you don't, arguments will break out when owners claim to have more money than they actually do.

Use these breaks to stretch and shake out the cobwebs. Your mind is working overtime today—let it stretch, too. Also use the breaks to keep your paperwork organized. This is crucial because the draft will move quickly. You may miss something.

Remember that your draft isn't just about filling your roster. You need to juggle information so you're always up-to-date. Here's a list of key things you need to constantly update:

Foul Tips

Use break time to tally everyone's remaining money and to keep your own paperwork organized.

1. Opponents' remaining cash
2. Opponents' remaining roster slots
3. Players still available by position

This is imperative. If you're halfway through the draft and one owner hasn't bought any middle infielders yet, you know it's coming. When it does, you'll be able to bid him up because he has to buy *someone*. And if he's low on cash to boot? You can price him out of the last decent player at the position (assuming you have room on your roster, that is).

This is meat-'n'-potatoes draft strategy. If you don't keep tabs on your opponents, you won't be able to utilize even the most basic power games.

Is it too much to think about? A helping hand may be just what you need. There's nothing wrong with having a teammate or assistant. One of you can be in charge of acquisition, the other can handle numbers. Just make sure you can coexist with this person. Brawling at the table with a teammate is a sure sign of strategic breakdown. Try to avoid it.

Personally, I will never, ever have an assistant. First off, I'm a control freak. Second, I don't need someone whispering in my ear telling me to bid on Uggie Urbina when I know darn well that I planned to do it in the first place. But that's just me. A teammate might be just the thing to put you over the top ... or over the edge.

Foul Tips

Does your league allow you to have a draft assistant or teammate? A helper could be invaluable.

The Waiting Game

If you've been smart and calm and patient, you should have plenty of money left in the late rounds of your draft to get just about any player thrown out there. It's okay to have money left over when your roster is full—but not too much money. A buck or two at most. Remember, you won't get change.

Overheard in the Dugout

Back in '98, I ruined my season on Draft Day. I played it so coyly that I found myself with $24 left in the final rounds. $24! Almost 10% of my total draft budget! It was a huge mistake. By the time I realized how much I had left, there was nothing I could do about it. All that remained were $1 scrubs. It was a long road to recovery. I ended up placing third for the season—not bad considering how stupid I was. It's a mistake I will never make again.

But what happens if you overspent? You need to figure something out, and quick. Let's pretend ….

You've had a pretty good day. You nailed down a baker's dozen of players you really wanted, and you got them all at value or lower. And the other players you landed aren't too awful. Might even make decent trade bait later. But you did overspend on pitching. Which means you have a problem.

You have $3 left. And you have three slots to fill: a pitcher, a utility man, and—big ouch—a third baseman. The math is as simple as it's been all day. Three bucks. Three players. You're out of the bidding because you have nothing to bid. All you can do is wait for your turn to call out a player's name. If someone decides to go to $2, you lose. So what do you do?

Play the waiting game. Throw out players that you know will be bid up. Don't kid yourself that you'll get them. You won't. The key to the waiting game is getting the rest of the league to fill their rosters. And I mean completely fill them. They will be done and you'll be sitting there with your three slots and three bucks like a doofus.

But you aren't a doofus. You're Captain Kirk. What you have effectively done is take a draft disaster—a no-win situation—and made it an advantage. You now have the equivalent of three extra reserve picks. How's that? Well, everyone's rosters are full. You actually get to pick your last three players. Name them and they're yours. No bidups. No arguments. No prisoners.

I won't lie to you: The pickings may be thin. But as you'll see in the next chapter, the reserve draft always produces at best, sleepers, and at worst, useful talent. You now get the first three picks for a buck and no one can do anything about it.

So who do you pick? This situation actually happened to me in the '99 draft. I'll tell you exactly how I handled it in Chapter 10, "Nothing Like the Real Thing: Zim's Draft, 1999." For now, I'll just say pick the best players available (duh). That's a bit of a copout, but think about it. You can pick anyone you want. A promising platoon third baseman. A stud rookie getting a shot to start. Or the best set-up reliever in the game. And maybe, just maybe, you'll throw out a prime *crickets pick*, which means that when a player's name is called, no one responds—all you hear is crickets. But after a few seconds of shock, the other owners realize that you snagged a great prospect, or an overlooked starter, or a potential sleeper. Then the cursing begins.

In the past few years, our league has seen its share of great crickets picks: Andruw Jones in '97; Bobby Abreu in '98; John Rocker and Damian Jackson in '99. All of them went for a buck. They're a real

Trash Talk

An owner throws out a **crickets pick** when the name in question elicits total silence from the other owners—all you hear are the crickets chirping—followed by cursing if the player is any good.

coup if you can snag one. However, if the silence continues—and the crickets don't stop chirping—you may have a useless player on your hands. But hey, them's the breaks, kid.

Strike Three

Seven words: Too much booze can hurt your draft. Preaching the evils of alcohol would be condescending and useless. But what I can preach is fatigue management. This doesn't just mean monitoring the effects of alcohol. This includes the mental wear and tear (boozing or not) you endure sitting in the same room for eight hours.

Drunks Are Funny ... on TV

It's time to talk about human nature again. As anyone who has ever built a beer-can pyramid knows, if you combine extended mental activity and booze, you get fatigue. You also get goofiness, slurring, frequent bathroom breaks, and violence. Depends on the person, you see. Beer's fine at a draft. In fact, if our league didn't have a half-barrel on hand, no one would show up. I believe it with all my liver.

Fatigue is unavoidable. Caffeine can help, but drinking six cups of coffee can be just as damaging as six cups of beer. (And you'll hit the head just as often.) Quite frankly, I'd rather get drunk than have a caffeine crash. You'll go nuts sitting in one place.

Nicotine is a similar option. How much can one person smoke in an eight-hour period? Make sure you bring your electronic voice box so the rest of the guys can hear your bids. The same goes for dip and chaw. If your lower lip falls off, you'll lose your bilabial fricatives. A bid might be misinterpreted, which is bad.

Overheard in the Dugout

Our draft generally begins at nine in the morning on a Saturday. A few guys always tap the keg before they sit down. Starting a beer I.V. this early in the morning is fine for some. I can proudly say that we have never had an alcohol-related behavior problem at our drafts. But only you know your booze threshold. Don't be an idiot and ruin everyone else's time by passing out at noon. You'll wake up feeling awful ... and probably tied naked to train tracks with the words "I'm a Bad Boy" painted on your chest. Consider yourself warned.

Obviously, the best route is to remain chemical free. Your head is clear and the only time your heart will race is when Salma Hayek's name is mentioned.

You may ask what I do to stay awake? Well, I don't need anything to stay awake. I love the game and the draft too much. In fact, I usually find myself wishing it would last longer.

But I do booze. Draft Day is a personal holiday, after all. I hit the keg a little after noon so's not to confuse the sun and my personal yardarm too much. I also bust out two big stogies as the day progresses. These are my vices. I don't recommend them, but you're not me and I'm not you and we're probably both very happy about that. How's that for good advice?

Recommended viewing: A good movie to watch the night before your draft? Not *Major League,* not *Bull Durham. Rounders.* Say what? *Rounders* is a great poker movie, and an auction draft has more to do with poker than with baseball. Throw in a viewing of *The Sting,* too. To have a good draft, you have to become a con man, a scoundrel, a rat. Well, maybe not to have a good draft, but a fun one.

Foul Tips

Use common sense: If you find that booze or caffeine is affecting your judgment (and no matter how deep the denial, you *will* know), slow down. Duh.

The Least You Need to Know

➤ The closer your draft is to Opening Day, the better.

➤ Be prepared: A 12-team draft will last an entire day.

➤ A draft-pick-style draft always goes faster and requires less preparation than an auction-style draft.

➤ Don't overspend in the early rounds.

➤ Always keep some cash for the late rounds—but not *too* much.

➤ Alcohol, caffeine, and nicotine are great fun, but overindulgence will hurt your draft picks.

Chapter 9

It Ain't over Yet: The Supplemental Drafts

—HUH?

In This Chapter

➤ Reserve energy for the reserve draft

➤ The talent pool runs deep

➤ You'll be happy you did the extra work

➤ Nothing minor about the minor league draft

Are you happy? Did your auction draft go as planned? I hope so. Because they usually don't. Everyone makes mistakes. Everyone deviates from his plan. Everyone ends up cursing and kicking things. It's okay. It's *natural*.

If you did well, you should have a respectable starting roster. Emphasis on *starting*. Why do I say that? As the season wears on, your roster will change. With injuries, trade offers, and other enticements, it's impossible to keep your Draft Day roster intact. I don't know anyone who can.

Which is why this chapter is perhaps more important than the previous Draft Day chapters. Your supplemental drafts can determine the success or failure of your team—for now and for the future. I'm talking about the reserve draft and the minor league draft. It is within the confines of these events where you shall find salvation ... or shinola.

The Reserve Draft

The *reserve draft* is a straight-pick system where each team selects a certain number of players in successive rounds to use as reserves for the upcoming season. In our rules, reserve picks have a salary of $5, which counts toward the salary cap. How many reserves you pick and what you pay for them is up to your league.

Our league picks five reserves. We allow a maximum of 13 reserves on our rosters at any given time during the regular season. You can tweak this number if you like, but

Trash Talk

The **reserve draft** allows owners to select a certain number (depending on your rules) of supplemental players as reserves for the upcoming season.

our system works well (for us). It's a pretty simple event. Everyone picks a player for as many rounds as it takes. The biggest hurdle you'll encounter is determining who picks first.

If your league is in its debut year, keep it simple: Draw numbers. However, if you're in an ongoing league, I suggest allowing the last place team to pick first, just like in the majors. Losing is bad enough—why punish the poor fool more than you have to?

This draft really moves. Once the picking commences, you'll have to think fast. Who do you pick? What do you need? Who's left? If you've done your pre-draft homework, these questions shouldn't be too hard to answer.

Depth, Depth, Depth

Foul Tips

In my league's rules, a player taken in the reserve draft has a salary of $5, which counts toward the salary cap.

That's the key word here: *depth*. Every team needs it. Look at the '99 Atlanta Braves. They lost Andres Galarraga, Kerry Ligtenberg, and Javy Lopez to season-ending injuries. Think about that: Their leading run producer, their closer, and their starting catcher. This would send most teams reeling. But the Braves won more than a hundred games and made the postseason for, like, the 50th consecutive year.

Why? *Depth*. They made no major trades. But the moves they did make brought them *more depth*. That is the sole purpose of the reserve draft.

A lot of guys reach this stage of the game, take a gander at the remaining players, and say, "You gotta be kidding. I hav'ta pick from this slush? Fuggetaboutit!" Well, my loquacious friend, as they say back on the farm, that's a load of weak fertilizer. There's *always* talent available. You just have to refine your thinking.

Picking the Litter, Part 2

Who exactly should you target in the reserve draft? Logic would suggest you take the best player available at any given time. But that may be oversimplifying things. See, in the reserve draft, you can pick any player, anywhere on the planet.

If you happen to be in a NL-only league, what about AL players? And vice versa? Trade rumors fly 24-hours a day. Good players are always on the verge of switching leagues. Why not take a flyer and pick one?

How about minor leaguers who you think will make the jump to the majors this year? This is a good way to get them cheaply in a deep league (and a good way to get a jump on the minor league draft). This is also a good way to tick off your fellow owners who wanted to draft minor leaguers in the minor league draft. You'll know when you pick one of these prized players. Everyone will curse at you. (Incidentally, the more times fellow owners curse at you on Draft Day, the better. It means you're doing your job.)

But be careful: This game has very specific rules about minor league rosters. If you pick a minor leaguer in the reserve draft, he is no longer eligible to be on a minor league roster. If you want to carry him over next year, you'll have to use a keeper slot. (See the next section on the minor league draft for more details.)

Foul Tips

The main purpose of the reserve draft is to achieve roster depth, finding players who will be productive and help you as the season progresses. Don't blow off this draft. If you pick without thinking, or simply don't prepare enough to know who to pick, you'll be wasting a draft that could mean the difference between contending and stinking.

Targets of Opportunity

Some good reserve draft targets are …

➤ Any position starter still available.

➤ Part-timers with a history of good production, or those playing behind injury-prone starters. They'll see a lot of action.

➤ Minor leaguers who will make the big club.

➤ *Swing men*—pitchers who will get some spot starts if another starter gets hurt. These guys can be incredibly valuable, especially the ones on playoff-caliber teams.

Trash Talk

Swing men are pitchers who can start or relieve. They can be incredibly good—and cheap—fantasy players.

➤ Set-up men—pitchers who usually set up the closers. These are also the guys who'll end up closing games if the closer gets hurt or stinks.

➤ Injured stars who might make a comeback this year. Or, if you're patient, you'll have a cheap star keeper for next season. (Andres Galarraga was a good example of this in our '99 reserve draft.)

As you can see, there are many reserve options even in a very deep league. The risk factor may be a little higher, but so is the reward when they blossom (talk about feeling like a genius). To prove I'm not full of it, here are some of the gems found in our '99 reserve draft, in descending order of selection:

Position	Player/Team	Key Stats
OF	Preston Wilson, Florida	(.280, 26 HR)
SS	Rey Ordonez, N.Y. Mets	(.258, 60 RBI)
SP	Rick Ankiel, St. Louis	(3.27 ERA, one hot prospect)
RP	Antonio Alfonseca, Florida	(21 saves)
OF	Jeffrey Hammonds, Cincinnati	(.279, 17 HR)
RP	Mike Remlinger, Atlanta	(10 wins, 2.37 ERA)
SP	Randy Wolf, Philadelphia	(116 Ks in 121 IP, a good prospect)
SP	Steve Parris, Cincinnati	(11-4, 3.50 ERA)
SP	Octavio Dotel, N.Y. Mets	(8-3, 85 Ks in 85 IP)
OF	Alex Ochoa, Milwaukee	(.300, 8 HR)
RP	Mike Williams, Pittsburgh	(23 saves)
RP	Dennis Cook, N.Y. Mets	(10 wins, 3 saves)
C	Eddie Perez, Atlanta	(.249, 7 HR)

Don't know them? Look up their complete '99 stats and see what I mean. Sure, none of them put up Ruthian numbers, but each and every one of them was a solid fantasy contributor in '99. At $5 each, Wilson, Ankiel, Alfonseca, Wolf, Parris, and Dotel are all arguable keepers. You can't do better than that in a deep league.

Baiting the Hook

Another use for reserve picks is trade bait. Our league allows the swapping of reserve picks, first round through fifth, at any time before the trading deadline.

Reserve picks are perfect as throw-ins when a deal is close, but not quite there. They are also great trade fodder late in the season when your team is out of it. Imagine what a contender would give you for an overpriced superstud you no longer need. If you plan to keep your league going next year, never stop planning for the following draft—even during the current one.

Never undervalue your reserve picks. Trading for them is always a good idea, especially if you acquire more than your allotted five picks. Remember, in these rules, we allow up to 13 reserves on the roster. Which means your reserve draft the following year can be pretty juicy. On the other hand, if you trade all your picks, you'll feel like a gunfighter who's suddenly out of bullets. So be careful. Try to find a nice balance (that word again!).

It's imperative that you take your reserve draft seriously. At it's best, it can bring you a potential superstar. On average, you'll get a useful fill-in. And at worst? You waive a guy. It's no big loss. But the gain can be bigger than you can possibly imagine—like, championship big. Think about that.

Foul Tips

Reserve picks make great trade bait in ongoing keeper leagues. But always be sure to keep some for next year.

Overheard in the Dugout

Back in '98, one owner traded for so many '99 reserve picks that he maxed out his reserve roster at 13 on Draft Day—all of them in the first two rounds. Seemed like every trade he made included a reserve pick as a throw-in. At the draft, he loaded up on outfielders. This gave him a ton of trade bait to work with. It was a good strategy, but in the end he fell out of the money for lack of pitching. Happens to the best of us.

The Minor League Draft

The *minor league draft* is similar to the reserve draft in that it's a straight-pick system. But the function is totally different.

The minor league draft is designed for ongoing keeper leagues. For me, maintaining the nucleus of a team from year to year is one of the most fun aspects of fantasy baseball. You truly get the flavor of what it might be like to run a real team. Minor leaguers add to that since you can draft any minor league player at any level (rookie league, Single-, Double-, and Triple-A). You can pick a super-hyped 23-year-old about to debut with the Yankees. Or you can pick a 16-year-old Dominican pitcher who was just assigned to rookie league by the Royals.

You're building your own farm system. If you're in the league for the long haul, so much the better. You can pick lower level prospects and watch them develop over the years. One day—with some luck—you'll promote them into productive roles on your active roster.

However, by its very nature, the minor league draft must have more specific—and stricter—rules than the reserve draft. The reserve draft allows you to draft virtually anyone you want. You could draft your mother, even if her fastball isn't what it used to be. But the minor league draft is just that: A draft for minor leaguers.

Here are the key rules and regs regarding minor leaguers in our league. Again, you can tweak them if you want, but we've worked long and hard on them and they work. I suggest you use them, too:

➤ No player is eligible for the minor league draft or the minor league roster if he appeared on anyone's active fantasy roster at any other time (a moot point in start-up leagues).

➤ Minor league salaries are $5—and you pay for them—but they do not count toward the salary cap. This last part was added to our rules to eliminate the risk of having to waive minor leaguers to stay under the salary cap. By removing them from the equation, we could keep them longer. (After all, you don't see major league teams dumping minor leaguers to shed payroll.)

➤ Minor leaguers may be carried on the minor league roster from year to year without having to use a keeper slot.

➤ Unlike reserve picks, minor league picks cannot be traded. Thing is, you'll never know how many picks you actually have until you declare your keepers next year. If you keep six minor leaguers, you'll have two picks left. If you keep three, you'll have five picks, and so on. If you allow trading of minor league picks, someone will eventually trade a pick that they don't have. Trust me, it almost happened in our league.

These are the biggies. I'll talk more about specific rules governing minor leaguers in later chapters. There's more to know about eligibility and promotions. For now, however, you're solid. Draft away.

Overheard in the Dugout

We removed minor leaguers from the salary cap in the '98 off-season. The sole reason for this was so owners wouldn't have to resort to waiving minor leaguers when they got crunched by the cap. I got wickedly crunched in my '98 bid for the money, and had to waive minor league second baseman Marlon Anderson. He's now a promising young in-fielder for the Phillies, which really sticks it in and breaks it off, if you ask me. But at least it won't happen again.

The Now vs. Later Debate

Our league has worked long and hard studying the minor league roster, draft, and the rules that govern them. Our debates had one common thread: Is the function of a minor league roster to be a secondary reserve roster—a place to stockpile help for this immediate season—or is it a bank account where prime prospects can be more easily protected and kept from year to year?

The debate still rages. If you consider the secondary reserve roster theory, then minor leaguers are drafted to be promoted. Pure and simple. You want guys who will help you this year, period. If you go the bank account route, then you want to keep your minor leaguers beyond one season. This encourages owners to draft from the lower-level minors as well as from the ripe prospects.

What do you think: promote them now or later? If you stick to the rules as our league plays them (see Appendix A, "A Sample Rulebook"), you'll find that they definitely lean toward the latter argument. We like to draft for the future. We like to keep our youngsters. So we wrote rules that make it easier for us to do so. If you want to play for now, draft players who you think will not just eventually get promoted to the Bigs this season, but those who will actually make an effective fantasy contribution.

Check out some of our league's minor league picks who went on to help out in the '99 season, in descending order of selection:

SP	Odalis Perez, Atlanta (6 wins before serious elbow injury)
RP	Kevin McGlinchy, Atlanta (7 wins, 2.82 ERA)
C	Ramon Castro, Florida (.179, but the C of the future)
RP	Jason Isringhausen, N.Y. Mets/Oakland (8 saves, the A's future closer)

RP	Guillermo Mota, Montreal (2.93 ERA)
RP	Mike Judd, Los Angeles (3 wins, a promising starter)
SP	Kyle Farnsworth, Chicago (5 wins, a promising starter)
2B	Joe McEwing, St. Louis (.275, 9 HR, utility man supreme)

None of them shook the pillars of heaven, mind you, but all showed flashes of promise. Sometimes that's all you can expect from rookies.

As I've said endlessly, you can do whatever you want. But if you're starting a league from scratch, you may not be too concerned about the future. Running a debut league is hard enough without having to strategize for three years down the pike. Make it easier on yourself and your fellow owners. Do whatever feels most comfortable. Let the rest of the cookies crumble where they may.

Prospect Potluck

The reserve and minor league drafts are where all your extra research pays off big time. You'll know exactly who is left and who is a potential gem. But you gotta know the plain truth: Prospects are a long shot. In a deep league, if you draft eight minor leaguers, consider yourself blessed (or just plain good) if more than two or three of them turn out to be somebody.

Don't get too upset if they don't pan out. And don't get too impatient, either. Sometimes it takes a while for a guy to blossom. If you promote a big-hype prospect who turns out to be a no-frills rookie flop, don't waive him. Don't trade him. Just stow him away on your reserve roster for a while. It's a long season and he may just surprise you.

Strike Three

Predicting which prospects will blossom is one of the hardest things in fantasy baseball—let alone real baseball. Don't be frustrated when your minor league picks fizzle. In fact, expect it. It saves on the heartbreak.

A recent example of this is White Sox first baseman Paul Konerko. In 1997, he was a major smash in Triple-A for the Dodgers. You couldn't hype a young man any harder. He was a future triple-crown threat—and '98 was the year! Well, two seasons, three positions, three teams, and about seven trips back and forth to Triple-A, Konerko landed with the White Sox. Just about every fantasy owner who drafted him had flown the coop. But in '99, it happened. He found a team who let him play every day, no matter what the consequences. Konerko calmed down. And he hit to the tune of .294 with 24 HR and 81 RBI. That's just the beginning for him. He's not yet 25. And some patient, good-hearted fantasy owner out there hung on to Paul—and is reaping the wheat, boy. Don't you wish it were you?

That street runs two ways, too. If you see a fellow owner cursing his rookie's good pedigree and bad stats, offer to take the player off his hands. You'll get him cheap and he could turn into the bargain of the year. Or at least the week.

Professional baseball scouts are not idiots. They don't pull punches when evaluating talent. Their general manager needs to know the bottom line: Can the kid play? When scouts go wild for a player, the hype rolls in like a tidal wave. And many times these super-duper players fall flat on their Nike swooshes. Does that mean that all the scouts were wrong? Not bloody likely. The talent is no doubt still there, even if it needs marinating. These fallen angels are low-cost—and therefore low-risk—investments that can pay off with a little patience.

Remember that. Take advantage of your fellow owners' disgust and anger. Because they're your buddies and they'd do the same for you.

Recommended viewing: *The Bad News Bears.* Perhaps the finest baseball film ever made, not because of what the kids do, but because of how the beer-swilling, curse-slurring grown-ups channel their aggression through the kids. Plus, it's darn funny.

Strike Three

If your fellow owner is getting impatient with a slow-developing prospect, offer to take the lad off his hands. Cheap. It could pay off big later.

The Least You Need to Know

➤ Use the reserve draft to establish roster depth.

➤ Go for part-timers who produce, swing men, set-up men, and injured stars who might make a comeback.

➤ A good reserve draft can make or break your season. Take it seriously.

➤ When drafting minor leaguers, you need to decide if you want players who will emerge this year, or in years to come.

➤ Don't be impatient with prospects. Sometimes they need time to blossom.

Chapter 10

Nothing Like the Real Thing: Zim's Draft, 1999

In This Chapter

➤ The benefit of hindsight

➤ Improvise, adapt, overcome

➤ My triumphs

➤ My tragedies

Most men like to tell stories. Fish stories, girl stories, hunting stories, and of course, sports stories. They are rarely true and always enhanced. With time, the three steps you fell down after four beers turn into three flights after 14 beers. "Didn't even cry, man." Okay, tough guy.

This, however, is a story worth telling. And worth hearing. It's the story of my '99 draft. Why is it worthwhile? Because it was far from perfect. I made some stupid mistakes that should have been avoided. But I also pulled a few rabbits out of my hat. Hopefully, I can give you a feel of what a draft is like.

I'd classify my draft as mildly successful. My best moves came later in the season on the trade front. We'll talk about them later. But for now, I think it would be useful for you to see how I handled my draft strategy, my bidding, and my supplemental picks.

Nothing like anecdotal evidence to prove a point. But don't think that I'm going to sugarcoat my mistakes. I'm as upset about them as anyone, but it serves no purpose to cover them up or ignore them. You'll hear it all.

The Big Day

I hacked my way across two states to find my destination: my hometown of Orwigsburg, Pennsylvania. Yeah, I know. Sounds like a bug. Most of the group met at Bob's Restaurant on Route 61. If you're ever there, have the toast. It's the best in the county.

After the usual early morning banter, we were off to our friend Scott's house. Scott and I have known each other for a good dozen years now, maybe more. We know things about each other that only good friends would know. Like what happened to him when he went to see the movie *The Abyss*. And what happened to me that night at the campground when we helped some people kick their keg of Genessee. Stuff like that.

Scott has been man enough to host our draft for the past two years. His living room is perfect for it. Just the right size so you aren't looking over each other's shoulders, but not so big that you have to screech your bids. The best feature? A bathroom less than five feet away (you can hear everything people say about you when you leave the room).

By nine in the morning, everyone was seated. The keg of Yuengling lager was indeed tapped, as were the coffee pot, the doughnut box, and the ring bologna link.

As Commish, I'm supposed to get the ball rolling, so I formally announce that our draft is underway. I turn the tables over to last season's champ, Jim, owner of the Gods. It's his privilege to throw out the first name up for bids on "The Price Ain't Right." That name? Mr. Greg Maddux.

Strike Three

Your war room shouldn't be so small that everyone is rubbing elbows. Remember, people like to look over each other's shoulders. Make sure you have some personal space.

My Keepers

As I'm sure you recall, our league is a 12-team, NL-only, 5 × 5 affair with a reserve and minor league draft after the auction. We're also a keeper league, with each owner allowed to carry over six players from the previous season.

The keepers were announced two weeks earlier, so owners would have a chance to cross them off their draft sheets and adjust the values of the remaining players. I hated that. Why? No suspense. I proposed a change to that rule during the winter so each owner could announce their keepers on Draft Day, just before the auction. To me, that would have added drama and last-minute value shuffling. Real think-by-the-seat-of-your-pants stuff. Alas, it didn't fly. The keepers were announced early, like always.

Foul Tips

If you are in a keeper league, when do you announce your keepers? My ideal time is on Draft Day, just before the auction. Talk about drama, tension, and last-minute planning.

Here were my '99 keepers:

2B	Craig Biggio	$31
OF	Sammy Sosa	$30
1B	Kevin Young	$16
OF	Rondell White	$10
SP	Kevin Millwood	$7
OF	J.D. Drew	$5

Not a bad crew. All of them were priced below market, especially Sosa and Young. Millwood would turn out to be a real coup, as well.

As you can see, I was heavy on outfielders. This was fine with me since outfielders are the most numerous position players. I could relax a bit during their bids and keep my paperwork in line. I honestly believed I had one of the top keeper lists in the league. All five hitters were five-tool guys (at least on paper). Millwood was a 17-game winner taking over the fourth starter slot for Atlanta. You couldn't ask for bluer chips.

These guys would be responsible for my whole draft … to an extent. At the very least, they would dictate what I would do in the middle rounds. So I had to come up with a plan …

My Initial Strategy

My conservative estimate for all five of my batters was 130 HRs, 450 RBIs, 400 runs, 100 SB, and a collective batting average not less than .280. That is one sweet core offense. By the league's '98 numbers, that put me halfway to first place in every offensive category—with only five players. Nice.

Naturally, my pitching draft would have to be a winner. Offense was no longer a priority. I had a list of several key batters who I *had* to have, as- suming reasonable cost. After that, it was pitch- ing, pitching, pitching.

My outlook on saves is now well known, but be- lieve it or not, I did have a plan. If it worked, I'd slam dunk the whole category for less than $15. If it didn't, I wouldn't be out that much money— and I don't like saves anyway. No biggie.

Strike Three

Your keepers will always dictate your initial draft strategy. But don't ignore what you don't need. If you're flush with catch- ers, you still should keep tabs on where the other catchers end up and for how much. Be thorough, for value never sleeps.

Foul Tips

It's a good idea to break down how much per position the average player will cost you. This will vary depending on your pitching/hitting breakdown (50/50, 60/40, and so on). Just divide the dollar total by the number of players you need to buy (13 hitters, 10 pitchers).

Starting pitching was the key. I wanted to nail down no fewer than seven solid starters. Emphasis on *solid*. No Rockies. No Marlins. No rookies. Price was a bit of an object, but I would be daring and allow myself to go as high as $130 on total pitching, 50 percent of my $260 draft budget.

My offensive keepers totaled $92, which left me $38 to fill eight batting slots ($130 − $92 = $38). That's less than $5 a slot. Not so good. But I was determined to build a first-rate pitching staff. Sosa and Biggio would have to carry the load.

Millwood was a paltry $7, so that left me with a potential $123 to spend on nine pitching slots, an average of nearly $14 a pitcher. Pretty generous—but that was good. If I spent wisely, I could then funnel some badly needed $$$ to my batting effort.

There you have it. That was my plan. Preliminary draft strategies ain't brain surgery, but they do take a little math and some reckless speculation. If you don't have any keepers to dictate your needs, your options are wide open.

Remember that this is just my personal plan for '99. Next season will be different. And I won't presume to tell you how to run your draft by saying, "Be like Mike." But illustrating how I arrive at my decisions (for better or worse) might make you feel better about arriving at your own. Or it might not.

The First Round (and My First Mistake)

The room came alive at Maddux's name: papers shuffled, throats cleared, and pens scribbled. The mystery of who would be called first was solved. Jim's opening bid was classic: $1.

Strike Three

Always open your bidding at $1, because you never know ....

The bidup was fast and furious. Everyone wanted to get his licks in, like a linebacker having butterflies until that first good hit of the day. In seconds, the price hit $30. That's when my ears perked up.

I had no intention of buying Greg Maddux in '99. I owned him in '98, and his final numbers were incredible. But the plain truth was that his second half had been rocky—so much so that it cost me the ERA title. I was still bitter about that. His '98 price had been $40 and I had him valued at that very same number for '99—but I just didn't trust him. For the first time ever, I had doubts about Mr. Greg Maddux.

But you have to be mindful of the kill zone for each and every player, no matter what you think of them. So I looked and I listened. "Thirty-two dollars ... thirty-three dollars ... thirty-four dollars." It was down to two owners now. I honestly don't even remember who. "Thirty-five dollars ... thirty-six dollars ...." Silence. I blinked. Silence? Another owner began the mantra, "Going once ...."

Foul Tips

Beware of early round hysteria. Above all, *stay calm.*

My mind hit puree. Mr. Greg Maddux for $36 in *this* league? No way. It couldn't happen. It didn't make sense. If he put up his usual numbers, it would be a good deal. Not a steal, but a good deal. "Going twice ...."

"Thirty-seven!" Everyone stared at me. I couldn't believe I said it. I didn't *want* Maddux! I couldn't afford to spend more than $25 on anyone! My mind still raced. It was just a bid up. Yeah, that's the ticket. The other owner will go to $38. It's still a fair price for Greg. No problem.

"Going once ...." C'mon, you moron, go to $38. "Going twice ...." Uh oh. "Sold for thirty-seven dollars! Zimmy draws first blood."

Uh, okay. So much for draft strategy. All I could do is shake my head. How did it happen? How could I be so reckless? There I was, the proud owner of Mr. Greg Maddux ... again. And with one bid, my very first bid of the day, my very first acquisition of the day, I destroyed my entire 1999 season.

The Frenzy Continues

The first round was exciting and predictable at the same time. The usual suspects went for the usual prices:

Bonds	$40
Piazza	$45 (!!!—a new league record)
Walker	$43
Schilling	$31
Larkin	$30
Urbina	$33
Beck	$31
Karros	$24 (a pretty good deal)

The bidding for Piazza got interesting. The previous draft salary record was set in '98: $44 for Larry Walker. Piazza is always a pleasure to own, especially in the second half. I stayed in for Mike until $35, then bailed. Three owners duked it out, driving the price up and up and up until it was a bloodbath. The rest of us winced with each bid.

Overheard in the Dugout

Some of these $40+ prices may seem insane, but our owners are not as crazy as they seem. The $40 player is a rarity in our league. The top '99 salaries were $45, $43, $40, and $37. The next highest salary was $34. That's only five players out of 432. The rest of the salaries were pretty close to where they should have been. You never know what people will *really* pay until the bidding begins.

There was one surprise in the first round. One of the new owners—a first-timer— raised all our eyebrows by tossing out the name Jose Lima. We all knew about Lima. A solid pitcher, if a little flaky. Pitched for Houston, a playoff team. But no one at the table thought of Lima as a first-round player. Oh well, the new owner was a little green. No problem.

The bidding started off tame enough. A buck. Two bucks. Soon the price hit $13. Then the roof blew off. "Twenty dollars!" declared the owner who originally called Lima's name. Everyone blinked, stunned. Whoa. Was he *nuts?* Lima was no $20 pitcher. Everyone at the table knew it. And everyone at the table knew that a first-time owner had just made a terrible mistake.

Trash Talk

A **scare bid** is the same as a pre-emptive bid. An owner throws out a bid so high that no other owner will dare top it.

This was a *scare bid,* a pre-emptive strike meant to chase off other owners so the new guy could have Lima, no questions asked. It worked. He got his $20 Lima. And everyone thought he was loco. I had Lima down as a $15 guy, no more. Judging by the expressions around the room, so did everyone else. But a strange thing happened in '99. Jose Lima emerged as one of the premiere starters in the league, winning 21 games. He ended up being a steal at $20. Maybe that new guy wasn't so dumb after all ...?

Wrong. Dead wrong. He made a grievous rookie error. When he lobbed his $20 grenade, Lima's bid was $13.

If the owner had been patient—not dramatic—he would have waded into battle and played the market. I truly believe that he could have gotten Lima for $18, maximum. Those couple bucks always mean a lot in the late rounds.

The fact that Lima blossomed is irrelevant. The owner was scared of losing the one player he wanted most, so he panicked. He didn't have the stomach to go in and fight for him. People, you *have* to fight for some players. Grind it out. Play the game. Don't waste your money on doomsday draft devices. You're only killing yourself.

The Middle Rounds

As the draft progressed, my roster began to fill. After Maddux ($37), I landed Dodger pitcher Chan Ho Park at $26—a little more than I wanted to pay. I really fought for him. Unfortunately, he tanked in '99. He became by far the most disappointing pitcher on my squad. Yeesh, two players, two whacks in the knee caps. It wasn't even 10 o'clock yet!

At the time, I wasn't too upset about getting Maddux and Park. Both were solid picks, though I knew I overpaid for both. In the '99 pre-season, you could've mentioned both guys as potential Cy Young contenders and no one would've laughed.

Strike Three

I don't recommend scare bids. Sure, they can get you a player you really want. But you might have been able to win a straight bidding war and gotten the same player for less than your scare bid.

Foul Tips

Don't bid more than $1 higher than the previous bidder. You could overinflate the price of a player and be stuck with him.

Next I snagged Reds first baseman Sean Casey for $22. Another dogfight. I'd hoped he would stay under $20, but I was willing to go as high as $25 (though it would've stung like a bullwhip). Twenty-two dollars wasn't a bad price. Casey would turn out to be a bargain and a keeper.

By now, however, I was spooked. I'd spent close to $90 for three players. I had a long way to go. So I sat back for a bit and let 46 picks go by. It's not like I sat there like a goof. I fought hard for some players and lost: Matt Williams ($26, a steal); Ricky Bottalico ($7, no way); Todd Stottlemyre ($18, too rich); Edgardo Alfonso ($24, nice price); Andy Benes ($19, yikes); Jason Schmidt ($17, double yikes); and Matt Clement ($11, too high at draft time).

My next coup, er, pick was worth the wait: Mike Hampton for $15. I drafted him expecting 15 wins. Talk about blossoming: 22 wins and a sub-3.00 ERA. Yee-ha! He and Kevin Millwood would anchor my staff for the whole year.

Next I landed a group of pitchers who I thought would be solid starters for decent prices: Bobby Jones (of the Mets, not Rockies), $13; Masato Yoshii, $10; and Bill Pulsipher, $5. At the time, they seemed safe. All turned out to fizzle. Luckily, as you'll see in upcoming chapters, none of these three stayed around long enough to do any damage.

I now had seven starting pitchers, my minimum goal. I spent a total of $113 to get them—a lot of scratch. You know, I was pretty happy with them at the time. But times change sooo fast.

The Late Rounds

The late rounds was where I did some of my best drafting ... and some of my most indifferent.

Offensively, I landed two cheap catchers, Bobby Estalella ($4) and Tyler Houston ($2). Estalella was coming off an injury, but I was convinced that Phillies starter Mike Lieberthal would get hurt. Well ... he didn't.

I was thrilled to get shortstop Pat Meares for $5. In his three previous seasons, he didn't hit less than .260 or drive in less than 60 runs. That's solid production for a shortstop. Of course, Meares got hurt.

I filled out my outfield with Todd Dunwoody ($6) from Florida, a solid prospect who looked to improve (he didn't). My utility slot was a bit of a surprise, however: catcher Angel Pena from L.A. I wanted him bad—he was a hot Triple-A prospect and starter Todd Hundley was coming off major surgery. Pena looked to be the man (he wasn't). I expected him to go in the reserve draft, but one sharp owner tried to sneak him through at $1. I topped him at $2 and took Pena home. What a disappointment.

The Saves Gambit ... Seriously

Now for my saves ploy. Everyone needs a good saves ploy. If it worked, I would be revered as a genius. If it didn't, I would be dismissed as a cheapskate and saver hater. I could live with either fate.

I went with the straight backup strategy, landing Wayne Gomes ($6), Jason Christiansen ($5), and Antonio Osuna ($1). Waiting in the wings on my minor league roster were Diamondback Ben Ford and Expo Guillermo Mota (as in Guillermota vs. Mothra). All were in line for saves if a closer got hurt. Ford and Mota were rumored to be impact guys. Christiansen and Gomes had already tasted some '98 saves. Osuna was as good a bet as any in L.A. if Jeff Shaw faltered.

So what happened? Gomes indeed became the Phillies' closer. He made me happy for the price I paid. As for the rest of my grand saves ploy? I have no comment at this time.

The *Really* Late Rounds

As I mentioned earlier, I played a classic waiting game at the end of the '99 draft. My spending spree on pitchers left me with $3 and three slots to fill: middle infielder, third baseman (ouch), and 10th pitcher. So I waited. And waited. Soon, everyone was staring at me. "What do you mean you have three slots left? C'mon, pick 'em!"

Guys were over the edge with fatigue. They wanted to get to the supplemental drafts as soon as possible. I stalled as long as I could, trying to make the best picks I could. It was tough under that pressure, but I fared okay. Each for a buck:

SS	Damian Jackson
3B	Aramis Ramirez
RP	Antonio Osuna

I mentioned Osuna before. He got hurt and never pitched an inning for me. Jackson and Ramirez, however, were wildcard picks—hot prospects with big impact potential. Both had an *outside* chance at winning starting jobs for San Diego and Pittsburgh, respectively.

As it turned out, Jackson stole 34 bases (while hitting .224, if you call that hitting). Still, steals are steals. I think he's a keeper at a buck. Ramirez never did start for the Bucs, but he had an eye-popping season at Triple-A. I ended up dealing him, which turned out good for me in the long run. We'll talk about that later.

All in all, the waiting game worked. Two out of three picks brought me quality in their own way. It's an endgame that I recommend highly (but don't tell your friends/enemies).

Foul Tips

Remember Clint's motto from the movie *Heartbreak Ridge:* Improvise, adapt, and overcome. Poignant words for when your draft strategy goes belly up.

Taking My Supplements

Thanks to a series of ill-fated '98 trades, I was left with only three reserve picks for '99, and none in the first round. I had to make them count.

My first pick was pitcher Mike Remlinger of the Braves. A good bet to vulch wins and maybe land a starting role if someone went down. As I said earlier, he turned out to be stellar in every way.

Soon it was pretty clear that a lot of owners were using the reserve draft to get an early start on the best minor league prospects. Guys like Rick Ankiel, Pat Burrell, and Ron Belliard were gone. There were two guys I really wanted, so I promised myself that if they were still available, I'd grab them now.

It was a risky proposition, since these guys would have to be carried as keepers if I wanted them next year. They were great prospects, but there was no guarantee that they would hit the Bigs in '99, let alone contribute.

Strike Three

You can never draft too many catchers. They always get hurt and owners will always trade for them.

I got 'em. Outfielder Lance Berkman of the Astros, widely regarded as one of the best pure hitters in the minors. And catcher Jason LaRue, a AA batting champ who was also a fine defensive backstop, something that boded well for playing time. Plus, you can never have too many catchers on the payroll. LaRue gave me four.

The minor league draft gave me an array of legitimate prospects, some of whom actually helped me out in the first half of the season.

Odalis Perez ended up the fifth starter for the Braves, which gave me eight starting pitchers (yippee-ki-yi-ay, mamacita). He would leave my squad in a trade that we'll discuss later.

Guillermo Mota (as in Guillermota vs. King Kong) was a dominant middle reliever for most of the year for the 'Spos. He, too, was traded, but not before putting up some good numbers for me.

The aforementioned Ben Ford was traded to the Yankees, which yanked my chain a bit. I thought I'd get some saves out of him since the D-backs didn't have a legitimate closer at the time. But that one fell through.

As I write this, I still have three blue-chip prospects on my minor league roster that I'm carrying into the millennium. I hope to see them next season, or the year after that. If they put up numbers like they did in AAA, I have every right to be excited.

I said it once, I'll say it again: Ya gotta love a keeper league!

The Mop-Up

My '99 draft laid a nice foundation, but my work was far from done. I was nowhere near being a contender and I knew it.

I spent $125 on pitching and $135 on offense. Which is pretty much what I expected. Maddux totally threw me off, but now that I had him on my roster, I didn't feel so bad about it. I mean, it's *Greg Maddux*.

I was especially happy with Sean Casey, Pat Meares, Angel Pena, Mike Hampton, and Wayne Gomes—all players that I deliberately pursued from day one of planning (for better or worse).

This is what my '99 team looked like:

Zim's Final Draft Day Roster

Position	Player	Price
Starters		
C	Bobby Estalella	$4
C	Tyler Houston	$2
1B	Kevin Young	$16 ('98 keeper)
3B	Aramis Ramirez	$1
CI	Sean Casey	$22
2B	Craig Biggio	$31 ('98 keeper)
SS	Pat Meares	$5
MI	Damian Jackson	$1
OF	Sammy Sosa	$30 ('98 keeper)
OF	Rondell White	$10 ('98 keeper)
OF	Todd Dunwoody	$6
OF	J.D. Drew	$5 ('98 keeper)
UT	Angel Pena (C)	$2
SP	Greg Maddux	$37
SP	Chan Ho Park	$26
SP	Mike Hampton	$15
SP	Bobby Jones	$13
SP	Masato Yoshii	$10
SP	Kevin Millwood	$7 ('98 keeper)
SP	Bill Pulsipher	$5
RP	Wayne Gomes	$6
RP	Jason Christiansen	$5
RP	Antonio Osuna	$1
Reserves		
RP	Mike Remlinger	$5
OF	Lance Berkman	$5
C	Jason LaRue	$5
Minor Leaguers		
SP	Odalis Perez	
3B	Chris Truby	
RP	Guillermo Mota	
SP	Wade Miller	
2B	Ralph Milliard	('98 holdover)

continues

Zim's Final Draft Day Roster   (continued)

Position	Player	Price
Minor Leaguers		
RP	Jeff Kubenka	('98 holdover)
SP	Courtney Duncan	('98 holdover)
RP	Ben Ford	('98 holdover)

Overall, I was satisfied. But a lot of work needed to be done, most of which I didn't even know about yet. That's the way it always is, though.

The gang had a good time and some good teams were built. We all had that post-Christmas buzz (and it wasn't just from the beer). When it was over, some of the guys went home to their families. Some of us stayed for poker and to regale each other with the day's excitement. Smoke a stogie. Kick the keg.

But all of us knew that this day was only the beginning. In a month or so, the regular season would begin. The real test. Then we could start separating the men from the moles. Until then, however, all that was left to do was sip our beers, puff our smokes, look at the peels of ring bologna skin on the floor, and smile.

Recommended viewing: *The Babe.* No, not the Pamela Anderson Lee version. I mean the one with John Goodman. One of the best performances of his career. And who can resist an overweight, alcoholic, womanizing Hall of Famer?

The Least You Need to Know

➤ If you suddenly spend more than you wanted to, don't panic. You can make it up in other areas.

➤ Don't bid more than you have to.

➤ Avoid using scare bids—sometimes they work, but they're generally a waste of money.

➤ The draft merely lays the foundation for your team. When the regular season starts, so does the real work.

Part 4

Managing Just Fine

By now you should have recovered from Draft Day. I hope it lived up to the hype for you. I also hope that you've been pondering your mistakes and successes, eyeing your roster with a sense of both pride and suspicion. That's natural.

In fact, it's a good sign. It means that your inner-GM is itching to start making moves. And you should make many, many moves. Transactions are a daily occurrence in major league baseball. Why should it be any different in fantasy baseball? There is always tweaking to be done. Shuffling. Fussing. Poking. You should never be satisfied.

This series of chapters will show you the finer points of transacting: trading, acquiring free agents, and dealing with injuries. Draft Day simply lays the foundation of your team. It's the mid-season management that wins championships. So let's check it out.

Chapter 11

I'll Trade Ya

In This Chapter

➤ Why are you making a trade?

➤ Is it a fair offer?

➤ The art of the steal, er, deal

➤ Throw-ins and future considerations

➤ When you should walk away

Everyone wants to be a General Manager (GM). In fact, it's the only reason fantasy baseball exists at all. Why is that? Ego? Competition? Jealousy? Nah. I just think it's a natural extension of being a sports fan. Nothing makes headlines like a blockbuster trade. Deals full of intrigue, drama, and suspense, everyone involved wondering if this is the swap that will put them over the top. The media jumps. Fans buzz. Trades are good for the soul.

That is, unless you're a player and suddenly have to sell your house, uproot your family, and ship off to a city you've only ever seen from the window of a chartered jet. Unless you're the GM who has to deal a hometown hero for three marginal prospects because the boss said, "Cut salary." Unless you're the incoming player who has to fill the shoes of that hometown hero.

Yes, trading is the lifeblood of baseball. The poetry of fast-talking hard sells, the fever of speed-dial, the chest-thumping importance of having to leave your cell phone on everywhere you go because you never know when you need to sell a skeptic on the skills of a part-time middle infielder. Mmm. Better than the smell of a new Porsche.

The Offer: Fair or Foul?

What constitutes a fair offer? Like the draft, swapping shortstops and their ilk is all about value. And as we know from our lessons, value is subjective. One man's fair offer is another man's final insult.

To make matters worse, once the season starts, evaluating talent becomes far more complex than it was for Draft Day. Back then, you based your dollar values on previous performance, reputation, and future performance. Injuries, trades, and playing time were factored in, as well.

You still have to consider all those factors. But you also have to throw the following criteria into the mix:

➤ Hot streaks and slumps.

➤ What your opponent wants and needs (two different things).

➤ How badly does he want or need it?

➤ How will the trade affect the standings (we'll discuss that in a minute).

➤ Most importantly: Does the deal improve my team?

Foul Tips

Value is subjective. Don't expect an owner to think a deal is fair just because you do.

This doesn't even address straight dollar value. You simply can't go by that. A $20 catcher is not worth the same as a $20 outfielder. But is a $20 outfielder worth the same as another $20 outfielder? Absolutely not. These are Draft Day prices. Things change. One guy could be on the verge of a career year while the other is on the verge of the bench.

Value changes with the wind, friends. And you know what they say about the wind: If it ain't broken, just go with it.

Strike Three

Beware of friends bearing trade offers. They are not your friends anymore. They are the devil with a pink carnation. They are the enemy. Don't trust them.

When Your "Friends" Come Knocking

Your friend Larry just called. "Amigo, listen up. I got a great deal for you."

You listen. Politely. But you're not sure what to think. Larry's one of your best buds. He wouldn't screw you over, would he? Not *Larry*. He got you drunk on your twenty-first birthday (you got arrested). He set you up with Betty Jean Bukowski (she broke your heart). He sprayed you with a fire extinguisher when you caught fire at Boy Scout camp (he lit the match).

Well, I don't know Larry from Adam. And you should pretend that you don't either. Fantasy baseball is not real life. Larry is *not* your friend. He is your deadliest enemy because he has your trust. Don't mess around. Whenever you are presented with a trade proposal—no matter who it's from—immediately ask yourself:

➤ Why do I need to make this trade?

➤ Why does my opponent need to make this trade?

➤ Why does he want to get rid of his player(s)?

➤ Why does he want mine?

Remember, he's your opponent, and while it is possible to help out both teams in a trade, he'll always try to beat you. Thus all the questions. If an opponent has taken the time to make you an offer, he has also taken the time to assess your roster, your needs, and your tendencies. He's going for your throat in a polite manner. If you expose the flesh, he'll gladly take a bite. Even Larry, amigo.

Foul Tips

A trade should always be an attempt to improve your team. Never trade for trading's sake.

When to Trade

Trade solely to improve your team. That's it. There's no other reason.

You'll run into all kinds of traders in your league. Some guys will always be open and fair. Some guys will be foolishly generous. Other guys will pass off the most insanely preposterous proposals like they're the deals of a lifetime. Like with everything we've talked about so far, the better you know your fellow owners, the better off you'll be.

My best advice on receiving trade proposals is patience. Think about the deal. Don't let an opponent rush you. If he does, he's probably trying to slip something past you.

Strike Three

Trading one superstar for a collection of lesser players is usually a bad idea, unless you have some dire need to fill (salary cuts, rebuilding). Instead of needing one proven star to deliver stats, you now need several lesser players to come through.

Keep Your Thief Detector Switched On

You should have an instinctive system in place that lets you analyze each offer quickly and thoroughly:

➤ **What's your gut reaction to the names on the table?** Are you intrigued? Excited? Insulted? Amused? If you know talent, chances are that your gut reaction is right.

➤ **What's your opponent's motivation?** Is he trying to pull a fast one? Or is he willing to negotiate?

➤ **How will the trade affect the standings?** Say an owner offers you a top-flight hitter for a top-flight closer—a pretty even dollar-value swap. Then you check out the standings and see that a 10-save jump will give your opponent six extra points in the overall standings. Hmmm. That hitter he's offering will maybe get you two points more in the standings ... but you'll lose three from lack of saves. He gets six points, you lose 1. Doesn't sound so fair now, does it?

➤ **How will the deal affect the rest of the league?** Upon further review, you realize that not only will that owner benefit from your saves, that outfielder he's offering will help you overtake a third owner in the home run category. The points that third owner loses will allow the first owner to catch him even faster. Guess what? The trade value of your closer just skyrocketed, my friend.

➤ **Do you really need to make the deal?** Look at your own situation. If your team is well balanced and performing as expected, you don't need to trade anybody for anything. So why do it?

Strike Three

If you're not an aggressive type, don't be intimidated by owners who are. They'll pull the hard sell and pressure you to take the deal. Don't cave. Ask for more. Or just say no.

These are just a few points. In a tight pennant race, every trade has a ripple effect across the rest of the league. You have to figure out who will be helped the most by an opponent's offer. Chances are it won't be you. If that's the case, ask for more. Or, even better, just say no.

But beware. If you're too tough to deal with, that owner will take his offer to someone else who won't be as fussy. He'll make the lopsided deal and then *you'll* be the one scrambling to make moves to stay in the race.

It's a juggling game. The bottom line is, don't be taken advantage of. You can't stop other owners from making bad decisions. But you can make sure every deal you make is as fair as it can be. Don't be a fool.

Make Them an Offer They Can't Refuse

Take everything I just told you about incoming offers and flip it. We're now talking about the offers *you* propose, and you should be doing everything I just warned you about.

This does not make you a bad person. Just competitive. Here's where you must truly become a used-car salesman. Not because you're trying to cheat the other guy, but because you're trying to sell him on the notion that your deal is the right thing to do.

When you make an unsolicited trade offer, you are effectively knocking on his door and asking him to buy something. Why should he do it? Or as the great Gordon Gekko once said, "Why am I listening to you?" You have to be the wily Bud Fox. You have to get past Gordo's snooty receptionist, his gold-leaf encrusted doors, his tough New York schmuck detector. How do you do that? Well, let's say you're jonesing for a starting pitcher on his roster.

Foul Tips

When you make a trade offer, you're acting like a traveling salesman knocking on an owner's door. The owner may not want any. You have to get your foot in the door and convince him he not only wants it, but *needs* it.

Here are some suggestions:

➤ **Look at his roster.** What does he lack? If he needs stolen bases, mention it to him. "I see you're a little on the slow side. Would you be interested in dealing for speed?"

➤ **Start with generalities.** Like speed, pitching, and power, for example. If your opponent is interested in talking trade, names will come up very quickly.

➤ **Be bold and put it on the table.** If you have a very specific deal in mind. I've sent many one-line e-mails that say nothing more than, "How about so-and-so for so-and-so?" You'll get a quick yes, no, or counter proposal.

➤ **Always start low.** Never give your final offer first. You never know when someone might just say okay to one of your initial offers.

➤ **Don't be afraid of being insulting.** Over the years, I've gotten so many silly, stupid, you-name-it bad offers that I don't even flinch anymore. However, if you know your deal is a little "off," be a pal and open the window to counteroffers.

Foul Tips

If you have the guts to make an insulting offer, let the owner know you're open to a counteroffer. Courtesy counts.

And if an owner says yes to your ridiculous offer? Cheer. Do not feel bad. Take the players and run. It is your responsibility to make a trade offer. It is the other owners' responsibilities to know the talent. If they screw up, it's their own fault.

Foul Tips

Future considerations such as players to be named, cash, old Christina Applegate posters, and other undefinable perks are prohibited in fantasy baseball.

Trash Talk

A **throw-in** is a marginal player included to help balance a nearly completed trade.

Strike Three

Reserve draft picks and minor leaguers are legal trade tender. Minor league draft picks are not.

But that's rare. Most owners know a bogus offer when they see one. If you chronically toss out these doozies without a hint of gamesmanship, your reputation will fester and guys will stop reading your e-mails. One of the worst fates an owner can have is to become a leper in his own league. So keep your trade offers fair and serious. Believe it or not, it is possible to be cutthroat and courteous at the same time.

Throw-Ins and Future Considerations

One of the most famous phrases in major league baseball is "a player to be named later." This usually translates into "some batless bozo to fill out the AA roster."

A *throw-in* is an undesirable player included in a trade simply to get rid of him. These guys are usually hard-throwing pitchers who never blossomed, five-tool failures, and other reclamation projects.

There have been some famous throw-ins in the majors over the years, guys attached to trades like barnacles simply to beef up the number of names—as if sheer numbers make a trade better. How about Ryne Sandberg? Jeff Bagwell? Mike Hampton? All were no-name minor leaguers traded for established veterans.

The throw-in has become a bit of an art form in the major leagues. If a GM can get mileage out of a throw-in, he looks that much smarter. And if the coaching staff is any good, it works pretty often since most failed prospects need only a change of scenery and some extra attention to tap their lost potential.

The Phillies' '93 pitching staff was a collection of cast-off hard throwers brought back to life by the incomparable pitching coach Johnny Podres. Tommy Greene, Terry Mulholland, and Curt Schilling all blossomed under Podres's tutelage.

Throw-ins have the same impact in fantasy baseball. However, players-to-be-named, cash, and so on, do not. Future considerations are too nebulous to be

allowed. You'll end up with more problems than you need—like when exactly will that player be named?

Reserve draft picks can be interpreted as future considerations—but they can be traded to your heart's content. They're tangible. The same thing with minor leaguers. But minor league draft picks? We talked about those already. They're a no-no.

So make your offers. Work your deals. And always try to improve your team. With time, making good offers will be as easy as doing *The New York Times* crossword puzzle while piloting a loaded 747 in high winds after a seven-hour bachelor party. Trust me.

> **Foul Tips**
>
> Throw-ins can turn into big-time lottery tickets, just like in the major leagues. Give them careful thought.

> **Overheard in the Dugout**
>
> My best throw-in in '99 was Denny Neagle. I was pulling off a large trade: eight players total. Neagle got me to do the deal. He started '99 awful, then was hurt for weeks. Worthless, right? But there was no surgery involved. I knew if he came back healthy, he'd be just fine. I was right: eight wins and a sub-3.50 ERA in the second half. So pay attention to those throw-ins, boys and goils.

When to Walk Away

Working a trade can be frustrating. Eventually there comes a time when you throw up your hands (or just throw up) and say, "Forget it, I'm spent." When is that? Only you know. A deal is only as good as you demand it to be. If you're chronically lazy, you won't do many trades. You won't work with other owners on their proposals, and you won't take the time to do up your own. What's the point?

I've heard a lot of guys whine about fellow owners, "He won't trade, he asks for too much, he's nuts, I can't get anything done." I just smile and nod because I know these guys aren't willing to do the hard negotiating. They won't flat out ask an owner, "Why do you think so-and-so is so valuable?" They just complain.

Sure, trading can be hard work. I've gone back and forth 10 times with an owner, offering, re-offering, pushing, and pulling. Why? Because it was worth it. You have to be just as willing.

Trading is the bread-and-butter of fantasy baseball. It's one of the main reasons you get into the game, to capture that authentic GM feel (sounds like a car commercial). Frustration is a part of that, as is banging your head against the door of an iron maiden (from the inside).

But the excitement you feel when you pull off something that you didn't think you could? Yee-*haw*.

Overheard in the Dugout

There is one guy in our league who always makes crazy offers. I personally don't mind because I know how his diseased brain works. He doesn't love to trade, he loves to *deal*. He truly is a used-car salesman. If you take his initial offers as gospel, then sure, you're gonna be insulted. But I know that you have to work with this guy. If you do, the trades will not only be fair, but will without a doubt be good for both teams. Remember, sometimes you have to work at a trade to get it right.

There is a time to walk away from a trade, but only when every avenue is exhausted—or when the deal no longer improves your team.

Behold the used-car salesman motif again. This time, however, throwing a tantrum in the showroom won't help. Your opponent doesn't have a sales manager to consult. Eventually you just have to walk away. If your opponent really wants the deal, he'll come back with a better offer. But if he doesn't, it was not meant to be. In fact, his silence may signal that he's waiting for *you* to come back. Don't do it: You won't be getting the best deal.

In all, your trades will be more important than any other transactions you make during the season. But there are no guarantees. You can make a trade that's so great, wonderful, and stupendous that other owners call to congratulate you. Then three days later the star you traded for tears up his knee riding his kid's tricycle on an off day. Your scream is heard for miles.

What do you do? I know what you do. You pick up the phone and try to make another trade. Because that's what fantasy baseball players do.

Recommended viewing: *Cobb.* Ron Shelton is our greatest living auteur of sports films. This opus is underrated, perhaps because the man Tommy Lee Jones portrays is a real, well, you pick the adjective. But Ty Cobb was still one of the greatest players of all time. And who can argue with a man who will do anything for a competitive "edge," including sharpening his spikes for sliding into middle infielders?

The Least You Need to Know

➤ Trades are the most important transactions you'll make in a given season. They can make a chump or kill a champ.

➤ Trade value is subjective—your fair deal is another owner's final insult.

➤ Be patient with other owners' trade offers. Don't rush to make a deal. Think. Analyze. Then renegotiate.

➤ Your own offers should start low, but still be fair. Always be willing to talk.

➤ Throw-ins like reserve draft picks and minor leaguers can be invaluable, as can lowly players you think will improve.

➤ The only reason to trade is to improve your team. Period.

Chapter 12

Ulcers, Hair Loss, and Other Season-Ending Injuries

In This Chapter

➤ Injuries hurt everyone

➤ Dealing with day-to-day aches

➤ The disabled list

➤ When your superstar goes down

➤ Healthcare options

There's nothing worse than seeing your star player go down on live TV. If the injury is bad, like Jason Kendall's compound ankle fracture in '99, live TV is a punch in the stomach even if you don't own the guy. Kendall, one of the top catchers in baseball, crossed first base on a close play and turned his ankle. At first it looked awkward, but not overly. Next thing you know, Kendall is down and his foot is dangling at an angle beyond normal human geometry. Chills.

When you take the time to value them, bid for them, and entrust them to your cause, any injury to any player ranks right up there with cheating girlfriends, dead grandparents, and kicks in the teeth. Unfortunately, sport is sport, and injuries happen.

All you can do is let time heal the wound. The player has surgeons, trainers, and massage therapists. You have aspirin, a pack of butts, and a bottle of tequila. Either way, neither of you is going to feel well for a while.

Bringing Out the Dead

The biggest problem with injuries may not be the loss of stats but the psychological abuse of knowing you are utterly helpless to do anything about it. When you draft a .300 hitter, you can reasonably expect that seven out of 10 times he's going to fail. You can *prepare* for it. It's no fun to watch him whiff with the bases loaded, but you know he'll get another shot in a couple of innings. But when a guy rips a gapper and pulls up lame coming into second base … man, that stinks (more poignant words beg to be used).

What do you do? First of all, don't panic—even if the player is Barry Bonds, who missed a huge chunk of '99 with an elbow injury. The fact is, your best player's head could literally explode and you'd still have 12 more batters or nine more pitchers who are healthy.

That's not to say that you should sit tight and do nothing. Of course you'll have to find a replacement if you don't have one lurking on your reserve roster (and let's hope you do).

Foul Tips

Injuries hurt (duh), but they are not the end of the world. You still have 12 hitters or nine pitchers who are healthy. Your job is to figure out how to replace that player's production as best you can.

Overheard in the Dugout

Barry Bonds's owner was devastated when he went down in '99. But this owner also was our league's most active trader. He soon had the situation in hand so well that he contended for the title all year long without Bonds. Which made it all the worse when Bonds returned to hit 35 home runs for the year, despite time served. The point is, injuries set you back, but if you're smart, they won't ruin you.

Your first order of business is to consult with your favorite media guru to assess the damage. How badly is the guy hurt? Only then will you know how much tequila to pour on your own wounds.

Ouch! Not *So Hard!*

What is it with some players? You have guys like Sammy Sosa, Craig Biggio, Albert Belle, and of course Cal Ripken who seem like they're made out of Teflon-coated PVC pipe.

Then you have guys like Ken Caminiti, Reggie Sanders, and Tony Gwynn who are made of balsa wood and low-grade papier-mâché. Sometimes they just play too hard: A guy like Caminiti, as breakable as he is, will stagger out to third base with a spear through his belly and a 10-pound sinker hanging from a ring in his nose. But Sanders and his ilk? You *have* to wonder. I mean, how many muscles can one man strain in a season?

Questioning a player's heart is perhaps one of the most dangerous games anyone can play. These men have been hard-core competitors their whole lives and they take their jobs very seriously. No one knows how bad a player hurts except the player. But still, you have a responsibility to put together the best team you can on Draft Day. Injury-prone dudes simply aren't that welcome—unless the price is right.

Does being an ouch-magnet make Tony Gwynn any less of a first-ballot Hall of Famer? Of course not. But most of your fantasy stats are based on volume. The bottom line is, a player has to play.

Foul Tips

On Draft Day, try to stick with players who have a history of good health. Only take injury-prone stars when they're at a great price.

Nicks, Cuts, Scrapes, and a Bat to the Head

"How is he, Skip?" "Day-to-day."

"When can he play?" "Maybe tomorrow. We won't know 'til then."

"Is he in much pain?" "We won't know 'til tomorrow."

"Your fly's open, skip." "He'll work with the trainer and we'll know more tomorrow."

Aaaaarrrrrgggghhhh! Minor injuries, a.k.a. the day-to-day syndrome, is the bane of the fantasy owner. You'd think we'd be grateful that the guy isn't limping off to an extended stay on the disabled list, but no. Why? Because a majority of leagues have weekly transactions, meaning they have one day a week to make roster changes.

Strike Three

When a player is day-to-day, do you reserve him? Dig up as much as you can on that player's past, the nature of the injury, and what the manager says.

Say your guy sits out a game Monday. The manager says he's day-to-day. Then he sits out Tuesday. Still day-to-day. Wednesday? Nope. Thursday's an off day. Still no word on so-and-so's condition. Will he hit the disabled list, Skip? *We'll know more tomorrow.* Grrr.

Finally, your guy pinch-hits Friday night. Then he sits Saturday and starts Sunday. That's a mere five at-bats in one week, all because the manager didn't know when the guy would be up to playing. You could've activated a scrub and gotten more playing time. That's the horror of day-to-day.

Some leagues allow daily transactions, which helps mightily with day-to-day injuries. But even then you have to depend on the player or the manager to let you know the guy's status. It's like sitting there on speed-dial trying to be caller 93—you'll waste more time than it's worth.

There are three major points to consider when trying to decide if you should reserve a day-to-day menace:

1. **The player's history.** Is he one of those guys who has a congenital need to sit every three days? Call it lack of heart, low tolerance for pain, or legitimate injury. Any way you slice it, they aren't in the lineup. This is also something you should consider on Draft Day.

2. **The nature of the injury.** Is it soreness, a mild strain, a twinge? Then it's probably nothing. But be afraid if you hear the words groin, hamstring, Achilles heel, or back spasms. These are day-to-day ailments that usually nag for months.

3. **What the manager or player says.** "We'll know more tomorrow" is an old favorite. But listen to the words. Read between the lines. Who's the replacement? If that guy's hot or favored in any way, the manager won't be so quick to bring the injured player back.

Should you avoid the day-to-day veterans of major league baseball: the Reggie Sanderses, the Rickey Hendersons, the Tony Gwynns? Not necessarily. Sanders still managed to hit 26 homers and steal 36 in only 133 games. Henderson hit .315 and stole 37. Gwynn hit .338 with 62 RBIs in 111 games. Hardly throwaway stats.

Owning any of these guys in '99 was a roller coaster. If you can take the nonsense, they're worth it in the end—to an extent. Price is the key. Don't pay for a 162-game projection on Draft Day.

If you can get a decent price, accept day-to-day reality, and keep a good backup on your reserve roster, you'll be okay. But if you don't, not even tequila and Pepto will be enough.

Be Kind to the Disabled

Okay. You wake up to read that your third baseman was put on the 15-day disabled list with a pulled groin. What do you do?

It's time to look for a replacement. Or is it? There are certain things to consider first:

➤ **How long will he be out?** Being on the 15-day disabled list doesn't automatically mean he'll be back in 15 days. Despite the usual sexual misinterpretations, a "pulled groin" is a bad thing. It hurts like knives and limits virtually every movement: swinging, running, and ranging for a ground ball.

➤ **What day is it?** If it's Monday, the day after transactions went in, you have to wait a whole week before you can reserve him. Is it worth replacing him? The guy may be out only one more week, which isn't an extinction-level event.

➤ **How good is your replacement?** If he's another starter, hoo-ya, master chief. Put him in. But if he's a part-timer, and your guy is expected back as soon as he's eligible, ask yourself if it's worth the risk. The part-time replacement might go hitless in 13 at-bats, which does nothing for your bottom line.

If it was me? I'd find an immediate replacement, a veteran third baseman who can hit. Injuries like the fabled groin pull are sometimes the worst because they nag. If your starter comes back too early, he could aggravate it. Which means back to the disabled list we go.

Your Surrogate Star

Where do you find your replacement? You have three options: your reserve roster, the free-agent market, or trade.

If you were fortunate enough to draft a reserve corner man on Draft Day, bully for you. That means you know the player and liked him enough to scarf him up. Plug him in and forget about him. If not, you have some legwork to do. The free-agent market is pretty cut and dried—either there's a useful third baseman out there or there isn't. Perhaps the answer lies on your own roster.

Who are your three starting corner guys? Do you have two third basemen? If so, move the second third baseman from the corner infield slot into the starting third base slot. This way you can look for either a third base or first base free agent to fill the now-vacant corner infield slot. Better still, is your utility guy eligible at the corners? Move him in. Now you can pick up anyone playing anywhere for your utility. Which is a lot easier.

Foul Tips

To give yourself free-agent flexibility, try juggling your roster according to position eligibility. If you can, your replacement options expand.

Strike Three

Don't dismantle your team trying to trade for a replacement player, especially if it's a short-term injury.

Alas, in deep leagues the only thing that may be available is a bum with a cracked bat living on playing time he won in a poker game with the devil. If you want a replacement, you're going to have to trade for one.

Make a clear decision. Do you want quality? You'll have to give quality and a whole lot more, because any owner you approach knows that you're desperate. Any third basemen they have will be expensive.

If you know your starting third baseman is coming back in two or three weeks—or even a month—don't mortgage the future of your team on another stud third baseman. Just find a band-aid guy. But if you hear the words "surgery" or "60-day disabled list," you might want to think about someone more permanent. Even then, I still say be conservative. Don't give up the farm, or the summer home, or the second Porsche.

Ticktock, Ticktock

Time can be your worst enemy at this stage. With weekly transactions, your life revolves around these seven-day chunks that become mini-seasons unto themselves. Something that happened seven days ago can seem like seven years.

Try to be patient. Two or three weeks is a drop in the bucket in a six-month season. You'll be feeling the loss of every potential RBI or strikeout the injured guy would normally produce. The media will enflame your pain by scrutinizing the player's rehab on a daily basis. What a double-edged sword: You want the info, but you hate hearing it.

Overheard in the Dugout

I acquired Met backup catcher Todd Pratt in '99. He's one of the better backups because he hits for average and power. Thing is, he has this guy Piazza playing in front of him. But for two weeks in April, Piazza went down. Pratt was the man. He went on a tear, hitting over .300 with three home runs and 12 RBIs while Mike sat. But soon his two weeks were up and the party was over. The point is, sometimes a starter's direct replacement is the best option—you *know* he will play.

He's Back!

Soon your player will return. A lot of times he'll be sent on a rehab stint in the minors to sharpen up. Monitor this as closely as you can, especially with pitchers. Sure, the talent level isn't the same, but your player's performance will tell you how he's feeling. If you keep hearing the words "on schedule" and "feels fine," smile and get ready to activate him.

Or wait. Huh? *Wait?* You've been waiting three weeks, why would you wait to activate him? A lot of times when a guy comes back—especially a pitcher—he gets shelled his first time out. You're simply protecting your roster from bad stats.

I hate doing this. I know it's the smart/prudent/ logical thing to do. But I draft players for *all* their stats, good and bad. If my guy comes back and kicks butt, I'll be kicking my own butt for being such a conservative wuss and waiting. But it's your choice.

Hopefully things will be back to normal soon. But what to do with the replacement when your guy comes back? If he's good enough, find a place for him on the active roster. If not, stash him on your reserve roster for next time. Because there's *always* a next time.

Foul Tips

When your guy comes back, stash his replacement on your reserve roster. You worked hard to find him and you may need his services again.

When Your Superstar Falls

Andres Galarraga … Barry Bonds … Kerry Wood … Jason Kendall … Javy Lopez … Alex Rodriguez …. All of them are among the top 5 percent at their positions. All are players you build around. And all of them were hurt for extended periods in '99, some for the whole year. They're virtually irreplaceable. But you have to do *something* when your superstar goes down.

The process isn't unlike what we just discussed. How badly is he hurt? When will he be back? Who will play in his place? The main difference with star players is that they are a cornerstone of your season's strategy, and possibly beyond.

You should reserve them, of course. But these players will no doubt be very expensive. As the season progresses, you will be crunched by the salary cap. If the player is out for the year, you will be forced into a heartbreaking decision: Do you keep the star for next year, or do you waive him for salary room and go for it this year?

Strike Three

If a pitcher is sent to a surgeon for an exam—especially docs named Jobe or Andrews—be afraid. It usually means something is seriously wrong.

That depends on where you are in the standings, as well as what time of year it is. If super stud goes down for the year in May, you'd be pretty foolish to pack it in. Waiving him might be the best decision, especially when you're talking about $30 to $35 of cap space. It's a bitter bullet to bite.

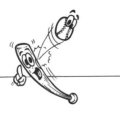

Foul Tips

If a fellow owner waives an injured superstar who is out for the year, pick him up as a cheap free agent and keep him for next season. It's a worthy risk.

Trash Talk

An **injured reserve list** operates like the major league disabled list. It keeps players free of the salary cap and can be a useful tool for retaining rights to high-salary players with major injuries.

All I can say is, if you do waive an injured superstar, Godspeed. Because I can tell you exactly what will happen: A fellow owner will pick him up at a bargain free-agent price and stash him away for next year. And there will be nothing you can do about it.

How do I know this? Because I have both Jason Kendall and Javy Lopez sitting on my roster waiting for the start of the 2000 season. Both were waived by their owners. Both were acquired by me for $15, a pittance. I look forward to their convalescence and return to form—for even if they come back at half-strength, I'm still a winner.

Healthcare Options

But what if you don't want to waive a superstar, effectively handing him over to a competitor at a discount? You have two options: Either take the pain and slap the guy on your reserve roster for the rest of the year, or establish an alternative storage system that relieves your salary cap of the superstar's super price. The former is how our league currently works. I carried the dead weight of Rondell White on my reserve roster for months when he got hurt in '98.

These salary cap debacles can be avoided, however. That's where the latter suggestion comes in. Our league is currently considering a new rule that would pull injured players' salaries out from under the cap.

Basically, it's an *injured reserve list* that works independently from your true reserve roster. If a superstar like Bonds goes down, an owner can put him on his injured reserve. If we had this in '99, that owner would've received a $40 break towards the salary cap. He also retains all rights to Bonds when he returns (restoring his salary under the cap as well). Naturally, any salary over the cap at that time would have to be shed.

There are some advantages and disadvantages, of course. An advantage is being able to replace and keep a superstar without having to worry about crunching salary numbers.

For this rule to work, the number of players allowed on the injured reserve at one time would have to be limited. Either that, or there would have to be a minimum length of stay on the injured reserve list, say one month. This would limit its use to players with major injuries. Plus, it would be unfair to carry injured-reserve list players into the off-season. Injured players would have to be returned to the main roster and the salary cap adjusted accordingly.

The disadvantages? The removal of risk. Major injuries are bad luck, and bad luck is a part of any sport. By establishing an injured reserve, you're giving an afflicted owner a free pass when it comes to salary strategy. Some people would say, "You lose a player, too bad. You feel abused by fate? Wear a helmet."

Foul Tips

An injured reserve list removes salary strategy from the picture, which allows an owner greater freedom when finding a replacement. This can be good or bad.

This problem doesn't exist in the major leagues because they don't have salary caps, so there really is no precedent. The injured reserve is but one suggestion among many. The limits of this game are the limits of your creativity.

I'm torn on the issue. I'm a big believer in karma, but I've also had my share of season-ending injuries over the years. I've had to waive more than one quality player. One—Javy Lopez—I was fortunate to re-acquire later when no one snagged him. It's up to your league to make up its own mind.

As for our league, man, I can't wait for the debate on this one!

Recommended viewing: *For Love of the Game.* More of a life story than a love story. And it's got Kevin Costner, the crown prince of baseball movies (except for Bob Uecker, of course).

The Least You Need to Know

➤ When a player is injured, you have three ways to find a replacement: your reserve roster, the free-agent market, and trade.

➤ Don't mortgage your team's future trading for a replacement.

➤ The trade price will be high because the league will know you are desperate.

➤ Try to get an injured starter's direct replacement—at least you know he will play.

➤ If a fellow owner waives a star who's out for the year, pick him up cheap as a free agent and save him for next year.

Chapter 13

The Replacements (Not the Band)

In This Chapter

➤ Finding mid-season replacements

➤ Knowing who's out there

➤ Losing a player to the other league

➤ The Free Agent Board System

➤ The Free Agent Budget System

Hopefully you're getting the swing of things when it comes to roster management. The mechanics of it are easy; picking the right replacements is hard. Unfortunately, the luck-skill relationship is love-hate. You can have all the knowledge and information in the world, and you can absolutely pick the best player available based on that. But you can't make him play, you can't make him perform, and you can't keep him healthy.

You need systems in place for free-agent acquisition and minor league promotion. Some call them rules. But like many of the rules in this modern instructional classic, you have options. So let's learn 'em, live 'em, and luv 'em.

What's out There?

You have to know where every player is at all times. A couple-three-four times every season in our league, an owner will put in for a free agent who is already spoken for (sometimes it's a player who's been on a roster since Draft Day).

I've done it. I'll probably do it again. There are so many players out there that you're bound to forget a few. In '99, I had this unexplainable habit of mixing up Brian Jordan and Brian Hunter of the Braves. When an owner tried to pick up Hunter as a free agent, I squawked back, "You own him already, fool."

Well, who's more foolish—the fool, or the fool who tells him he's an idiot? *C'est la vie.*

As you monitor major league transactions, make notes on your player value sheets. This should become a part of your daily routine—you shouldn't even think about it. The list should include minor to major injuries, benchings, and minor league ups and downs.

Foul Tips

Your mid-season lists should be a natural extension of your Draft Day lists, with up-to-date values of every player left unclaimed. Update regularly.

Overheard in the Dugout

Roger Cedeno flew below everyone's radar in our league's '99 draft. When I was looking for some outfield depth the week before Opening Day, imagine my surprise when I saw his name—a guy who might actually get me a dozen steals was still available! Well, he went on to get me many dozens of steals. The point is, when I revisited my draft sheets, his name was still there. Just because the draft is over doesn't mean that you can blow off your player value sheets. It's your primary source of unclaimed players.

The theory behind all this is making your replacement process quick and painless. After all, you've had the pain (your player's injury). And you must be quick, lest someone else snatches your replacement from the jaws of your roster.

This is especially vital if you're playing NL- or AL-only rules. When a good player switches leagues, you need to jump on him like a fly on a water buffalo. Alas, this may be a useless gesture depending on which rules you adopt (as you'll soon see). But knowing what's on the ticker tape first is always a good thing.

Losing a Player to the Other League

Let's say you play in a deep NL-only league like the one I'm in. Our rules are simple: If one of your players is traded to the AL, you lose him. Too bad, so sad, eat a nice meal, and take a long walk into a short bullpen.

I admit, this rule is tough. It hurts. Just about every owner has lost a guy to the other league with no compensation. This adds yet another element to your draft: Bid on players who are stable. However, in this day and age, when A-Rod and Junior can be regularly mentioned as trade fodder, no one player is safe.

But as always, you have rule options regarding cross-league trades. Here are three:

1. **The owner loses the player outright.** Cut, dried, and smoked. No mercy. This is the tough stance, but it adds its own intrigue and cautionary strategies—like trying to deal a player to another owner before he switches leagues.

2. **The owner has dibs on the players who come over in the trade.** Our league did this for a while, but it can get very sticky. For instance, in the '98 Randy Johnson trade, three minor leaguers came over in return. Does The Unit's owner get dibs on all three players, or just one? Can he put all three on his minor league roster, or does he have to carry them in reserve? There are so many "what ifs" with this rule, which is why we eliminated it. I include it here because you may be able to make it work.

3. **The owner retains the player's stats in the other league.** You simply carry them over. Seems fair, but it does eliminate draft strategy when you have trade rumors swirling around a certain player.

Overheard in the Dugout

The tough you-lose-him rule deeply affected our '98 draft. Bret Boone was endlessly rumored to be dealt to the Indians. Everyone avoided him. He eventually got picked up in the reserve draft for $5. Not only did he not get traded to the AL, he went on to have a career year. See what I mean about strategy? You never know what's going to happen, even if all the so-called experts tell you.

If you want to avoid this problem on your own roster, watch out for players in the final years of their contracts on low-revenue teams—especially the guys in line for a big raise. Their teams may not be able to resign them, so they trade them to make sure they get something in return (rather than losing them to free agency and getting bubkus). It happens so often nowadays it's almost heartbreaking. How do you think Randy Johnson's AL-only owners felt in '98?

Perhaps the easiest road is option #3, keeping the cross-league stats. There's no paperwork to fill out. You don't even have to make a roster move. And if you're lucky—as with The Big Unit—his stats in the other league will be 20 times better than the ones in his previous circuit. The bottom line is deciding how cruel you want to be to each other. It's up to you and your opponents.

Whatever you decide, you will eventually come to a dangerous fork in the road: Several owners will try to get the same player at the same time. In our league, this happens whenever a good player comes over from the AL. Naturally, everyone wants the guy. But who gets him?

Trash Talk

The Free Agent Acquisition Board (FAABoard) allows owners to pick up free agents based on their rank on "the Board"; the highest owner on the Board gets dibs on the player. **The Free Agent Acquisition Budget (FAABudget)** gives owners a finite money reserve to bid on potential free agents. The highest bid gets the free agent. These designations are pretty common fantasy terms, even though their initials are the same.

Which System Works for You?

Once again, you have options. You can use the *Free Agent Acquisition Board* (*FAABoard*) system, or the *Free Agent Acquisition Budget* (*FAABudget*) system. Both work. Both are intriguing. Both add dimension and character to your league. Both have the initials FAAB, which can drive you nuts. But once you adopt a system, you'll have a strategic friend for life. Here's why ...

On Being Chairman of the FAABoard

Foul Tips

If only one owner claims a free agent, he gets the player without dispute. If a player has multiple claims, use the Board.

Our league uses the Board, short for tote board. If only one owner claims a player, he gets that player automatically, without dispute. But if you have multiple claims on the same player, you go to the Board. It's simple: The FAABoard is a list of every team in the league—it has nothing to do with the standings. If more than one claim is staked for a player, the highest owner on the board gets the player. That's it.

In this system, free agents are paid a flat free-agent salary depending on the time of year:

> **Before the All-Star Break:**
> $20 for a normal free agent
> $15 for a free agent replacing an injured player at the same position
>
> **After the All-Star Break:**
> $25 for a normal free agent
> $20 for an injury replacement

There are three stipulations to this system:

1. All free agents are frozen on the acquiring owner's active roster for two weeks. They cannot be reserved, traded, or waived during that time.

2. In accordance with the two-week rule, no free agents may be acquired during the last two weeks of the season, since the off-season does not count as active duty. This makes last-ditch September replacement efforts interesting.

3. If you decide your free agent is a keeper, his salary becomes $15 for next season. This is how our league likes to do things. You can keep his salary at its current level or not. Your choice. But if you think reducing a free agent's price when he's a keeper is making things too easy, think again. We've found over and over that $15 is a real threshold, should-I-keep-him price. Many owners agonize, wondering if the player will go for less in the next draft. Tough call.

There is no limit to the number of free agents an owner can acquire, as long as he is in compliance with the salary cap. And trust me, if you pick up a few noninjury free agents, those dollars add up fast. (See Appendix A, "A Sample Rulebook," for salary cap guidelines.) The winning dude now owns the player for the normal free-agent salary. He can do whatever he wants with the player (but no rough stuff) after the two-week active roster freeze.

Here's the key to the Board system: If multiple claims come in, the owner who wins also is moved to the bottom of the Board, moving everyone else up a notch. For example, here's what the fictional Arizona Stall League looks like before multiple claims:

Fedora Brigade	The Unbearable Rightness of Being Rush
The Monty Hall Bangers	Fanny's Tequila Shooters
R.J.'s Tobacco Suits	Ks R Us
The Chosen Ones	The Surgin' Generals
Runs 'N' Noses	The Dead Cat Swingers
Bill's Partisan Scum	The Jennifer Love Hewitts

It's 1998. Britney Spears is only a twinkle in *Billboard*'s eye. *Armageddon* is #1 at the movie house. Ah, nothing like the old days.

Randy Johnson just came over to the Astros in a trade that everyone thinks sewed up the National League pennant. We know now that that's not true, not even close. But The Unit is landing, and everyone in the 'Zona Stall League wants him, especially the Love Hewitts, for obvious reasons.

But look! The Fedora Brigade's owner, Mike Zimmerman, is on vacation in southern Sri Lanka (hunting the elusive pipsquack bird). The Monty Hall Bangers haven't been in touch since May, when they lost four starters to injury. R.J. of the Tobacco Suits puts in his claim at $20 (the injury discount for a post–All-Star pickup). The Hewitts put in at $25, as do the Noses, Generals, and Swingers.

According to the Board, R.J. gets The Unit. But he moves to the bottom of the list, while everyone below him jumps up a notch—like so:

Fedora Brigade	Fanny's Tequila Shooters
The Monty Hall Bangers	Ks R Us
The Chosen Ones	The Surgin' Generals
Runs 'N' Noses	The Dead Cat Swingers
Bill's Partisan Scum	The Jennifer Love Hewitts
The Unbearable Rightness of Being Rush	R.J.'s Tobacco Suits

Nice and simple, right? You'll find that even if you're last on the list, you'll move up rapidly. Free agents are scarfed up like M&Ms.

You can establish the initial Board order on Draft Day by random drawing, picking numbers out of a hat. Or you can go by standings, last to first. You can carry the Board order from year to year, or redo it fresh every Draft Day. It's all up to you.

Foul Tips

Board positions are perfectly tradeable. The #1 slot is especially valuable as the major league trading deadline (July 31) approaches.

One last bit of advice about the Board system: Board positions make great trade bait. The #1 slot is especially valuable as the major league trading deadline (July 31) approaches. Cross-league trades are more apt to happen in the weeks leading up to the big day. Good luck, and happy acquiring.

Budget Talks

The FAABudget works differently. At the beginning of the season, each owner has a supplementary budget of $100. When multiple claims are staked on a player, the Commish alerts the owners interested. They must then submit a confidential bid for the player.

Minimum bid is $1. Maximum bid can vary, depending on your league. You can make it $52, the individual player salary cap that our league uses for Draft Day. You can make it however much is left in that owner's FAABudget. Or you can make it something else. It's up to you. Whoever has the highest bid wins. The winning bid then becomes the free agent's salary for that season. It applies to the salary cap just like any other player salary would. In the event of ties, the Commish simply tells the players involved to up the ante.

This system brings its own strategies and caveats. If you spend early and often, you'll be shut out of the big bids for good players who cross leagues. If you play it conservative, you'll have a big pile of useless $$$ (no carryovers to next year, big guy). The only advantage is not having spent it in the first place.

Strike Three

If you blow your FAABudget early, you won't have any money left to compete for a big player who comes over from the other league.

This system also keeps the spirit of the draft alive:

➤ The bidding continues. There's nothing more suspenseful than a sealed-bid auction. Did you bid enough? Did you bid too much? Only your conscience knows for sure.

➤ You can find incredible bargains by anticipating key call-ups and replacements. Going for a player early can mean the difference between paying $1 now or $20+ later. Going early also runs the risk of picking a guy before he's ripe. Timing is of the essence.

➤ Bidding wars mean that free-agent salaries will be closer to fair market value (or at least what your league's market will bear). This makes sense for the big-ticket guys who come over from the other league. In the FAABoard system, Randy Johnson was acquired and kept for $15. A coup for the owner who got him, but not a very realistic price.

Foul Tips

The FAABudget is a great system for padding the kitty. The higher the bids, the more $$$ the league collects.

And if this isn't enough for you? If the FAABoard and the FAABudget don't float your free agent boat? Try this …

Using Both Systems Simultaneously

The Board and the Budget both work well. So well, in fact, that they can be used simultaneously, or to complement each other. Take a look:

Use the FAABoard for regular pickups and the FAABudget strictly for players who come over from the other league, when the demand will spark bidding wars. You'll have to keep track of two systems, but you also get the best of both worlds. Twice the drama! Twice the venom! Half the sanity!

Foul Tips

You can use the FAABoard for regular pickups and the FAA-Budget strictly for players who come over from the other league.

Use the FAABoard system before the All-Star Break and the FAABudget system after the All-Star Break, when the free-agent market heats up. This will establish closer-to-market prices for big-ticket players who make the crossover.

On the FAABoard side, you can play with free agent prices, keeper prices, and deadlines. On the FAABudget, you can fiddle with restrictions, luxury taxes, whatever. The beauty of this game is the endless experimentation you can perform.

You can create any number of variations on these systems to suit your league. Ask around in fantasy baseball chat rooms on the Web. Guys will give you endless advice on how their own system suits their league.

The Price of Pain

Everything has a price. Men. Women. Children. Beer. In fantasy baseball, it's transactions. And when you're talking about players? The salary cap.

Every little move you make should cost you. Not much. But just enough to make you remember the money game. Our league charges the following fees:

➤ **Reserving/activating a player:** 25¢

➤ **Trades:** 25¢ per player

➤ **Free agents:** no charge except salary

For example, if a team reserves one player and promotes another from the minor league roster, the total transaction would cost $1 (25¢ for the reserve, 25¢ for the promotion, and 50¢ for the minor leaguer's salary). Remember, we play with a $260 draft budget. Your numbers will vary depending on where your decimal point lands.

Play with the fees, but I wouldn't charge more than pocket change. You don't want guys thinking about cost when contemplating roster moves—except where salary is concerned. Which brings me to salary caps …

Overheard in the Dugout

In '99, our league's accumulated transaction fees added up to nearly $350. That gave our kitty a lot of extra scratch. Your total will depend on your decimal debate and how much you decide to charge for each move. Remember, it all adds up.

Our league uses a salary cap of $40. This does not include minor leaguers. They are paid for on Draft Day, and their salaries do not kick into the cap until they are promoted to the active roster. I urge you to think hard on the cap. If it's too strict, you won't be able to move players freely. If it's too generous, owners will stockpile free agents on their reserve rosters, which can really hurt a deep league. Forty dollars works well for us, but every league is different.

Strike Three

Don't confuse salary cap with draft budget. You're allowed to spend $260 on Draft Day. After that, you may acquire players so long as your total team salary does not exceed $40, or whatever cap your league settles on.

As always, I recommend using the systems of roster management I've outlined, simply because these methods are tried and true. But ask around. I'm not the only bush burning in the grotto. The realm of fantasy baseball is a big ol' forest fire full of experts. Just don't burn yourself.

Recommended viewing: Any baseball blooper reel, whether it be ESPN's most recent compilation on *Baseball Tonight*, or the Dire Straits *Walk of Life* video (if you're ancient enough to remember it). There's nothing better to put you in the mood for baseball.

The Least You Need to Know

➤ Your mid-season free agent lists should be a natural extension of your Draft Day lists, with up-to-date values of every player left unclaimed. Update them regularly.

➤ If you play in an NL- or AL-only league, establish a system for who gets dibs on players coming over from the other league.

➤ When multiple owners claim a free agent in the FAABoard system, the owner highest on the Board gets the free agent.

➤ When multiple owners claim a free agent in the FAABudget system, a secret-bid auction is held. The highest bidder gets the player.

➤ Your league can use either the FAABoard or the FAABudget system, or both. They can complement each other and add strategy.

Part 5

It's a Long, Hot Summer

Are you ready for some baseball? By the time your league has had its draft, the first trading blood has been drawn, and the free-agent pool has been drained, Opening Day can't come soon enough. It's a lot like a scene from Excalibur *or* Braveheart—*all your soldiers lined up and ready to do battle. Their replacements—should you need them—sweat it out on your reserve roster. Now all you need is some guy in a blue shirt to scream, "Attack!" or "Play ball," as it were.*

These next chapters will take you step by step, month by month, through a fantasy baseball season. I'll peddle the usual good advice, and I'll also tell the story of my own team, the Fedora Brigade 1999.

I'll show you my moves and what I was thinking at the time. I'll also tell you what I'm thinking now—and they ain't the same things. You'll see for yourself how a team is run, how things sometimes don't go as planned, and how sweet it is when they do. I think you'll learn something useful. I know I have. So get ready—Opening Day is here.

Chapter 14

April and May: Opening Day Jitters and the Virtue of Patience

> ### In This Chapter
>
> ➤ Don't panic when you see the numbers
>
> ➤ Stats that will make you crazy
>
> ➤ Is it a career year ... or just a hot start?
>
> ➤ Zim's saga begins

Superstition will kill you. You know what I mean: You tune in to an Opening Day game that features one of your pitchers or one of your hitters. You say proudly, beer breath huffing, "My pitcher's first pitch will determine what my season will be like." At which point he throws it to the backstop.

You bury your face in your hands, not realizing how silly you look and how stupid you sound. That one pitch is not your whole season anymore than is a leadoff man's first at-bat. Heck, many times a player's first *month* is a write-off.

You can take all your superstitions and paranoia and stuff them in a sock, mister. Then shove them under your bed and forget you ever had them. Silliness like that affects your judgment. You need to be cold, objective, and as bitter as a downsized executioner. You're a General Manager now. Act like one.

The First Time Ever I Saw Your Stats

The worst mistake any fantasy owner—novice or expert—can make is to panic. This statement is true at any time during the year. But never is it more true than in the misty, chilly nights of April. Say your team tanks in every category. Maybe only one or two guys are off to hot starts. Every strategy you set up is collapsing before your eyes. Your season—a triumphant dream only a few weeks ago—is now in flames.

You e-mail every owner with prospective deals. Every pitcher with an ERA over 5.00 is available, even though their names would make any baseball fan drool. Every batter with an average under .200 can be had, too, including a couple of future Hall of Famers. You don't care. You have to do *something* to stop the bleeding.

Foul Tips

Don't panic: April and May are not the time to judge your season. Let your players hit their strides.

Meanwhile, a few sympathetic owners—guys who really want to help you out—offer to take some of these disappointing players off your hands. To prove their generosity, they bear gifts: pitchers who have won their first three decisions and batters who have hit .500 for the month. Hey, not bad. You snag yourself a couple of performers. You start to feel better about yourself and your skills. Maybe you're not so stupid after all.

Then May rolls around. Those guys you traded for have stopped winning. The hitters have stopped hitting. And the solid players you gave up? Exploding across the league like a Gulf War light show.

Strike Three

The standings will fluctuate as much as the batting averages in April and May. Ignore them.

Do *not* panic when you see your team's stats in April and May. Sit back. Take a deep breath. Think. After that, if you're still convinced a player has gone south for the summer, then reserve him, deal him, or waive him. But if you have any doubts—if the player is a veteran and a proven performer, or if his job is not in jeopardy—hold on to him with both hands.

If you have an alternative at his position, fine, reserve the guy for a while. Ride out his misery. If you don't, the buzzards known as your competitors will be waiting for your call, drooling at the prospect of picking up an undervalued performer. Don't fall for it.

In the early goings, the standings will fluctuate as much as the batting averages. Ignore them. Seriously. I mean, you'll know where you're lacking just by who you have on your squad. Say you're down 10+ stolen bases on May 15. *Relax*. If you drafted speed, the speed will come. Have faith. There could be a hundred reasons why a guy doesn't perform in April. To name a very few …

➤ **Weather.** Some guys like it hot. April is not.

➤ **Rhythm.** Despite spring training, the routines are not yet there. It takes some players time to get comfortable.

➤ **Timing.** Everyone slumps. It just looks worse statistically in April because there are no previous numbers to keep things respectable.

The beauty of baseball is the length of its season. Sure, we call them the boys of summer. But they play through two months of spring and a few weeks of autumn, too. Six months. Twenty-five weeks of regular season. From the first week of April to the first week of October.

And you're worried about a few bad days? Shame on you. You should know better. Thankfully, now you do.

The Law of the Street: Sell High

Maybe the secret of this game *can* be boiled down into one sentence: Be a vulture. Substitute any animal you want. Lions, tigers, and bears are a bit blasé. Try wolverine, Tasmanian devil, jackal, or barracuda. Anyway, you get the point. For every bit of advice I give one way, the opposite also applies.

If I say don't panic and trade a proven performer, what should you do? The opposite: Go out and find the guy who is panicking and steal away his fallen stars in lieu of your shooting stars. Offer the journeyman pitcher who has no right being 4-0, or the slow-batted outfielder who's clubbed seven April homers. These guys will look like Koufax and Killebrew in comparison, and their value will never be higher. In June, when the books begin to balance themselves, those supermen will have had their kryptonite chaser while you're riding a slow starter all the way to Labor Day.

> **Foul Tips**
>
> Be a cold-blooded scavenger. Be an opportunist. Just be there when you sense fear in another owner. Use it to make him do something he wouldn't do in his right mind.

It's not unusual to see a batter maintain a .500 average into May. Or a pitcher sporting a sub-1.00 ERA. Or any other stat you can think of. Hot starts are par golf in this game. The numbers are so perverted, they'll make you crazy. So either take advantage of them, or sit back and enjoy them.

Panic is for the weak. And the weak are eaten like caviar before the hot meals of the summer.

Career Years and Other Freaks of Human Nature

It does happen. Some players explode for amazing seasons when no one else sees it coming. We call them sleepers. If you have one, burn some incense and sacrifice a jelly doughnut to the gods for smiling upon you. But how can you tell—especially in April and May—the difference between a career year and a hot start? Tough call. There are a few barometers to monitor:

➤ **Past performance.** The pitcher's never won more than five games in a year. His ERA's never been below 5.00. Good clues.

➤ **Age.** Is the guy a journeyman hurler/pinch hitter? Or is he a 27-year-old former-stud prospect who has finally blossomed? Don't be fooled: Even a 33-year-old can bust out.

➤ **The word on the street.** What are the experts saying? His manager and teammates? The sportswriters? For example, in '99, I knew I had a sleeper supreme in Roger Cedeno when Mike Piazza said, "Something's different. He's *faster* this year." Piazza would know—he knew Cedeno from their L.A. days.

> **Foul Tips**
>
> Sell high. Players off to hot starts are like over-valued stocks. Trade them now while the paper value is high.

Overheard in the Dugout

Probably the most unlikely pitcher/hitter combo to break out in '99 were Kent Bottenfield (Cardinals) and Luis Gonzalez (D-backs). Bottenfield's line: 18 wins, 3.97 ERA, 89 walks in 190.1 innings. But his WHIP was 1.503. Had I owned him, I would've traded him by his ninth win. Gonzalez's numbers: .336 in 614 at-bats, 26 home runs, 111 RBIs, 112 runs, 9 stolen bases. My thinking would've been, "He's a one-half wonder."

Everyone in real and fantasy baseball waited patiently for these two to come back to Earth in '99. Neither did, although Bottenfield's numbers suggest that he dodged some bullets. The bottom line is, no one could've predicted these breakouts or how long they'd last.

Hot starts generally fizzle as the year progresses, but there is no set timetable. April? May? The All-Star Break? You can only monitor the player's performance, consult the experts, and go with your gut.

Cinderella Story? Going for Choke? My Tale of Woe

Well, here we go. Am I ready to stare into the mirror and scream? Yes—I do it every day. But now there's something at stake. Like I did in the Senate hearings, I need to tell the truth about what happened. Why it happened. It's the only way to prevent future mistakes, even though there are always new ones to make.

I'm an active owner. Sometimes hyperactive. I love to trade. I love test-driving free agents for their two-week freeze period. For me, a week without a transaction is like a magic show without a rabbit. This season is no different. I pulled an array of moves before Opening Day, jockeying for position at the gates. If you remember my Draft Day roster, you also remember that I had a lot of work to do before the season began:

Strike Three

Hot starts almost always peter out. You just have to predict when. All you can do is monitor the player's performance, consult the experts, and go with your gut. You will make mistakes. Prepare for them, deal with them, and do not dwell on them. Repair the damage and move on.

My Draft Day Roster

Position	Player	Price
Starters		
C	Tyler Houston	$2
C	Bobby Estalella	$4
1B	Kevin Young	$16
3B	Aramis Ramirez	$1
CI	Sean Casey	$22
2B	Craig Biggio	$31
SS	Pat Meares	$5
MI	Damian Jackson	$1
OF	Sammy Sosa	$30
OF	Rondell White	$10
OF	J.D. Drew	$5
OF	Todd Dunwoody	$6

continues

My Draft Day Roster   (continued)

Position	Player	Price
Starters		
UT	Angel Pena (C)	$2
SP	Greg Maddux	$37
SP	Chan Ho Park	$26
SP	Mike Hampton	$15
SP	Bobby Jones	$13
SP	Masato Yoshii	$10
SP	Kevin Millwood	$7
SP	Bill Pulsipher	$5
RP	Wayne Gomes	$6
RP	Jason Christiansen	$5
RP	Antonio Osuna	$1
Reserves		
RP	Mike Remlinger	
C	Jason LaRue	
OF	Lance Berkman	

Only nine of those batters were going to see regular playing time. That's a lot of dead weight in prospects and injuries. Estalella, Ramirez, Pena, and Osuna had to go. Jackson was iffy—I didn't know if he was going to make the Pods squad yet. I was also iffy on Masato Yoshii. Liked him on Draft Day. Not so crazy about him now.

Where to begin? Like the man said: at the beginning.

Spring Cleaning

My first trade happened on March 20. I sent outfielder Todd Dunwoody ($6) to the Philadelphia Phantoms for third baseman Aaron Boone ($4).

The Strategy. At the time, I figured that their stats would be a push. Both had some power and speed. However, I needed a third baseman more than I needed an outfielder. Now I could reserve Aramis Ramirez and start Boone. Good deal.

What Really Happened. Boone tanked in a big way in the first half, getting sent to Triple-A. But this story isn't over yet …

A week later, I traded SP Bobby Jones ($13) to the Phantoms to retrieve Dunwoody.

The Strategy. Upon further review, I needed offense more than I needed pitching. Jones had been offered initially, so I offered him up again. The Phantoms bit.

What Really Happened. Bobby Jones tore a muscle. Dunwoody spent most of '99 in Triple-A. And Boone went on to have a blistering second half, resulting in a respectable season. He's now a rising star.

As you can see, these moves were based on pure speculation. The season hadn't started yet. Should I have been making these deals at all? Should I have been waiting for the season to begin? It's a good debate. But like I said, I tweak my rosters almost endlessly. At the time, these were very real deficiencies that needed to be filled *immediately*.

My first free-agent pickups came the same week. I snagged relief pitcher Stan Belinda ($20 regular free-agent salary) of the Reds and outfielder Roger Cedeno ($20) of the Mets.

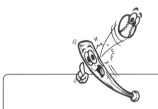

Foul Tips

Make your moves with confidence. Second-guessing can come later. Questioning your decisions now will only paralyze you, and you could miss an opportunity.

The Strategy. Belinda was a mainstay in my '98 bullpen. He'd been around for a while, always picked up some saves, and struck out a batter an inning. A good inning burner who would add some depth. Cedeno we talked about earlier in the book.

What Really Happened. Belinda was the first real mistake of the year. Several days later, he went on the disabled list, diagnosed with multiple sclerosis. A crushing blow to a respected player. He was out for a long, long time. And thanks to free-agent rules, stuck on my active roster for the first two weeks of the season. Yeesh. But Cedeno? Woo-hoo!

I made a trade offer to the Reading Reds on March 25. Greg Maddux for Brett Tomko and either Edgardo Alfonso, Carl Everett, or Mike Cameron. It didn't happen.

The Strategy. Offense. I needed a good young bat, either an outfielder or a middle infielder. Tomko would've filled Maddux's slot, but not his shoes.

What Really Happened. Had this deal gone through, it would've been good for both teams. Alfonso, Everett, and Cameron are now legitimate stars. Oh well.

Two more transactions closed out the pre-season. I dealt SP Masato Yoshii ($10) to the Shepherds of Fury for outfielder Jermaine Allensworth ($5) of the Mets, and picked up free agent relief pitcher Doug Henry ($20) of the Astros.

The Strategy. More depth. But more to the point, Masato Yoshii had a horrifying spring training. Plus, he was rumored to be headed to the AL. I no longer wanted any part of him. I figured Allensworth to get good at-bats with the injury-plagued Rickey Henderson and Bobby Bonilla ahead of him. Doug Henry was a respectable inning-burning middle reliever who could add depth.

What Really Happened. Yoshii was a roller coaster all year, ultimately disappointing everyone. Allensworth was useless, dumped in Triple-A for the year. And Henry? I don't know. I cut him loose after two ludicrous weeks and never looked back.

As you can see, this is just a sampling of the constant wheels and deals that spin behind the scenes. Mine was one team of 12. Everyone else was doing the same thing. And the season hadn't even started yet. Anyway, at the time I felt a little better about my squad. I had no idea what the future would bring, but at least the season could now, finally, at long last, begin.

April Showers, or Where Most of My Pitchers Were Sent by the Third Inning

Boy, did it begin. By April 7, I was mauled by an injury epidemic:

➤ Shortstop Pat Meares: wrist, surgical candidate

➤ Relief pitcher Antonio Osuna: elbow, disabled list

➤ Relief pitcher Mike Remlinger: back, disabled list

➤ Relief pitcher Stan Belinda: multiple sclerosis, disabled list

➤ Catcher Bobby Estalella: shoulder, Triple-A

➤ Third baseman Aaron Boone: stomach pains, condition unknown

In one week, all my pitching depth was erased. I immediately did some major-league free agent shopping: In one day I nabbed third baseman Dave Magadan of the Padres, jack-of-all-stuff Dave Berg of the Marlins, and catcher Todd Pratt of the Mets—all for the free-agent discount of $15 each.

The Strategy. Depth. Pure and simple. I knew none of them would break any batting records. But I also knew that all would give me respectable batting averages.

What Really Happened. Pretty much what I wanted. All hit well, but played sparingly. They were band-aids, and they lasted about as long.

Great Quotes from Zim's Notes

April 9   Probably have to deal a starting pitcher. Millwood or Hampton. Wouldn't want to deal anyone else.

April 9   Damian Jackson could take over short and steal 30. But I don't have that kind of luck.

April 21   Brett Tomko will probably be better than Mike Hampton (you'd hope).

April 21   A couple of rookies, Joe Nathan in San Francisco and Todd Ritchie in Pittsburgh, got called up and started well. But they are booby traps sent to tempt me. I must remain pure.

To make matters worse, two weeks into the season, no one was hitting except first baseman Sean Casey (who led the NL). Check out these two-week wonders:

2B	Craig Biggio	.136
3B	Aaron Boone	.000
OF	J.D. Drew	.111
OF	Roger Cedeno	.200
OF	Todd Dunwoody	.190
OF	Sammy Sosa	.095
C	Tyler Houston	.143
OF	Rondell White	.174
1B	Kevin Young	.261 (Wow! A hitter!)

Those numbers, above any other piece of evidence I have provided, are living proof of this chapter's axiom: *Don't panic.*

If anyone had a reason to panic, it was me. My entire lineup had a case of the yips. But most of that crew are proven performers. I wasn't worried about them, long-term. In the short-term, however, there were some deals brewing …

Outfielder Rondell White ($10) has always been a fantasy enigma. Huge talent. Huge injury risk. In '98, he was on pace for a 30-30 season. But as always, he managed to go down for the year in the middle of a peak performance. Now, in '99, he was playing every day. But danger lurked in the wind: He'd had enough fluid drained from his knees to fill a beer stein. But he was surging toward .300. Unfortunately, .300 would not be enough from him. I needed power and speed, and his creaky knees sapped both. Still, his name and his batting average would go a long way—or so I hoped.

165

I immediately sent out a league-wide e-mail extolling the virtues of the now-available-for-a-limited-time Rondell White: .300 hitter; healthy (legally); low price of $10; 30-30 candidate (in April, even Orel Hershiser is a 30-30 candidate). As I thought, the interest in White was lively. I received the following offers:

From the Wilson BigDogs: White for Cub closer Rod Beck ($31) and minor league outfielder Milton Bradley (almost worth acquiring for his name alone)

From the Reading Reds: White for Padres SP Matt Clement ($11) and Mets set-up man Armando Benitez ($7); or White and Mike Hampton for Clement, Benitez, and SP Brett Tomko ($13)

From the Sculp's Hill Seminoles: White and Hampton for Dodger gazillionaire Kevin Brown

There were three other offers, but these were the ones that were the most serious. As you can see, everyone had a jones for Mike Hampton, whom I ultimately held on to (good move). At the time, I was interested in moving only White—for two players, if possible.

With the benefit of hindsight, the Clement-Benitez deal is the no-brainer. Talk about a steal. But at the time, Armando was squarely behind John Franco in the Mets' bullpen. He just didn't seem worth it. Plus, saves are a cancer in the belly of this game. Begone, saves!

With some further negotiations, I traded White to the Reds for starting pitchers Matt Clement and Brett Tomko.

The Strategy. I get two quality starters for one injury-prone outfielder. In my mind, I made out like a bandit.

What Really Happened. Tomko tanked. He showed sporadic flashes of brilliance, but ultimately ended up in the bullpen by way of Triple-A. Clement performed admirably for a first full-year guy, and I later packaged him for a much better player. We'll talk about that later.

This story of my trades has two morals, as I see it:

1. Take a page from the media: hype works. When you get the entire league involved in a trade proposal—and everyone knows it—pound for pound, the offers will be more serious and open to negotiation.

2. Always take Benitez.

By the end of April, I hadn't panicked too badly. I still believed most of my moves would bear fruit, albeit rotten. As for the standings? Solidly in eighth place, 44 category points out of first place. Hey, no one said it would be easy.

Overheard in the Dugout

My team officially hit bottom on April 28, 1999. My team's box score for the day amounted to a .189 batting average, two RBIs, one run scored, a token steal, an ERA of 11.25, and a WHIP of 2.333. It couldn't get any worse than that. Could it?

May Flowers, or How My Team Blossomed

My first trade of May turned out to be one of the best I made all year. On May 3, I dealt relief pitcher Antonio Osuna ($1) and my second round 2000 reserve pick to the Shepherds of Fury for Reds starting pitcher Steve Parris ($5).

> **The Strategy.** Tomko was sent down to Triple-A and his direct replacement in the rotation was Parris. Parris's numbers in '98 were respectable even though he was a part-timer. When he did get a chance to start, he pitched well. It seemed like a decent risk.

> **What Really Happened.** Parris became a mainstay in the Reds' rotation, winning nearly a dozen games. Osuna tried a few comebacks, but eventually shut it down for the year, facing surgery. Which means I essentially got Parris for a second round reserve pick. Which is nice.

May witnessed the beginning of my team's surgence. (You have to have a surgence before you can have a resurgence.) As predicted, many players began shaking off the rust and contributing. But alas, it wasn't enough. The first week of May I slipped into ninth place. Totally unacceptable.

What did I do? I put a quarter in the hype machine again. I sent out a league-wide e-mail saying that if my team didn't see marked improvement by May 15, I would begin wholesale changes to the roster. (How's that for not panicking?) My reasons for doing this were twofold:

1. I wanted to see if anyone would take me seriously. Who knows what kind of offers I'd get for Sosa, Biggio, and the others.

2. I also wanted to generate buzz for buzz's sake. This kind of thing keeps everyone interested, their blood pumping, their brains rattling. Was I serious about dumping my team for different personnel? Maybe. Maybe not. Like I said, you never know what people will offer.

Foul Tips

Things getting stale in your league? Offer up your entire team for trade and see what happens.

Ultimately, this gambit went nowhere. Everyone assumed I was dumping my team for prospects in preparation for next season. Not true, I told them several times. I'm still playing for this year; I just want better players!

On May 14, Aaron Boone was sent to Triple-A and shortstop Pat Meares went in for surgery, out for the year. *That* hurt. Now I had holes at shortstop and third base that were too big for band-aid free agents. I needed bats and I needed them fast. I went on an offer tear, sending out more feelers than a body snatcher in a bordello:

To the Haven Bulldogs: Greg Maddux and Todd Dunwoody for outfielder Larry Walker ($43).

To the Shepherds of Fury: Maddux for third baseman Chipper Jones ($32).

To the Dallastown Black Crackers: I want catcher Javy Lopez ($23) and third baseman Vinny Castilla ($33). Name your price.

And so on. For my efforts, I was rejected by all. I managed to make two timely free-agent pickups: first baseman Kevin Millar ($20) of the Marlins and outfielder Jeffrey Hammonds ($15) of the Reds.

The Strategy. We spoke about Millar earlier in the book. Starter Derek Lee was sent to Triple-A and Millar got his shot. I trumped the league and put him at utility. Hammonds, who was seeing decent playing time, replaced Dunwoody in the outfield.

What Really Happened. Millar played well. He was a mainstay on my roster for the rest of the year. Hammonds was solid, contributing power and average. He was later packaged in a deal for a better player.

More Great Quotes from Zim's Notes	
May 7	My entire early season planning now hinges on Brett Tomko and Bill Pulsipher.
May 14	Remember the name Kevin Millar.
May 26	Ron Gant still seems like my best bet.

In all my scrambling for trades and free agents, a funny thing happened. My team started to play. And I mean *play*. Sosa boomed home runs, Cedeno stole every base in sight, Casey roped line drive after line drive, and Hampton, Millwood, Parris, and, yes, even Brett Tomko started pitching well. Check out these numbers, as of May 24:

OF	Sammy Sosa	.268, 14 HR
1B	Kevin Young	.327, 27 RBIs
C	Tyler Houston	.391, 4 HR
2B	Craig Biggio	.288, 12 SB
OF	Roger Cedeno	.330, 21 SB

Not bad. The slackers were still J.D. Drew, Todd Dunwoody, and Aaron Boone. I hardly noticed, I was so busy writing and answering trade e-mails. Then, on Monday morning, May 30, exactly two months into the '99 season, I printed the stats and standings like I did every week. What did I see?

I was in fourth place.

Zim's Roster as of May 30

Position	Player	Price
Starters		
C	Tyler Houston	$2
C	Todd Pratt	$15
1B	Kevin Young	$16
3B	Dave Magadan	$20
CI	Sean Casey	$22
2B	Craig Biggio	$31
SS	Damian Jackson	$1
MI	Dave Berg	$15
OF	Sammy Sosa	$30
OF	Roger Cedeno	$20
OF	Jeffrey Hammonds	$15
OF	J.D. Drew	$5
UT	Kevin Millar	$20
SP	Greg Maddux	$37
SP	Chan Ho Park	$26
SP	Mike Hampton	$15
SP	Brett Tomko	$13

continues

Zim's Roster as of May 30   (continued)

Position	Player	Price
Starters		
SP	Kevin Millwood	$7
SP	Odalis Perez (from minors)	$5
SP	Steve Parris	$5
RP	Wayne Gomes	$6
RP	Jason Christiansen	$5
RO	Mike Remlinger	$5
Reserves		
SS	Pat Meares	(DL)
OF	Todd Dunwoody	(AAA)
3B	Aaron Boone	(AAA)
OF	Jermaine Allensworth	(bench)
SP	Bill Pulsipher	(DL)

Fourth place. Not a bad starting point for the rest of the season. But there was so much season to go. A lot more would soon happen.

Recommended viewing: *The Natural.* A classic from the Sundance Kid. Makes you believe that you can play this game, too. Even though you can't.

The Least You Need to Know

➤ Don't panic: April and May are not the time to judge your season. Let your players hit their strides.

➤ The standings will fluctuate as much as the stats in April and May. Ignore them.

➤ Sell high. Players off to hot starts are like over-valued stocks. Trade them now while their value is higher.

➤ Hot starts will fizzle, but there is no set timetable. You can only monitor the player's performance, consult the experts, and go with your gut.

Chapter 15

Things Heat Up: June to the All-Star Break

In This Chapter

➤ Do you have a morning routine?

➤ Your season begins to gel in June

➤ All-Star reflection time

➤ Get ready for the second half

➤ Zim's mistakes mount

June is a great time for baseball. Memorial Day weekend has officially cracked a champagne bottle on the prow of the summer with barbecues, camping adventures, and beer-laced trips down short-term memory lane. In June, you can leave the jacket at home for night games (unless you live in San Francisco, in which case you can leave the parka but take the army blanket). You can walk the dog in the morning without shoes and the dew feels good. You can plant yourself on the front porch with a jigger of lemonade, listen to a ballgame on the radio, doze off, and not have a care in the world.

That is, if you are just a regular baseball fan. If you're a fantasy owner, you may know it's June because of the calendar, but chances are you don't even know if the sun's out. You're still locked in your basement wondering in the sweet name of Griffey Jr. why the owner of the Dogtown Fire Hydrants hasn't returned your e-mail re: Boone for Batista.

June has its own atmosphere in fantasy baseball. The season is well on its way and many surprises are already out of the bag. But not all of them. Hopefully you've been patient, vigilant, and quick to take advantage of your foes. For now is the time to size up their throats.

Rise and Whine: Your Morning Routine

If you managed to avoid the highlight shows the night before, there is nothing more suspenseful than opening the morning paper. You toss aside the other sections in favor of the really important headlines like "Phils Eke Out Win vs. 'Spos."

The box scores are spread before you like some ancient Egyptian manuscript and you're Indiana Jones looking for Pharaoh Jim's Lost Anubus Trading Card Collection. You casually glance at the scores, but not that closely. You seek out only the players you own. What did they do? Why didn't they play? Oh no, are they hurt? Coffee … *more coffee!*

This is your morning routine. By now, on June 1, it should be a vital part of the waking up process—so much so that if it's disrupted by vacation, visitors, or a lax paperboy, you'll be quite the time bomb 'til lunch. Like breakfast, your morning baseball routine is the most important mental meal of the day.

If you're an owner worth his salt, you'll accomplish more before 9 A.M. than most people do all day. A solid, faithful morning routine enables you to react immediately to news, update player values, plot transactions, and basically run your team the way it should be run.

Foul Tips

By June, your morning routine should be in place, enabling you to react immediately to news, update player values, plot transactions, and anything else that needs your attention.

Overheard in the Dugout

My morning routine lasts all day. I log onto the Internet first thing in the morning. There I get box scores, player news, and overnight e-mails. I then send my own e-mails with trade props, counterprops, and so on. I log on again at lunch, after dinner, and right before bed for updates and more scores. Am I insane? Close … darn close.

My morning routine lasts all day, especially in June when the competition is heating up. Here's a timeline for my average day, including the places I go for information:

> 6 A.M.: Go online. Check ESPN for box scores and news. Proceed to Rotonews to check on league standings and individual player updates. Print them out once a week to add to my notes. Answer e-mail. Ignore family.

> 8:30 A.M.: Read *USA Today* cover to cover to remind me that the world turns during baseball season (thus explaining why we have both day and night games). Spend extra time with box scores and team notes.

> 1 P.M.: Go online at work to *USA Today*'s Internet baseball page for anything I missed, including Roto Roost, a daily online fantasy column. Proceed to Rotonews for updated player updates.

> 7 P.M.: Check e-mail, verify who's pitching that night.

> 11 P.M.: Check in-progress box scores at ESPN online, answer e-mail, try to sleep.

If this seems excessive, maybe it is. But I'm never, ever out of the loop when it comes to injuries, benchings, trades, rumors, and anything else that you need to know to stay on top of this game. One of the beauties of baseball—as opposed to football and hockey—is that you have new stats flowing every single day. Someone is always playing. There is always something to react to. Always news to read.

Get a routine. Stick to it. It's not hard if you need morning box scores like you need oxygen. Like some half-baked exercise infomercial, all it takes is five minutes a day.

It's important. Trust me.

Strike Three

If you're not dedicated to daily information, then you're probably not dedicated to your league. Why play if you're not trying to win?

What Makes June Gel

June could be perceived as a middle-of-the-road month and not very meaningful. That couldn't be more wrong. June will tell you more about the final outcome of your league than you could possibly imagine. By now you'll know which owners are in it for the long haul. The others? Let me guess: They have gradually slipped away, not answering phone messages or e-mails, and when they do, they're not much interested in trading to help themselves—let alone you.

Overheard in the Dugout

By June '99, our league had lost two owners to resignation. A third was virtually incommunicado by the All-Star Break. One guy had a personality conflict, another didn't realize how involved the league was, and the third fell out of contention and lost interest. We luckily found replacements so the league could continue with 12 owners. But as you'll see, you'll know who's serious by the time June 1 flips over on the calendar.

Why does this happen? Some guys are draft moles. Some guys are lazy. Some may not have realized how involved this game really is. When they see their team falling in the standings, they think it's all over. They don't know where to begin to stop the bleeding. There isn't much you can do about these people. You can replace them if you find gullible, er, suitable subs. Or you can go on without them. Either way, it's a shame.

On the Field in June

June is also when players hit their stride. Take a page from '98: In June, Sammy Sosa broke the monthly home run record with 20, assuring his place next to Mark McGwire as a serious threat to Maris's season mark.

Strike Three

League standings begin to solidify in June, so don't get left behind. If you need to make a big move to get in the race, now's the time to start scheming. June is too early to give up. There's more than half the season left!

You'll notice that in April and May, the league standings fluctuate daily. An especially bad or good day by your team can move you a couple of places either way. But in June? Nope. The stats—like pouring cement for a foundation—will have accumulated enough that the standings solidify. Now it takes a trend rather than an anomaly to move you up or down.

What does this mean? Well, if by June 15 you find yourself in the bottom half of the standings, it's time to seriously consider a move. If you wait too long, you'll be buried. You may be frustrated, but do not, I repeat, *do not* quit. The temptation to *dump* will be great. Resist it. By dumping, I mean trading high-salary stars to contending teams for low-cost keepers, minor leaguers, and reserve picks.

The majors do it, and you should, too. But not in June! It's far too early to quit. You could be in last place, 60 points out of first, and I guarantee you it is possible to finish in the money. A good trade here, a key free agent there, and suddenly you're a Surgin' General. Some reasons why it's too early to dump:

➤ Any hot prospects you trade for now may be cold fish by October. The same goes for cheap keepers.

➤ Half a season is an eternity—plenty of time for a savvy owner to turn his team around.

➤ Most important: By joining the league, you swore an oath to try to remain competitive until the bitter end. Sure, eventually you have to face reality if you have a bad team. But June is far too early for that.

> **Trash Talk**
>
> A **dump** takes place when an owner trades away all his star talent in favor of keepers and draft picks in preparation for next season. Also known as quitting.

I've always craved the challenge of taking a dead-last team in mid-season and seeing if I could turn it around. In a way, that would be more of a measurement of fantasy skill than drafting a team from scratch. In a matter of a few months you'd be able to see just how well you judge talent, predict performance, and trade. But dumping in June? That's like folding in seven-card stud with only two cards showing.

Leading Up to the All-Star Break

Okay. It's June 15. The All-Star Break, baseball's traditional halfway mile marker, is right around the corner. It's time to think. And think hard. You could be in first by 10 points or in last by 75 points. Either way, you need to start planning for the second half. If you're a contender, what's it going to take for you to win? If you're a loser (figuratively), what will it take to get you in contention? And if you've sipped the cup of cowardice and decided to dump, who will you trade and who will you seek?

Above all: Be objective about your roster. What do you have? What do you need? It's easy to say, "trade from strength for what you lack." That's oversimplifying things. Performance is unpredictable, no matter how much we study.

You'll no doubt have several players who, despite good health, have disappointed you on every level. You'll want to replace them—but should you? They may be in line for a second-half breakout.

> **Foul Tips**
>
> The All-Star Break is the perfect time to reflect on the first half and what you need to win/contend/survive.

How about those first-half sleepers who dazzled you every morning, making you smile and tell your children that they live in a fair and just world? Chances are they are ripe for a slump … maybe. That's the problem with prognostication: not being able to tell the future.

Here are but a few factors you have to consider:

➤ **Which players will fade?** First-year stars, high-inning/high-appearance pitchers, and everyday catchers are prone to second-half swoons.

➤ **Which ones will rise up?** Disappointing vets, proven high-average hitters, and Mike Piazza are all good second-half bets.

➤ **Free agents go up in price** in the FAABoard system. This makes the salary cap an issue.

Tread—and trade—carefully. Do some research on players and how they perform historically in the second half. And most of all, circle your opponents' rosters like the vulture you are and try to get them to let go of a first-half disappointment. A player who will be so good in the second half that you'll finally be able to add "Super Genius" after your name on your business cards.

A Tribute to Mike Piazza

Mike Piazza breaks all the known rules of the second half: He's a catcher playing 140 to 150 games a year for nearly 10 years and he has shown no signs of slowing down. But his second-half stats for the past three years have been utterly mind-boggling:

	AVG	AB	H	HR	RBI
'97 first half	.357	300	107	16	51
'97 second half	.367	256	94	24	73
'98 first half	.308	302	93	14	48
'98 second half	.351	259	91	18	63
'99 first half	.302	248	75	16	47
'99 second half	.304	286	87	24	77

That's a man to think about at the All-Star Break.

For you, the All-Star Break should be just that: a break. You'll have three days to dislodge yourself from endless pitching rotations and lineup shuffles. However, you'll be up to your lapels in injury reports and trade rumors, which always seem to escalate at that time of year.

Still, after all your data is analyzed, after all your first-half washouts are wrapped with trade-scented bows, after your last devious plot has been warmed to the verge of hatching, take an All-Star Break. Watch the home run derby. Take in the festivities. Soak up the sentiment. Enjoy the midsummer classic as it was meant to be enjoyed: beer in fist, cigar in fingers, and gleam in eye. You've earned it.

Zim's Favorite Mistake

On June 1, I'm in fourth place. In the money. That's nice, but I must say that being in the money in June is nothing to crow about. It means that your work has just begun. It means that you are merely in the ballpark, as it were. You have won nothing.

So far, the Fedora Brigade is solid in batting average, stolen bases, ERA, WHIP, strikeouts, and wins. Which means I have stellar pitching (Hampton, Millwood, Parris) and a bunch of line-drive hitters (Casey, Kevin Young, Biggio). I'm lousy in the power categories, home runs and RBIs. So what do I do? I think. It's June 1. I'm in fourth place. I have a real shot at this thing if I make the right deal. So I think some more, and then some more.

Strike Three

If something is wrong with your roster, don't flirt with the problem. Carpet-bomb it. Make a blockbuster trade for a superstar.

As if reading my mind, the owner of the Dallastown Black Crackers sends out a league-wide e-mail that he's decided to play for next year. He's dumping assets faster than a credit-strapped sugar daddy. And as much as I hate it when owners throw in the towel that early, it is music to my ears. Because I have another definitive fantasy philosophy: If something is wrong with your roster, don't flirt with the problem. Carpet-bomb it.

I traded a "platinum futures" package to the Crackers: starting pitcher Odalis Perez ($5), starting pitcher Matt Clement ($11), third baseman Aaron Boone ($4), super-prospect outfielder Lance Berkman ($5), and my first and third round 2000 reserve picks. In return, I got Colorado third baseman Vinny Castilla ($32), plus throw-in starting pitcher Denny Neagle ($21, on the disabled list at the time).

> **My Strategy.** I needed a big bat. Boone was a first-half washout at third base. Castilla was one of the top three in the league. Like I said, carpet-bomb. If he performed close to his career norms, I could expect another 25 home runs and 100 RBIs from him. And Neagle? I didn't expect much. But if he eventually got healthy, I knew I'd have a solid pitcher on my hands.
>
> **What Really Happened.** Castilla fell short of his career norms, but was still a solid producer. Neagle got healthy and won eight games (3.13 ERA for me) in

177

the second half. Odalis Perez blew out his elbow. Boone's now a potential rising star. Clement turned in a promising second-half performance, while the Crackers eventually waived Berkman for salary cap reasons. All in all, I believe I came out ahead.

At the time, I thought I was giving up too much. Vinny Castilla's name was enough to send ripples through the ranks of the contenders, but still … six players for two? I told myself not to look back. Castilla was still one of the top three third basemen in the majors. It would be worth it.

My move worked in the short term: As of June 6, I rose to second place! Sure, it lasted for only two days. But I tasted what could be mine. I was on the right track. All it would take was a few more well-placed, well-timed moves.

Strike Three

When you make a trade—for good or bad—don't look back. Regrets will cloud your future decisions.

I had to start with my pitching, which was now thin. Trading was not an option. Since I was trying to bolster my RBI and home run output, I couldn't really spare anyone on offense. I also didn't want to dip into my prospect bag—Aramis Ramirez, Damian Jackson, Angel Pena—any more, at least not immediately.

That left free agency. So I went out and acquired the last two starting pitchers available: Milwaukee's Bill Pulsipher (who I had waived earlier for salary cap reasons) and Bobby M. Jones of the Rockies (as opposed to the Bobby Jones who pitches for the Mets). The first of two major June mistakes.

To Thine Own Self Be True, Stupid

Argh. Right there it is in black and white. I broke my personal moratorium on Colorado Rockies pitchers. In retrospect, I should have had a moratorium on Milwaukee pitchers, too, but that's another story.

I really thought I had something with Bobby M. Jones. I watched him carefully, strictly because he was available. He had strung together three straight quality starts—more than six innings, giving up three runs or fewer. I checked up on what the experts said about Jones in the preseason. After the normal Colorado warnings, they all said he had a good arm and would be a solid pickup if he pitched anywhere outside of the Mountain time zone. A potential sleeper.

In my own defense, Jones was pitching well at the time. The wins and strikeouts ka-chinged in my eyes. I said "phooey" and went for him. Pulsipher I knew about, since I'd drafted him. He was coming off a back injury, but pitched extremely well in two Triple-A rehab starts. Seemed safe enough.

Choose your cliché: "famous last words," "eat his words," "words to the wise," "curse words." I used them all.

The Strategy. Simple. Pitching depth. In our league, free-agent starting pitchers are rare (that they were available to begin with should have been a warning sign). After trading Odalis and Clement, I needed innings.

What Really Happened. Bobby M. Jones's string of quality starts ended and never began again. I cut him loose after 20+ innings (9.15 ERA!) and considered myself stupid, but alive. Pulsipher wasn't much better (5.98 ERA for me), but he did win five games and pitched well from time to time. In all, these were two very sloppy, very ill-advised gambles that tore a hole in the seat of my trousers. They very nearly tore flesh. I know better now, but even worse, I knew better then.

Strike Three

Never compromise your beliefs. By signing a Rockies pitcher, I broke one of my personal rules and I got hosed. You will too.

Which leads me to my second major mistake of the month …

I Should've Fired Myself

I love Greg Maddux. You read my previous tribute. A great pitcher. A classy competitor. A nice person (so I'm told). Aside from Roger Clemens, he'll probably be the last pitcher to win 300 games in a long, long time. He was a mainstay on my pitching staff in '98 and, despite my Draft Day recklessness, I welcomed him aboard the happy barge with open arms in '99.

But something happened on the way to victory lane. Maddux forgot how to pitch. He got hit on harder than the last cocktail waitress at a computer programmer convention, routinely giving up 10+ hits per start. Which brings up the ultimate fantasy baseball performance question: Exactly how long should you wait for an underperforming player to turn it around?

Foul Tips

How long should you wait for a player to turn his season around? Depends on the player. Stars will almost always come around.

The situation with Maddux was serious. Feature stories began to run with headlines like: "What's Wrong with Maddux?" and "Is He Done?" Maddux himself and the Braves coaching staff laughed it off, saying that his health was fine. He needed only to improve location.

There was also speculation that the umpires—in reaction to a major league mandate—were enforcing a different strike zone. Maddux (and an equally ineffective Tom Glavine) were no longer getting that vital outside strike call. As a result, they were bringing the ball closer to the plate and getting clobbered.

Foul Tips

Yet another factor affecting player values: umpiring. In '99, the league's "improved" strike zone may have squeezed players such as Maddux and Tom Glavine.

All good theories. Mine? I think it had less to do with the strike zone than with the "catcher's box." It has always existed in the rules, but in '99, umpires demanded that the lines be drawn behind the plate. Catchers were not allowed out of their box. Javy Lopez and Eddie Perez couldn't set up outside to make those outside balls look like strikes.

But all of that is moot. The bottom line was that my best pitcher was now my worst pitcher. It was the most frustrating thing I've ever dealt with as a fantasy owner. Earlier in the season, I'd explored trading Maddux, but only peripherally. They were attempts to see what I could get for him at full value. But now? With an ERA near 5.00 and a WHIP over 1.500? He was just another struggling arm.

Once again, our league's resident psychic, the owner of the Black Crackers, came calling. His offer was a siren's song in the dark of night:

C Javy Lopez ($23) straight up for Maddux ($37).

The drool poured from my lips. Visions of an improved ERA and WHIP, along with the 15 home runs and 60 RBIs Lopez would bring, danced in my head like drunken Shriners. I made the deal instantly. A monumental mistake.

The Strategy. Trading a negative roster force for a positive one. Maddux had been pitching poorly since August of '98. Was he done? Sure looked like it. Javy Lopez was a pretty good trade-off at the time.

What Really Happened. Check out Maddux's numbers:

Greg Maddux Before Trade

W-L	IP	H	BB	K	ERA	WHIP
6-4	92	124	14	57	4.40	1.500

Greg Maddux After Trade

W-L	IP	H	BB	K	ERA	WHIP
13-5	127.1	134	23	79	2.97	1.233

The Crackers' owner gave me—and subsequently all of you—an object lesson on striking while the iron is hot and a man is down. You can't ask for a better textbook example of stealing a disappointing first-half star for less than he was worth.

Is Javy Lopez that bad? Absolutely not. He's one of the top five fantasy catchers in the majors. He was hitting over .300 for the season and looked to be on his way to a career year. Then he got hurt. And I don't mean just hurt: He blew out his knee, perhaps the most devastating injury a catcher can have. Gone for the year two weeks after I acquired him. Just like that. Meanwhile, Maddux smiled and waved at me from the Crackers' roster as he turned in yet another Cy Young-caliber performance.

Like any other stupid move, it seemed like a good idea at the time. In fact, had Javy stayed healthy and put up career-normal numbers for me, I still would've considered it a fair deal simply for the dollar savings. At $23, Javy was $14 less than Mad Dog. His 2000 salary would jump to $28 because of our keeper rules (to be discussed later), which was still a good price for him. Healthy, that is.

I spent months recovering from this trade. But I did—enough to where it really didn't affect the outcome of my season. I had to scramble, though, and take more risks. Luckily, I made the right choices. Had Javy remained healthy, I might have even looked smart.

Hmmm, maybe I am after all. I later waived Javy. He rode the waiver wire for over a month, so I snapped him up at $15. I plan on keeping him for 2000, assuming his knee is 100 percent. Not bad damage control, if I do say so myself.

My Life Without Greg

So I traded Greg Maddux, Odalis Perez, and Matt Clement and added Bobby M. Jones, Bill Pulsipher, and a lame Javy Lopez to show for it. Ugh. By June 15, I slipped back to fourth place.

But I noticed something in the standings. The ERA and WHIP categories had become extremely tight. Only a small margin separated half the league. (Remember what I said about performance categories being competitive?) If I could get my pitching staff to go on an ERA/WHIP mission, I'd make a quick seven- to eight-point jump in the overall standings. That's *huge*. And the numbers were so close that it could've happened within two weeks.

Naturally, Greg Maddux had begun his resurrection. Right after my trade, he went on an amazing run of five straight starts giving up two runs or less. He could've single-handedly given me that ERA/WHIP boost I desperately needed. I tasted the powder of my grinding teeth every day.

Foul Tips

When trying to improve your team, concentrate on the tighter categories where several owners are closely knotted together. If you surge, you can have a multi-point jump in a short amount of time. This could be crucial if you have a shot at one of the money slots. Because time is money.

I'd have to do it the hard way. Blood-'n'-guts. I made it not just a two-week mission, but a season-long quest. The ERA and WHIP categories would be mine, and I'd do it

Foul Tips

Remember, when trying to improve pitching, starters will help in four categories, closers in only one.

Strike Three

If you find yourself stonewalled on every deal, don't panic. Take some time to reassess your offers, then try again. If that doesn't work, try different deodorant. Not every owner will want to trade every time. Be persistent, but also know when to quit. If you're a known pest, owners will jack up values on principal.

with starting pitchers, not relievers. In the process, I'd rack up wins and strikeouts like crazy. And in the end, even without the mighty Maddux, I'd be on top of four out of five pitching categories.

How to accomplish this? By now, Hampton and Millwood were as dominant as starters could be. Parris was just fine. Tomko had emerged as an acceptable pitcher, but he could no longer be counted on (as the rest of the season would prove). Chan Ho Park was a fantastic disappointment, but I would not fall into the Maddux trap with him. He'd remain on my roster until they shipped him back to Korea.

But these pitchers wouldn't be enough. Bottom line, I needed at least two solid starters, preferably from playoff-bound teams. A tall order, but not an impossible one. I had to become Captain Kirk and find a way to beat the no-win scenario.

My first trade offer was to the Haven Bulldogs. He had Tom Glavine in the third year of his contract, which meant he couldn't be kept for 2000. The Bulldogs were fading fast in the standings, and I figured they might be in the market for young keepers. Glavine was a good target. Like Maddux, he was improving. At the time, his ERA for the last month was 3.38. Looked like he was back.

Alas, the Bulldogs did not bite. My next target: the Silver Bullets and their stash of under-appreciated hurlers Steve Woodard, Sterling Hitchcock, Jon Leiber, and Andy Ashby. The Bullets also had super-stud prospect Rick Ankiel on their reserve roster. I made a play for all of them and came up empty.

I don't know what it was. Perhaps they weren't eager to deal. Perhaps my refusal to part with Damian Jackson—who had recently stolen five bases in one game—was a factor. Any way you slice it, I was shut out. The Bulldogs dangled the Mets' Rick Reed. I responded with a marginal offer and was refused. Reed wasn't what I was looking for.

I was starting to feel like a real major league GM, in that I needed pitching when there was no pitching to be had. I refused to be desperate, and I especially refused to panic. My ERA/WHIP numbers were actually improving without any help. However, my lack of depth would soon show in the volume stats.

I had the All-Star Break to come up with a solution. Three days. Then it was back to work with a vengeance. How could I turn the following roster into a championship squad?

Zim's Roster as of July 10

Position	Player	Price
Starters		
C	Tyler Houston	$2
C	Angel Pena	$2
1B	Kevin Young	$16
3B	Vinny Castilla	$33
CI	Sean Casey	$22
2B	Craig Biggio	$31
SS	Damian Jackson	$1
MI	Dave Berg	$20 (free agent)
OF	Sammy Sosa	$30
OF	Roger Cedeno	$20 (free agent)
OF	Jeffrey Hammonds	$20 (free agent)
OF	J.D. Drew	$5
UT	Kevin Millar	$20 (free agent)
SP	Chan Ho Park	$26
SP	Bill Pulsipher	$20 (free agent)
SP	Mike Hampton	$15
SP	Brett Tomko	$13
SP	Kevin Millwood	$7
SP	Steve Parris	$5
RP	Wayne Gomes	$6
RP	Jason Christiansen	$5
RP	Guillermo Mota	$5
RP	Mike Remlinger	$5
Reserves		
OF	Todd Dunwoody	$6 (AAA)
SP	Denny Neagle	$21 (DL)
C	Javy Lopez	$23 (DL)
C	Todd Pratt	$20
SS	Pat Meares	$5 (DL)

On July 10, I returned to second place, 15 points out of first. Not an insurmountable lead. It could be done. It would be done.

It *had* to be done.

Recommended viewing: The All-Star Game and related festivities, like the Home Run Derby. Take a break. Enjoy some real baseball that doesn't count. You've bloody well earned it.

The Least You Need to Know

➤ Events in June can tell you more about the outcome of your league than you think.

➤ By June, your morning routine should be in place, enabling you to react immediately to news, update player values, and plot transactions.

➤ If you're not dedicated to daily information, you'll have a hard time being dedicated to your league.

➤ As league standings begin to solidify in June, it's time to start scheming. If you need to make a big move, now's the time to get in the race.

➤ June is too early to dump and quit. You have half a season to turn your team around.

➤ No matter how your team is performing, use the All-Star Break to reflect on your season.

Chapter 16

The Dog Days:
July and August

In This Chapter

➤ Time for objectivity: Can you win?

➤ To dump or not to dump

➤ The trading deadline

➤ Don't forget about next year ... unless you're winning this year

➤ Zim makes his final bid

Ah, the dog days. The temperature on the field during day games reaches 150 degrees. Sweat runs in dark bands around the wool caps of the pitchers. The catchers flip off their saturated masks to snag a foul pop and a spray of droplets flies off with them.

For fantasy owners it is different, but oh so much the same. Moisture drools down the basement walls, feeding the water bugs and centipedes. As we pound the keyboard, sweat drips from the pits behind our knees. The air conditioner rattles and clanks, giving off more heat than cool. The fans in our computer towers buzz like tireless bees. Sound familiar? Who needs real life? Have another pork rind. They're all protein.

In the dog days, things get interesting. Time slowly chisels away at the stone tablets, making your league's standings more permanent each day. Your hackles should be up on end, your teeth bared, prepared to clamp on the throats of your opponents.

You still have work to do. Decisions to make. Paths to choose. Pennant races are heating up all across the country, and now is the time to assess the damage that has been done—either by you or to you. Ready? We're going in anyway.

Can You Win?

Good GMs and managers make the tough choices. They aren't always right, but at the time they are staunch in their belief that their experience, intelligence, and guts will make everything happen. You should feel the same.

As the second half progresses, there will come a time when you must ask yourself once and for all: "Can I win?" If so, what will it take? Be objective. You can't afford sentiment, stubbornness, or plain old wishful thinking. The deals you make should now be designed not only to help yourself, but to hurt your closest opponents. Roster moves become even more crucial, with their timing sometimes meaning the difference of a point in the standings. You can't afford to lose that point.

If you're in the bottom half of the standings, use the same objectivity. Can you climb back into the money? If not, who can you trade for grade-A keepers? And who should you trade with? Being a spoiler can be deviously fun.

Foul Tips

Now is the time to be objective: Can you win? If you can't win, you still have two important jobs: prepping for next year and acting as the spoiler.

Strike Three

The deals you make this time of year should be designed not only to help yourself, but to hurt your closest opponents.

But we're getting ahead of ourselves. Let's start with the money slots.

If You're a Contender

Now is the time for careful review of each stat category. Where are you? What are the margins separating you from the other teams? Those margins could be the key to your season.

For instance, say you're fourth in saves. Is it worth it to fight for the top three slots? If the teams above you lead by only a handful of saves, sure, it's definitely worth trading for another closer (assuming you can land an elite closer without gutting some other category). You can make up those points with one hot player.

However, if the third-place owner is 10 saves ahead of you, it's probably not worth it. Ten saves is a month's work even for a red-hot closer. Tight categories offer the best opportunities for advancement, especially this late in the game.

As for trading, last-place teams will dangle their superstars in exchange for keepers, picks, and prospects. Any one of those studly five-tool gods would look great on your roster. The beauty of trading young talent for stars is that you'll get the immediate help you need. If you think you can win, *absolutely go for it at all costs*. Worry about next year when next year comes.

But choose your battles. Trading for McGwire or Sosa doesn't make much sense if you're already among the top three in home runs. Target key categories where you can win the most points in the shortest amount of time. Remember, you now have less than three months to climb the standings.

Also, don't just concentrate on improving your own team. Help other teams take points away from your closest competitors, which will allow you to advance. "How do I do that?" you might ask. I'll tell you.

If you're in the thick of the race, you'll probably try to strike a deal with a losing team for one of their pricey vets. In the midst of this negotiating, see where this losing team is in each category. Are they duking it out with one of your competitors? If so, you might be able to help yourself by helping the losing team.

For example, let's say that you're carving a deal with the New Orleans Hangovers for Chipper Jones. Ol' Chipper will help you in five categories, which you need for the stretch. The Hangovers are willing to deal him for minor leaguers and reserve picks, which makes you drool.

But wait. You notice the one category in which the Hangovers *didn't* stink is saves. In fact, they're third place in that category. Hmmm. If the 'Overs could rack up six extra saves, they would take over the category. Double hmmm.

The Lincoln Tunnel Turncoats, your nemesis all season, are second in saves. If the Hangovers were to knock them back a point, maybe even two, so much the better. So you get back to the owner of the Hangovers: "Instead of those two minor leaguers, would you take Uggie Urbina at $28? Could be a keeper." The owner likes the idea of playing spoiler—at least his team can have some impact on the outcome of the league. And Uggie's a borderline keeper at $28. So he says, "Yes, it will be done. Bring Uggie to me. I will deal with the Turncoats myself."

Foul Tips

If you think you can win, go for it. Don't mess around. Remember, the whole point of being in a fantasy league is winning it.

Strike Three

Choose your battles carefully. Just because you trade for three superstars doesn't automatically guarantee a title. Target key categories where the most points can be won.

Foul Tips

Trading a player to one team to take points away from another is a good strategy, but don't trade away so much that you lose points and defeat the purpose.

Strike Three

You have less than three months to climb the standings. Long-term plans no longer exist.

Bam. Not only do you have Chipper Jones to help your offense, the Hangovers are indirectly working for you.

Be careful, however. Don't trade a player like Uggie Urbina unless you can afford to. How will his absence affect *your* saves? Losing a couple points to gain a couple is a useless gesture, and could actually hurt you.

The key is to remain in control at all times, even if lousy teams are having fire sales. Recklessness will burn you like sunlight on Dracula. Sure, there are times when it's better—and more fun—to carpet-bomb your problems. But surgical strikes have their day in court, too. A good owner knows when to use either one. Or both at the same time ...

Dumping on Deadline

There's an old joke that asks, "What do you call a guy who graduates last in his medical school class?" *Doctor.* No one goes into a major endeavor—especially something that they think they're good at—and expects to fail. But what if you do? What if you stink?

Overheard in the Dugout

The major league "free" trading deadline is July 31. After that, a player must clear waivers to be traded. Most fantasy leagues base their own trading deadline on that date. My league has set the date as the Sunday following July 31. This gives owners a chance to react to last-minute major league deals, which can be especially useful if you lose a player to the other league.

Every 12-team league has a 12th team. What if it's you? Heck, you could even be as high as fourth and get nothing, depending on how you structure winnings. Someone has to stink. If it's you, it may not be your fault. Your squad could be decimated by injuries. You could lose key players to the other league. Your wife could leave you. Anything can happen.

If *everything* happens—if your season resembles a train wreck near a toxic waste dump in the middle of Death Valley—then the dog days are the time to make things right. Or at least save a little face. How do you do that? By dumping, of course. I know I equated dumping with quitting earlier, which is true to a certain extent. Dumping is an acknowledgment that you can no longer remain competitive. The timing determines if you are a quitter or not.

Dumping in June is quitting. No two ways about it. But dumping in late July or August is a strategic godsend to a team in the gutter. The timing will depend on when (or if) your league established a *trading deadline*. Will your league have a trading deadline? You certainly don't have to. But it makes for some interesting second-half scheming. I'm definitely a fan. Just don't make it too late in the year or it will serve no real purpose.

For this discussion, we'll assume that your league indeed has one. The major league deadline is July 31. In the weeks leading up to that date, rumors fly like teeth at a hockey game, and big-time cross-league trades dominate the headlines. It's an exciting time that carries over into fantasy leagues with equal fervor.

Your dumping will revolve around that date. Your first step is simple: Slip another quarter into the hype machine. Send league-wide e-mails announcing your intent to dump. Tell them which players are available. Tell them what you want in return. Then wait for the offers to pour in. If you have two or three good to great players on the payroll, you'll have no problem finding interested contenders.

Trash Talk

The **trading deadline** cuts off league-wide trading for the season after a certain date. It's an optional rule, but one I recommend. The ideal time for a fantasy league trading deadline is sometime in August. Not too early, not too late.

Strike Three

Don't make your league's trading deadline too late in the season, or it will serve no purpose.

A league-wide announcement has its advantages:

➤ **Open availability can spur a bidding war.** You could find yourself playing monkey-in-the-middle between two ever-sweetening offers from desperate contenders. Just don't lie about previous offers to get another owner to increase his.

➤ **Open availability prevents unseemly accusations.** If everyone has a fair shot at your players, no one can accuse you of playing favorites. But if you do take an inferior offer, be prepared to answer for it. Owners don't like to lose out when they've made a stronger offer. And collusion is such an ugly word.

➤ **Open availability eliminates useless players from the equation.** When you tell the league exactly who you want, the other owners won't waste your time by offering their fringe "prospects." An even better idea is to attach a team-by-team "want list" to your announcement, telling each owner exactly who you covet on their rosters.

Foul Tips

A dumping owner is always in the driver's seat. Contenders need your stars more than you need their prospects.

Strike Three

Look at fair-value trading from a major league standpoint. What would a superstar's real team ask for in return?

You certainly don't have to send out a league-wide announcement. If you have specific prospects/keepers in mind, by all means approach their owner directly. However, that puts you at an instant disadvantage *because you came to him*. He'll try to squeeze you. If you throw your players out to the league, the owners will come to you. And *you* can squeeze *them*.

The key to any trade—be it on April 1 or August 31—is getting fair value. Now, value is subjective. But if you're sitting on a Ken Griffey Jr., you should get a lot more than a few token prospects. Look what the real-life Seattle Mariners got in exchange for Junior.

Be nasty when it comes to dumping. You're in the driver's seat, so be Mad Max. The contenders need your stars more than you need their prospects. You may be fighting for next year, but they want to win *now*. Use that desperation. Don't make it easy for them.

Dumping your roster can be an honorable act, as long as you act honorably. No one likes a quitter. But everyone respects an owner passionate enough to stay involved, be a spoiler, and position himself for next season. Do it up right and you'll be drooling for the next Draft Day.

A Dirty Deadline Deed, Done Dirt Cheap

If you are in a NL- or AL-only league, listen up …

An interesting prelude to the major league trading deadline is the flurry of rumors you hear. According to the papers, A-Rod, Mike Piazza, Mo Vaughn, the Big Hurt, Vinny Castilla, and Curt Schilling were all switching leagues in July '99. They went nowhere. A useful strategy—especially if you're languishing in the bottom half of your league's standings—is to go out and acquire all the rumored trade bait in the other league. Meaning that if you're in an AL-only league in '99, you'd have picked up Schilling, Piazza, and Castilla. In an NL-only league, A-Rod, Mo, and so on.

Note: I don't recommend this strategy to contenders. If it backfires, you'll have a useless player frozen on your roster for two weeks, which can be crippling. You also would've come up empty. But if you're a bottom feeder, you have nothing to lose.

Why should you do this? You'll have these superstars sewn up at ludicrous (read: keeper) free-agent prices. The key to this strategy is timing. It can work in either the FAABoard or FAABudget system, but you have to put in your claims and bids before everyone else. Which means monitoring the rumor mill like it's a TV tuned to the Laetitia Casta channel.

In the FAABoard system, the #1 slot on the board is a real power throne. You can hold it all year, lying in wait for the big star to cross the transom. When he does, *bam,* you'll be there to trump any other claims. That is, unless some last-place owner didn't claim that star two weeks earlier when the cross-league trade was only a rumor.

Overheard in the Dugout

In mid-July '99, the owner of the Black Crackers made a pre-emptive strike on the cross-league trading market. He claimed Juan Guzman, Kenny Rogers, Andy Pettite, Tony Clark, Frank Thomas, and Kevin Appier as free agents, waiving a slew of dead weight to fit everyone under the cap. Only Guzman and Rogers came over, but that's a pretty good ratio.

If your roster can take the risk, why not try it? At worst, you have a dead position on your active squad for two weeks. At best, you have a superstar keeper on your hands and the only thing you gave up was the time it took you to put in the claim. And remember, you can do this at any time during the season.

In our league, Randy Johnson and Mark McGwire are two perfect examples of cross-league superstars who have been claimed this way over the years. Not bad, eh?

Zim Makes a Few Good Moves

As the weather got hotter, my team got better. I fluctuated between second and third place every week. But over the break, I did some soul searching and realized that I have no soul. I also realized that I could make a serious run at the championship.

The Phantoms had ridden the top slot the entire season, but the Fedora Brigade, Sculp's Hill Seminoles, and Reading Reds were chipping away at his point total each week. Something had to give. If I made the right moves, I might just pull it off.

What Did I Need?

Two good starting pitchers, minimum. The ERA, WHIP and strikeout categories were the tightest—I could make a seven- or eight-point jump very quickly. Two premium starters would give me a total of nine. Which would beef up my volume stats nicely.

On the offensive side, I also needed some serious home run and RBI help. None of my young, cheap Draft Day catchers were seeing any action. J.D. Drew had disappointed in a big way. Vinny Castilla wasn't himself. Something had to be done.

Once again, a frustrated owner came through. The Shepherds of Fury announced their second annual Furious Dump. This one was all the harder to swallow for the Furious One because he wasn't that far out of the money. But his pitching had collapsed to the point where Orel Hershiser was his ace. That's tough. Still, the Shepherd had a nice stable of pure power hitters: Mike Piazza, Chipper Jones, Jeromy Burnitz, Gary Sheffield, and Ryan Klesko. If I could get my hands on any one of them …

One? Screw that. I needed help. I had prospects. I had potential keepers. It was time to make the Big Deal.

It Was Time to Do Whatever It Would Take

First I asked about Piazza. I dealt for him in the second half of '98 and knew what a terror he was in the dog days. Alas, the Furious One had already dealt him. Hmmm.

I offered first baseman Kevin Young ($16, nice keeper price), third baseman Aramis Ramirez ($1), outfielder Jeffrey Hammonds ($20), and minor league pitcher Jeff Kubenka for Jones ($32), Hershiser ($20), and Sheffield ($15). He bit.

> **The Strategy.** Young was having the best season of his career and was a keeper at $16. You couldn't find a better third base prospect than Aramis, who kept his Triple-A batting average above .325 most of the season. Kubenka was unhittable at times at Triple-A, but a failure so far in the Bigs. Hammonds was a fine fill-in, but not much more. In Chipper, Sheffield, and Bulldog, I got an MVP, a star hitter, and an inning-burning pitcher on a playoff staff.

> **What Really Happened.** Chipper blossomed beyond my wildest expectations, hitting .332 for me and contributing in all five categories. Sheffield quietly hit .297 for me with 49 RBI, which was unexpected. And Hershiser? 4.11 ERA in 70 innings. Not too terrible these days.

This was the big deal I needed. I may have come out on top in this one, which was nice after the Maddux deal. But I wasn't done. The shopping list still had some names on it.

A Tough Choice ... but a Good Choice

I've only ever made two memorable prognostications in this game.

The first came in '98. I'd drafted Andy Ashby for $9 and he went on to have his breakout season. I stuck with him for 13 wins (he eventually won 17) and a sub-3.00 ERA (he finished at 3.34). But I had a gut feeling. I don't know what triggered it, but it told me to dump Ashby—and fast. At $9, he was an attractive keeper. So I dealt him and a high-round reserve pick to a dumping team for a $44 Mike Piazza. Soon after the deal, Ashby got hurt and lost his bid for a 20-win season. I got off his bandwagon in the nick of time and got Mr. Second Half in return.

The second one came in '99, right after the Chipper deal. I'd ridden Roger Cedeno at the top of the stolen bases category all year. But my gut screamed once again: *Trade him.* I don't know why. There was no reason to. Cedeno was hitting .315 at the time with 56 swipes. Still, the voice commanded ...

I checked on the steals category. Even if I dealt Cedeno, I'd lose a point, maybe two. On my roster, J.D. Drew, Biggio, Damian Jackson, and now Chipper were all regular base-stealing contributors. Cedeno didn't drive in runs, so I really could afford to deal him.

I approached one of the season's quieter teams, the Stogies, and asked if he was interested in Cedeno. He was. I also checked to make sure that even if Cedeno stole 30 bases for the guy, it wouldn't affect my place in the stolen base scheme of things. Cedeno was a breakout star and a no-brain keeper at $15 (his free-agent price). I wanted two pitchers in return: Scott Elarton of the Astros (one of the best young arms in the game) and Francisco Cordova of the Pirates. Alas, it was too stinky for the Stogies. He passed.

I then approached one of the league's nefarious dumpers: the Black Crackers. I respected what he did with all the AL free agent pickups and wanted to deal for pitcher Juan Guzman. He'd just come over to the NL and I foresaw a nice initial tour of duty in the second half. No one in the NL had ever seen him, which usually bodes well.

Strike Three

Sometimes your gut will tell you what to do. If you and your gut have a good history, I'd listen to it. If not, sit down and have a long talk with your gut. Chances are you two just aren't communicating. Guts can be incorrigible, but in this game you need yours. Feed it, rub it, do what-ever it takes to be on good terms with it.

Foul Tips

If a player switches leagues, his initial trip around the new league will probably be good, especially for pitchers.

I changed tactics in my negotiations, however. I pride myself on being a forward-thinking owner. I try to always see the big picture, which I imagine is a direct link to my preference of wide-screen video rentals.

Anyway, I'd traded three of my five 2000 reserve picks earlier in the season. All I had left were my fourth- and fifth-round picks. Unacceptable. So I offered Roger Cedeno for Juan Guzman and two second-round 2000 reserve picks. (The Crackers had stockpiled an extra second rounder.) The Crackers said sure thing, daddy-o.

> **The Strategy.** Guzman gave me another starting pitcher. Add him to Hershiser and I was near my goal. The two reserve picks gave me peace of mind for the 2000 draft.

> **What Really Happened.** My gut was right about Cedeno. He stole only 10 bases in the last two months. He was still a nice keeper, but I was playing for this year. I got out when the stock was hot. Guzman pitched brilliantly for me, winning six games with a 3.12 ERA in 69 innings. And the two reserve picks are tucked in my vest pocket awaiting Draft Day 2000.

This deal proved to be the best of both worlds for me. It gave me the starting pitcher I so desperately needed, plus it beefed up my reserve draft for next year. I know this flies in the face of the "win now" mantra, but if you're in a keeper league you must think wide-screen at all times—whether you're on top or sucking scum off the bottom.

Still Not Done

I was now in full-trade mode heading into the deadline, determined to eliminate from my roster all potential keepers that I didn't absolutely need. I wanted quality in return and salary was no object.

This is another strategy I enjoy: the *max-out*. See, in a six-team league, you'll probably have a starter at every active roster position. But in a deep 12-team-or-more league, you won't. It's almost impossible. Unless you max out. It's a powerful late-season ploy that puts all of your talent on the playing field, as it were. It's simple. You max out your salary cap, making sure that every dollar is on the active roster. No reserves unless absolutely necessary.

This gives you three advantages:

1. You can acquire unkeepable high-priced superstars from dumping teams and not worry about the cap.

2. You can eliminate high-priced, free-agent bench players. They weren't helping much anyway. It's late in the season and you need starters at every position.

Trash Talk

A **max-out** is when you put every salary cap dollar onto the active roster, maxing out both the cap and your production.

3. It simplifies your management in the September stretch. If every slot on your active roster is filled with a full-time player, your roster is running on all cylinders. In a deep league, this is a huge advantage.

The max-out isn't always possible to pull off, but the closer you can get, the better. I decided now was the time if I was going to make an honest run at the title.

First on my list of bye-byes: Wayne Gomes, $6. At the time, he was a keeper. He had a solid hold on the Philadelphia closer role and was my primary provider of much-hated saves in '99. He had to go. I shopped him mercilessly. But no one would bite. I ran into an age-old problem: My closest competitors were the ones who needed him most. I couldn't help them beat me, could I?

I changed tactics once again, offering Gomes to the Reading Reds for a futures package: Braves second base prospect Marcus Giles and two 2000 reserve picks. The Reds went for it.

My Strategy. Once again, thinking wide-screen. This deal would give me six total reserve picks in 2000, plus a two-time minor league MVP in Giles. And Gomes? My gut said he was done.

What Really Happened. My max-out plan was off to a lousy start. I got no immediate help for Gomes, which was my goal. Still, I managed to snag some great future help. I felt good about the deal, for I was right about Gomes: He saved 13 games for me. In the last two-plus months, however, he saved only six more. And his job is in jeopardy in 2000.

I still had some decent, cheap prospects to deal: catcher Angel Pena, $2; catcher Jason LaRue, $5; and Guillermo Mota, $5. Pena's value dropped significantly in recent months. He fizzled at the plate and his conditioning was questioned. He got sent back to Triple-A and became untradeable.

The other two, however, remained viable and valuable. And I had one more major deal up my sleeve …

Strike Three

When you're shopping a player, sometimes the only owners who want him are your closest competitors. *Don't* help them no matter how much you want to trade the guy.

My Last Trade of the Season

I returned to the garden of the Furious One, who is always hungry for prospects. I knew he would grant me an audience. I was right.

I offered him Mota and LaRue for future Hall o' Famer and all-around nice interview, outfielder Tony Gwynn ($13).

My Strategy. Get the best bat those two prospects would buy. Gwynn had been in and out of the lineup all year, missing almost a third of the season to nagging injuries. But he had just come off the disabled list, had logged his 3,000th hit, and could now proceed as before.

What Really Happened. Mota and LaRue remain two promising youngsters. Gwynn stayed healthy the rest of the way, hitting a ruddy .364 for me, tossing in five home runs and four stolen bases for fun.

This is a perfect example of a max-out trade. It worked out well for me. Time will tell how the Furious Shepherd tends to his flock, but it looks good.

By now, the trading deadline had passed. My max-out plan was in the books. Whew. Man, I was exhausted. Much of the wheeling and dealing isn't mentioned in these pages. For every trade I pulled off, there were 10 deals that died. But I was pretty happy. I'd spackled over the hole left by the exit of Greg Maddux and could once again sail on. Remember, I also acquired injured catchers Jason Kendall and Javy Lopez at $15 each to keep for 2000. I couldn't pass them up at that price.

You might be thinking, "For a guy making vows to win, win, win in '99, he made an awful lot of moves preparing for 2000." You're right. But I shopped around as hard and thoroughly as possible. The bottom line is that not everyone is willing to deal the right players at the right time just to please you. I improvised, adapted, and overcame these prejudices to put the best team I could on the field. If I couldn't get a win-now starter, I hustled a win-later pick or prospect. Remember: Think wide-screen.

Meanwhile, I added Chipper Jones, Gary Sheffield, Tony Gwynn, Juan Guzman, and Orel Hershiser to my active roster in return for Roger Cedeno, Kevin Young, Aramis Ramirez, Jeff Kubenka, Jason LaRue, and Guillermo Mota. Throw in four 2000 reserve picks and Marcus Giles, and I'm a happy guy at the trading deadline.

Zim's Roster as of August 31

Position	Player	Price
Starters		
C	Tyler Houston	$2
C	Javy Lopez	$15 (DL)
1B	Sean Casey	$22
3B	Chipper Jones	$32
CI	Vinny Castilla	$33
2B	Craig Biggio	$31
SS	Damian Jackson	$1
MI	Pat Meares	$5

Position	Player	Price
OF	Sammy Sosa	$30
OF	Gary Sheffield	$20
OF	Tony Gwynn	$13
OF	J.D. Drew	$5
UT	Kevin Millar	$20
SP	Chan Ho Park	$26
SP	Denny Neagle	$21
SP	Orel Hershiser	$20
SP	Bill Pulsipher	$20
SP	Juan Guzman	$15
SP	Mike Hampton	$15
SP	Brett Tomko	$13
SP	Kevin Millwood	$7
SP	Steve Parris	$5
RP	Mike Remlinger	$5

Reserves

C	Javy Lopez	$15
C	Angel Pena	$2

Max-Out Stats

$376 on active roster

$17 on reserve, $7 free

94 percent of $400 salary cap is on active roster

Not a bad max-out. I say bring on the stretch run. It's time to win this thing.

Recommended viewing: *Rookie of the Year.* Sure, it's a kiddie flick, but no matter what your age, who wouldn't want to bust their arm and suddenly be able to throw 110 m.p.h?

> **The Least You Need to Know**

➤ Mid- to late-July is the time to be objective: Can you win?

➤ If you can, make a commitment to do everything it takes to pull it off.

➤ But remember, you now have less than three months to climb the standings. Long-term plans no longer exist.

➤ Tight categories offer the best opportunities for advancement, especially this late in the game.

➤ If you can't win, you still have two important jobs: prepping for next year and acting as the spoiler.

➤ If you decide to dump, you're in the driver's seat. Contenders need your star players more than you need their prospects.

September Panic

Ah, the throat. Poets have written about the erogeneity of it. Vampires have worshipped the life within it. The magnificence of the flesh, the majesty of the nape, the mystery of the wattle. Sonnets, love letters, reams of gushing tribute to that one telling piece of anatomy. But you? The only thing you should be asking yourself about throats is, "How doth I tear my enemies' out?"

It's September, fool. I can't sum up life more succinctly than that. If you want to win, you must now chill your heart, boil your blood, and become one with the spirit of Rambo. Win by attrition. Suck the marrow out of life and spit it in the face of death. Eat things that would make a billy goat puke. Stuff like that.

But seriously: Is your killer instinct intact? I hope so. You'll need every ounce of strength you have left from this marathon season. If you're running on empty, now's the time to plug in that reserve tank. There is still much work to do. So grab an energy bar, a laptop, two aspirin, and follow me.

Going for the Throat

Time is running out. As of September 1, you have less than five weeks to operate. Pennant chases, like Poe's ever-descending pendulum, are in full swing. September call-ups clog the clubhouse. It's a busy time in the majors and in fantasy.

Foul Tips

Some leagues freeze newly acquired free agents and promoted minor leaguers on the active roster for two weeks. If so, you must cease these transactions two weeks before the end of the regular season.

We'll assume that your league is using a trading deadline. If so, trading's long gone by September. The only avenues you have left for acquiring new personnel are free agency and your minor league roster. I advise you to milk those systems for all they're worth.

The rules—as our league uses them—will squeeze you. Our rulebook states that both free-agents and minor leaguers must remain frozen on your active roster for two weeks after you acquire/promote them. During that freeze, you cannot trade, waive, or reserve them. This means that these types of transactions must cease two weeks before the end of the regular season. Why? To keep things neat, basically. Who wants to deal with frozen roster spots all the way into next season? Not me.

Be Offensive: Attack!

You need to be prepared. If you're in the middle of a dead-heat dogfight for first place—or sixth, eighth, eleventh … anyplace but *last* place—your action or inaction in September could make all the difference in the world. Every strategy you have used or thought of using can help in September. If you were saving something, now's the time.

You must attack everything and everyone: your opponents, your players, the very game itself. Dump your toy box on the floor and catalog *everything*. Leave no possibility unconsidered. No path unexplored. Every strategy you've employed so far will help, and your scrutiny of players should be jacked up exponentially. Issues such as injuries, playoffs, and rookie playing time factor in. You need to be up on even the tiniest line on the back page of the most obscure sports section in the country. What else is there to live for?

You Can't Win if They Don't Play

Contending major league teams have their own problems. If they're running away with their division, they might sit their stars to rest them for the post-season. (Heck, even Biggio took a few innings off in late '99.) How will that affect your production?

Foul Tips

News updates and player trends are more important than ever this month—read the paper, surf the Web, and watch the tube.

How about the tight races? If a team is fighting down to the last game of the season, who are their best bench players in the clutch? One of them might be available as a last-minute pickup.

What about last-place teams? Are they facing off against contenders in the final two weeks of the regular season? Will they roll over or stand tall and play spoiler? If you own players on those teams, watch them carefully for signs of giving up. Sure, these guys are pros, but chronic losing takes a toll—especially when it has been slathered on for the past six months like thick coats of lead paint. By September, some guys just want to go fishing.

And, oh yeah, you need to know everything yesterday. Every week in September, your transactions should be well thought out and designed to move you up the standings. With a shortened free-agent timetable and no more trading, your options will be limited. In fact, there will be a lot of things beyond your control even on your own roster. So let's talk about what you *can* control.

Squeezing Out the Extra Win, Save, or Steal

The key to September is *productivity*. Before the sarcasm erupts, I'm not pretending that productivity is unimportant the rest of the year. Duh … you know what I mean.

It always happens: When the final stats are tallied in October, a couple of the volume categories like steals, wins, and saves are decided by one. *One.* If you think that's harsh, performance categories like ERA, WHIP, and batting average will come down to *thousandths of a point.*

Everything counts, folks. Early in the season it's easy to slack off and leave an injured or inactive player hanging around your active roster for lack of a decent replacement. That ends now. If you have a hole in your roster come September and you're fighting for a money slot, it's time to fill the hole with *someone* who will put up numbers you need.

This hinges on what's happening in the individual categories. If you need volume, pick the bag with the least scum and plug him in. Numbers, numbers, numbers. Any will do.

If you're okay in the volume stats but lousy in the performance categories, you need to manipulate them. The best way to avoid a sinking batting average or a rising ERA is to have only the best players active. Why tempt fate with a .200-hitting shortstop or a bum starting pitcher? Here's a radical idea: Acquire some injured or inactive free-agents and plug them in. The dead space can't hurt you—but *do this only if you will not suffer in the volume categories!*

Strike Three

Some volume categories will hinge on one save or steal. Some performance categories will come down to thousandths of a point. Don't get caught short.

Foul Tips

With the trading deadline past, the only way to change personnel is through free agents or your minor league roster. Use them.

All this may seem Brady-Bunch-keen, but where exactly do you find these miracle roster plug-ins this late in the year? Well, like a cement union worker with a sledge-hammer, you have to pound some pavement.

The Bottomless Barrel

Don't be fooled: Every barrel has a bottom. You may have reached yours. What talent is left out there will depend solely on how deep your league runs. Are you in a 15-team, NL-only bloodbath? Every player will be sucked dry. I can't help you there. But are you in an eight-team mixed league? There will be tons of talent available (relatively speaking).

Assess your situation:

➤ **How desperate are you?** Will any old journeyman do? Probably not. Don't pick up a sentimental favorite or a 40-year-old on a last-place team and expect him to play (unless he's Joe Carter, and I'll tell you about him in a minute).

➤ **How desperate are your opponents?** What do they have to do to beat you? Examine their rosters and try to predict their moves, like gunning for the same player you want.

➤ **How lucky do you feel?** If you're fortunate enough to have several players to choose from, go with your gut. As you now know, information and predictions go only so far. Eventually, it's going to come down to you and your conscience.

Overheard in the Dugout

Back in '98, Joe Carter crossed leagues to the Giants in a late-season trade. I picked him up for my September run simply because I needed offense—any offense. Luckily, the Giants were in a pennant race and landed Carter for his bat and experience. He batted over .300 for me with 20 RBIs in a few short weeks. However, that did not relieve him of his '93 Phillies-killing World Series home run.

What if all the established talent is gone or not worth the risk? To further beat a dead metaphor, if the apples at the bottom of the barrel are rotten, go to the tree.

Major Minors

It happens every September 1. The majors call on their minors to bear the standard (or the stigma) of a team's youth movement. Some of these guys arrive only for their obligatory cup of coffee. Some make unexpected impressions and help win pennants. Some prove to be all they are supposed to be. And some don't.

On this fateful date, you should immediately make a list of every minor leaguer who is called up to his big league team. Why? Because you don't want any names to slip through. Sure, a lot of these guys will be well-known to the fantasy baseball freak, but one or two always cruise under the radar. Hopefully, a few will already be on your reserve and minor league rosters. If so, congrats—your supplemental drafts paid off with free plug-in talent.

If not? They're probably on someone else's roster. Cross off every player who is unavailable. Hopefully, you'll be left with a small pool of talent to pick from. (A pool made even smaller depending on your specific needs.) If you see a minor leaguer who does what you need and looks likely to play, snap that guy up faster than a deviled egg at a Penn State tailgate party. There may be ramifications later (we'll talk about this is a minute), but you shouldn't care if a money slot is on the line.

Foul Tips

The value of a minor league call-up depends solely on playing time. If a guy doesn't play, he can't help (or hurt) you.

Just remember a few plusses and minuses about September call-ups:

➤ **They're unknown.** No one has faced them yet, so sometimes they perform well the first time out (especially starting pitchers). This is perfect in a confined time/space continuum like September.

➤ **They're nervous.** On the other hand, if they haven't been called up before, they'll tend to sweat the details. Like breathing.

➤ **They're hungry.** They'll try to impress their manager the same way they'd try to impress Angelina Jolie on a first date. This can inspire glorious success or humiliating failure, depending on the makeup of the prospect. Be careful (especially if you're Angelina Jolie).

Predictions don't go as far here. The bottom line is that minor leaguers are more unpredictable than their major league brethren, even if they're destined to become the next Mickey Mantle. Take their scouting reports with a grain of sand. Put it in your shorts and you'll chafe. Put it in an oyster and you'll get a pearl. Life's a gamble.

Overheard in the Dugout

On Draft Day '98, I picked up J.D. Drew in the reserve draft and carried his dormant butt all year. Then, in September, the Cardinals called him up. Thanks to a certain home run hitter elsewhere in the Redbirds' lineup, Drew went practically unnoticed, belting five homers, 14 ribs, and hitting well over .400 in a little over two weeks. Remember: September call-ups can have a real impact.

To Call or Not to Call?

Let's pretend …

It's September. You've done a splendid job this season. Your roster is flush with talent and a dazzling array of potential keepers. In fact, you may have too many keepers, which is a painful thorn in the back of your mind; you don't want to think about the off-season in the middle of a pennant race, but you can't help it.

Thinking that way is healthy. Natural. Even with the championship still up for grabs in September '99, I still had the forethought to pick up injured superstar catchers Kendall and Lopez strictly for the 2000 season.

Foul Tips

Players on the minor league roster can be kept from year to year without counting toward a team's keeper list—so long as they are not promoted and have not appeared on any other active roster.

But wait, we're pretending …

You're in third place. With a nice spurt of pitching, you could jump to second. Winning it all is impossible, unfortunately. Still, second place is nice—and within reach. The best part? Two pitchers on your minor league roster have been promoted by their major league teams for September, and both have been promised at least two starts.

Your heart jumps. This could be the pitching you so desperately need. It's even more fortunate since there is nothing available on the free-agent market. Instinct says promote these two pitchers immediately. Get 'em active. Get 'em wet. They could net you some extra cash since the difference between second and third place winnings is substantial.

You type the e-mail. You position the mouse. But your arrow freezes on the "send" button. You can't do it. Why? You know why. Players on the minor league roster can be kept from year to year without counting toward a team's keeper list—so long as they are not promoted and have not appeared on any other active roster. If you promote them, they are no longer protected.

These pitchers are prime prospects. If they stay healthy, they are projected as top-three hurlers in their respective rotations. If you leave them un- touched on your minor league roster, you can carry them to next season without a hitch. But if you promote them, you will have to put them on your keeper list. And you're already flush with keepers. What do you do?

It's a tough call. Some things to consider …

➤ **Your place in the standings.** If you're fight- ing for the crown, make the move. Do *any- thing* to win. But if you're fighting for a consolation slot and know that the league will continue next season? It might be better to let the prospects stay where they are.

➤ **Your alternative talent.** If you can find a suitable free-agent instead, do it.

➤ **Your keeper situation.** Do you have a full complement of keepers? More? Less? Try to be objective.

If you're not in a keeper league, hey, forget I said anything. But if you are, take it to heart. Keepers are the vital organs of an ongoing league. Good prospects on your minor league roster are equally valuable. If you have to expend them, do it for the only good cause there is: victory.

Foul Tips

If you can win it all, do it. Make any and all moves necessary and worry about the consequences after the ticker-tape parade.

Strike Three

Once called up, minor leaguers can never again appear on a minor league roster. Come next season, you must make them keepers or waive them. What's worth more: the help the minor leaguer will give you now, or the help he'll give you next season?

Last-Minute Strategies

Sure, everything we've talked about in this chapter is a last-minute strategy. The en- tire pace, tone, and theme should reek desperation. Because you *will* be desperate. But there are a few final tidbits I can tell you that may help.

It's all going to come down to one or two categories for you. I've already told you how to manipulate the performance categories. But the volume categories can't be bribed, bought, or befriended. You have to pile up the numbers, period. In the spirit of last-minute gift ideas, here are a few hints on where to find ...

Steals

If Greg Luzinski taught us anything, it's that anyone can steal a base. But you want better odds than that. Check the free-agent market. You might get lucky and find an Otis Nixon or an F.P. Santangelo out there who could get you a steal or two in September. These are guys who you wouldn't be interested in early in the year but who could help in a pinch. Better yet, look at the unclaimed minor league call-ups. Are any of them speedy? If so, they'll be puttin' on the spikes to impress the skipper. Bleed their speed for everything you can get.

Wins

This can get dicey. If you grab every rookie call-up who's set to start a game, your ERA and WHIP will suddenly look like the NASDAQ index after a Yahoo-eBay-AOL merger. Rookie pitchers are scarier than the Blair Witch. Your best bet is to stick with as many vets as you can. Sure, some rookies will surprise and pitch well, but the good ones will have been drafted long ago.

Saves

There's no substitute for an elite closer. But September is a strange month. Some rookie call-ups and established set-up guys will get save chances, especially on runaway play-off teams who need to rest their closers for the post season. All you can do is some re-search and hope for the best (read: an injury).

In the end, when the sand runs out, I hope you can look in the mirror and honestly say you did everything you could do. It's all about effort. Transact until your fingers bleed from typing. If you come out on top, rejoice with great gladness and furious dancing. If you don't, despite your best shot, don't be too devastated. Like the cliché says, the Yankees weren't rebuilt in a day and there is always, forever and ever, a next year. Unless your league collapses. Then you're screwed.

What Happened to Zim

By September 1, I had pretty much painted myself into a corner. Or coronary. Take your pick. August was my max-out month, and as you saw at the end of last chapter, 94 percent of my salary cap was dedicated to my active roster. I didn't have enough cap room to pick up a free-agent and I had no minor leaguers to call up. I hit a dead end.

This wasn't exactly a disaster. I was happy with my roster, for the most part. Every position was producing *something* except an injured Javy Lopez in the second catch-er's slot. Tyler Houston would eventually be dealt from the Cubs to the Indians in a late-season waiver deal, but his contributions to my team in the second half had been marginal (which is a kind way of saying he stank up the barnyard).

It didn't matter. The way our league's stats were shaking out, the only categories in which I could gain anything were batting average and steals. Home runs, RBIs, and runs were all but cast in stone.

So ... how could I advance in those two categories?

Strike Three

Don't freak out if you find yourself with no moves to make. If you're happy with your roster, go with it and don't look back.

> **Batting Average:** I had done all I could do. I had Casey, Gwynn, Chipper, Sheffield, and Biggio all hitting over .300. The rest of the roster cancelled them out and there were no free-agents out there who could help.

> **Steals:** The trade of Roger Cedeno really didn't hurt me like I thought it would. What I gained in pitching from Juan Guzman was much more valuable. I'd sat atop the stolen bases category for most of the year, but the Phantoms were yapping dogs nipping at my Milk-Bone heels.

That's All She Wrote

In retrospect, even if I had some cap room for a free agent, there wasn't anyone out there who was playing enough to impact batting average. And steals? Yeah, right.

Our league is always tough in the late innings. Good players get sucked up into our vacuum faster than dog hair. By September, all one can do is hope to get lucky with a cross-league waiver trade or a surprising rookie call-up.

The point is, you may not have any moves left to make. Don't be alarmed. This is natural. At some point, like the parent of a high school draft pick shipping out to rookie league camp, you will have to cut the cord, sit back, and let your talent work. If you've fought bravely and are happy with your squad, don't look back. Enjoy the last few weeks of the season: the drama, the fantastic finishes, and hopefully, the long, lonely journey down victory lane.

Foul Tips

Despite all the late-season scrambling, you should see a sharp decline in the number of weekly transactions in September. This is natural, but in no way should it prevent you from doing what you have to do.

And the Winner Is ...

So what happened to me? It was a dogfight, all right. The Phantoms entered September with a

16-point lead over the second-place team, the Seminoles. On August 29, 1999, the race looked like this:

	BA	HR	R	RBI	SB	ERA	K	S	W	WHIP
Phantoms	12	12	12	12	11.5	9	11	10	10.5	5
Total: 105										
Seminoles	7	4	8	6	10	10	12	8	12	12
Total: 89										
F. Brigade	11	7.5	9	7	11.5	11	9	2	10.5	10
Total: 88.5										
Reds	9	11	10	11	8	7	8	5	9	6
Total: 84										

Remember, this is a 12-team league, therefore 12 points is first place in any given category. We were the only four teams in the race to the end. The fifth place team—the Diapers—was 20 points behind the Reds, and not a factor.

For me to make up 16.5 points in one month seemed like a tall order. But I was optimistic. All my players were in place. I would've loved to have a few more, natch, but who wouldn't? Suddenly, an interesting thing happened. My team started pitching. I mean, really pitching. Millwood, Hampton, Neagle, Guzman, Parris, Hershiser, and even the immortal Chan Ho Park turned in one winning start after another. I was euphoric.

A week later, September 6, 1999, the standings looked like this:

	BA	HR	R	RBI	SB	ERA	K	S	W	WHIP
Phantoms	12	12	12	12	11	8	10	10	9	5
Total: 101										
F. Brigade	11	9	8	6	12	11	9	2	11	12
Total: 91										
Seminoles	7	4	8	8	10	10	12	8	12	10
Total: 89										
Reds	10	10	11	11	8	7	8	5	10	4
Total: 84										

Suddenly, it's a 10-point lead. My WHIP dropped from 1.373 to 1.363, enough to take over the category. (See what I mean about thousandths of a point?) Not only that, my home runs popped, too, which was a nice surprise.

But this fight was just beginning. Waterloo, Little Big Horn, Bunker Hill, the ice planet of Hoth—all were small potatoes compared to the climactic bloodbath at hand. Could the Brigade surge even further? Could the stellar pitching continue? Only the Great Owner glaring down from the Luxury Box in the Sky knew for sure, and he wasn't telling.

Two weeks cruised by, a blur of magic-number dramatics and late-season fades. But not my Brigade. Witness the standings on September 21, 1999:

	BA	HR	R	RBI	SB	ERA	K	S	W	WHIP
Phantoms	11	12	12	12	11.5	8	10	10	9	5
Total: 100.5										
F. Brigade	9	11	8	7	11.5	11	11	2	12	12
Total: 94.5										
Seminoles	8	5	9	9	10	10	12	8	11	11
Total: 93										
Reds	10	10	11	11	8	6	8	4	10	4
Total: 82										

Six points! Could it happen? Was there enough time?!

My pitching continued to flourish. The July/August stockpiling of starting pitchers finally broke through, propelling me to second in strikeouts and wins. And all those quality starts? *Bam,* first place in WHIP and ERA, baby. I knocked the Seminoles from their pert little perch and assumed command of the mound.

At this point—two weeks to go—all of my pitching strategies (the overpaying, the ignoring of closers, the dumb trades) finally bore fruit. It was my best save of the year (an easy call if you look at my score in that category).

My home runs continued to surge thanks almost single-handedly to Chipper Jones. But check out that batting average. A two-point swoon—.28802 down to .28684. Who was responsible? Damian Jackson, J.D. Drew, and a few others. Like I said before, there was nothing to be done. All I could do was cross my fingers and watch the numbers.

September 28, 1999, one week left:

	BA	HR	R	RBI	SB	ERA	K	S	W	WHIP
Phantoms	12	12	12	12	12	7	10	10	9	5
Total: 101										
F. Brigade	9	10.5	8	7	11	11	11	2	12	12
Total: 93.5										
Seminoles	8	5	9	8	10	10	12	9	11	10
Total: 92										
Reds	10	10	11	11	8	7	8	5	10	4
Total: 82										

Look at the batting average tumble. Down from .28684 to .28623. Those little ten-thousandths of a point cost me two slots in the standings!

This week also marked the beginning of the end in steals. My guys just stopped running while the Phantoms ran even faster. My pitching held its course. (Man, were Millwood, Hampton, Guzman, and Neagle fun to watch in the second half!) But there was only one week left to make up 7.5 points.

Could I do it? Did I believe in miracles? Could the Cinderella story from Orwigsburg achieve the impossible? Nope.

The Day After

The final standings of our league, October 4, 1999:

	BA	HR	R	RBI	SB	ERA	K	S	W	WHIP
Phantoms	11	12	12	12	12	7	10	10	9	5
Total: 100										
F. Brigade	9	10	8	7	11	11	11	2	12	12
Total: 93										
Seminoles	8	5	9	9	10	10	12	9	11	10
Total: 93										
Reds	10	11	11	11	8	6	9	5	10	4
Total: 85										
Diapers	3	9	10	10	9	5	5	11	2	7
Total: 71										
Lions	12	6	4	5	3	2	8	12	8	3
Total: 63										
Bullets	5	1	1	1	1	12	7	6	7	11
Total: 52										
Stogies	7	2	5	3	6	9	2	3	3	8
Total: 48										
BigDogs	4	7	7	8	7	3	1	8	1	2
Total: 48										
Bulldogs	2	4	3	4	2	8	3	7	4.5	9
Total: 46.5										
Shepherds of Fury	6	8	6	6	5	14	4	4.5	1
Total: 45.5										
Black Crackers 1	3	2	2	4	4	6	1	6	6
Total: 35										

Thus is history written.

Ties May Bind, but Winning Keeps You Regular

A tie. How do you run this six-month sanity gauntlet and end up tied? That's like tying for second in the New York Marathon. What are the odds? Pretty good, apparently.

The real heartbreak here is that our league has no tie-breaker system. That's a huge lack of foresight on our part—but there had never been a tie. No one ever thought about it (*big* note for the next winter meeting).

I thought I had those scumbag Seminoles. Ol' Leroy kept dogging me, though. And Kerry, the notorious Phantom, deserves a tip o' the *chapeau*. He rode first place almost from post to post. He very nearly swept the offensive categories. That's impressive in any league.

His advantage? He picked the right has-beens. Alex Fernandez, Matt Williams, Tony Womack, and a bunch of veterans who took their depreciated values and beat the rest of the league over the head with them. An even scarier thought: He did his offensive damage without Barry Bonds for much of the year. All the rest of us could do was scramble to keep up.

Strike Three

Make sure your league has a tie-breaker system in place. I suggest an obscure category like triples or pitchers' combined batting average.

What Cost Me the Title

A cursory glance at the standings suggests that saves did me in. I disagree. I finished with 17 saves. Had I acquired one solid closer by midseason—the Lions dangled Uggie Urbina several times—I could've at least doubled that number. And you know what that would've gotten me? *A lousy three points.* The seventh-place team in that category (worth six points) finished with 45 saves. I would've needed 29 more saves to achieve a fourth point overall.

Three words: *not worth it.* Why? Let's say I traded for Urbina. The Lions were asking for a top-flight batter in return. A Sean Casey. A Craig Biggio. I say again: *not worth it.*

My saves strategy depended on luck. I had Gomes, who came through, albeit marginally. (Thank God he did his worst deflating after I traded him.) But nearly every expert out there thought Jason Christiansen would see more save ops in Pittsburgh. Ditto for pre-trade Ben Ford. And Guillermo Mota (if Urbina had been dealt by the 'Spos, as was widely rumored). Had the planets

Foul Tips

When it's all over, take a break before overanalyzing what happened. You have all winter to beat yourself up.

come into line, I could've been sitting on 40+ saves for chump change. At least I made an effort—a more detailed thought process than simply going out and spending $35 on a Rod Beck or a Kerry Ligtenberg. One more time: *not worth it.*

To an objective observer, I probably seem to be in deep denial about the importance of saves. But I don't think so. I'll reinforce my stance by directing your attention to the teams that topped out the save category. Look where they ended up in the standings: fifth and sixth. Saves eat up so many resources for so little return. Only the Phantoms truly capitalized on saves, and they hit the lottery with Rookie of the Year Scott Williamson. That's how it happens sometimes.

No, I died by the bat. Somehow I managed to have Sammy Sosa, Vinny Castilla, Chipper Jones, Tony Gwynn, Gary Sheffield, Sean Casey, and Craig Biggio on the same roster and finished only in the middle of the RBI and runs pack. I'm still puzzling over that one.

Strike Three

Don't be a sore loser. Be man enough to congratulate the person who stomped your guts out and showed everyone how stupid you are.

Strike Three

Injuries are, bar none, the worst thing that can happen to a fantasy owner. Don't get upset about circumstances beyond your control.

My late-season swoon in batting average sucked the life from me as well. It was unexpected because I was on top of the category for most of the season. Just couldn't hold on—even with all those superstars. I have bare spots from scratching my head.

Javy Lopez was a big factor. He would've delivered 12+ home runs and 50+ RBIs had he stayed healthy. Add those numbers to my totals and I gain five points. That doesn't take into account his impact on runs. And what if he had hit over .300? He could've single-handedly been responsible for my winning the title.

Injuries are—bar none—the worst thing that can happen to a fantasy owner. You make all the right moves and *bam,* down goes your best catcher. Crying about it won't help. But it doesn't hurt, either. 'Cause you're feeling *lots* of hurt.

The Maddux trade was another turning point for my team. I ended up just fine in pitching, but that trade set off a chain reaction of other trades to compensate for Maddux's and Lopez's losses. For all intents and purposes, I waived two superstars. Got nothing in return but heartbreak. Ain't that a country song?

Anyway, as a direct aftershock of the Maddux trade, I also dealt Roger Cedeno and many of my active roster prospects for pitching. Had I kept Maddux, I wouldn't have made those deals. Or would I? See, no matter what happens, you can't predict the future. So don't try. Maddux Schmaddux. Lopez Schlopez. I made all the right moves—from an "educated guess" standpoint. Most of them made sense. If they would've panned as planned, I would've won in a landslide.

As it stands, however, I engineered a heck of a run at a juggernaut of a team and came in second. Okay, I *tied* for second. But I wouldn't trade the excitement, the challenge, the controlled insanity of the 1999 season for anything. Well, maybe for one thing. The title.

For your viewing pleasure, my final roster:

My Final Roster

Position	Player	Price
Starters		
C	Javy Lopez	$15 (free agent)
C	Tyler Houston	$2
1B	Sean Casey	$22
3B	Chipper Jones	$32
CI	Vinny Castilla	$33
2B	Craig Biggio	$31
SS	Damian Jackson	$1
MI	Pat Meares	$5
OF	Sammy Sosa	$30
OF	Gary Sheffield	$20
OF	Tony Gwynn	$13
OF	J.D. Drew	$5
UT	Kevin Millar	$20 (free agent)
SP	Chan Ho Park	$26
SP	Denny Neagle	$21
SP	Bill Pulsipher	$20 (free agent)
SP	Orel Hershiser	$20 (free agent)
SP	Mike Hampton	$15
SP	Juan Guzman	$15 (free agent)
SP	Brett Tomko	$13
SP	Kevin Millwood	$7
SP	Steve Parris	$5
RP	Mike Remlinger	$5
Reserves		
C	Jason Kendall	$15
C	Angel Pena	$2

Was I disappointed? Of course. My team ended the season in the middle of a huge surge. Another two weeks at the same performance level, and I would've had a real shot at the title. But that's not how it works. I should've taken care of business earlier.

But that's life in the cold, hard world of fantasy baseball.

Recommended viewing: *Bull Durham.* Another candidate for best baseball movie ever made. You probably need it after a long season. Crack open a cold one and recite the dialogue. You know you know it.

The Least You Need to Know

➤ Every strategy you have used or thought of using can help in September. If you were saving something, now's the time.

➤ Some volume categories will hinge on one save or steal. Some performance categories will come down to thousandths of a point. Don't get caught short.

➤ After the trading deadline, the only way to change personnel is through free agents or your minor league roster. Milk them.

➤ September call-ups can make a difference. Keep your eyes open for surprises.

➤ If you can win it all, do it. Make any and all moves necessary and worry about the consequences after the ticker-tape parade.

Part 6

How Did You Do?

Your living room looks like the wrap party of Caddyshack. *Your computer has armpit stains. Your dog ran away. When you finally get up from your work chair, it sounds like duct tape being peeled off a cow's backside. You open the shades. The leaves are changing. The sun's rays pierce the front window at a different angle. Is that the Jones kid across the street? When did he learn to drive? You may have ruined your life, but …*

No—*that's wrong. You* liberated *your life. You broke free and plunged into a world of hard-core sports that most fans only dream of. You created a virtual reality of baseball ownership so real that it hardly seemed like a game.*

But now it's time to assess the damage. Do an autopsy—a performance postmortem, if you will. You need to know what worked and what stank during your season. What cost you? What spent you? What snatched victory from your greedy little paws? It's time to find out.

WHERE DID I GO WRONG?

Chapter 18

Time to Reflect

In This Chapter

➤ You can learn from the good and the bad

➤ Don't dwell on luck

➤ What worked and what sank

➤ What to do with this information

Before I knew I was going to write this book, I had habits. I kept meticulous records of my fantasy baseball dealings—trades, waivers, and the more colorful e-mails. Also, each season I try to maintain a brief but telling journal. In it are ideas, strategies, trade dreams, and commentary on league affairs. For my eyes only, of course. These black three-ring binders now clog my bookshelves with annual regularity.

Upon re-reading the '99 edition of my records in preparation for this book, I was constantly amazed at the never-ending subtext of anger within. It was like I was on a six-month rage bender, frothing at everything from Greg Maddux's WHIP to Sean Casey's inability to hit .400. Maybe it helped me cope. I dunno. But I don't remember any kind of catharsis, which probably means I'm still a ticking time bomb. Oh well.

The point is, I hope you have kept some kind of ongoing record of your team's season. If you plan to forge ahead year by year, it's vital. Why? Knowing what you've already done will help you figure out what you're going to do.

So what *did* you do?

What Categories Did You Hit/Miss?

It all comes back to scoring. Some categories you no doubt conquered. Some you tanked. The question is, how many tanks invaded?

As you saw last chapter, my league's cham-peen soo-preem, the Phantoms, scored a flat 100 points to take the crown. In a 5 × 5 league, that's an average of 10 points per category. Which, oddly enough, means that you can come in third place in every category and still end up first overall. Isn't it ironic? Don't you think?

Printing out weekly stats and standings will allow you to chart these categorical trends, anomalies, and facts. Even in the final month of the '99 season, our teams were still in constant flux within each category. This is why it is so important to keep records. There are other reasons, too:

➤ **You'll forget.** Oh, yes you will, the same way you can't remember who lost the '98 World Series. Sure, you might recall your big trades, but the fringe stuff will evaporate from your mind faster than a boring dream. And it's that fringe stuff that tells you the most about your own subconscious tendencies—the stuff that kills you in the long run.

➤ **You'll keep info you never knew you had.** For instance, if you're in a stable league for a few years with the same people, imagine what you might learn about them by charting their long-term transactions. Maybe they lean toward certain players. Maybe they have set patterns you wouldn't see in one season. Maybe they're not very good but just plain lucky. Pretend you're the FBI. Keep files on people. It'll serve you well.

➤ It's fun. Much like a photo album full of bad hairstyles, you'll see your lack of sophistication, your stupidity, and your naiveté. You'll also see your genius. I usually take some time to review past seasons before an upcoming draft.

Now we'll take a category-by-category look at what happened to me in '99. You should do the same for yourself. You might be surprised what you learn.

Slam Dunks

I nailed a few categories better than I ever dreamed I would. Some by luck, some by design. I'll take success any way I can get it, dude.

Home Runs

I knew I'd be competitive, but I didn't really surge in the category until August and September. Based on my early results, placing third (10 points) was a nice surprise.

What Went Right. Sammy Sosa, duh. Sean Casey hit seven more dingers than I projected. Chipper Jones was a second-half monster. Vinny Castilla, while seeming *sooo* mortal, still swatted his share.

What Went Wrong. Kevin Young, J.D. Drew, Kevin Millar, Rondell White, and Todd Dunwoody were all disappointments in the home run category. I fully expected Young to hit 30 (not to denigrate the rest of his season, which was superb). And Drew? He came up a good dozen short. If even one of these guys had performed to expectations, I might have finished even higher.

Steals

Like I was in batting average, I was at or near the top all season. In the end, I fell to second.

What Went Right. Roger Cedeno. No one predicted his speed explosion. Some weeks it seemed like he stole three bases a day. J.D. Drew sped up in the second half. Damian Jackson emerged as well, though his batting average crushed me. But 34 steals? I'll buy that for a dollar (and did).

What Went Wrong. Trading Cedeno was not the problem (I got all but 10 of his total steals). The Phantoms had Tony Womack and Reggie Sanders, who ran all over the place in the second half. Biggio, Drew, Chipper, and Damian were no match for them. It was a dogfight and I lost. Still, second place ain't no stink bomb.

ERA and WHIP

I stayed in the top three most of the year, but really turned it on in the last two months. Nailed 'em both, a fact I'm truly proud of.

What Went Right. Kevin Millwood, Mike Hampton, Juan Guzman, Denny Neagle, Mike Remlinger, Steve Parris, and Orel Hershiser. And you know what? All of them were pretty mortal until the All-Star Break. After that, they were unstoppable. If only it were this easy to pick a staff every year.

What Went Wrong. I really thought this would be Chan Ho Park's year. And I wasn't alone. Everyone went after him in the '99 draft, which is why I had to pay $26. He eventually won 13, but they were ugly wins. I also thought Bill

Pulsipher would turn it on this year. He's shown flashes of quality, but the man just can't stay healthy. And Bobby M. Jones, Doug Henry, Odalis Perez, Brett Tomko, Jeff Brantley? Ugh, better luck next year.

Strikeouts and Wins

Like ERA and WHIP, I really didn't surge in these categories until the second half. But surge I did, winning wins and placing strikeouts. The only team that could beat me in strikeouts had Randy Johnson.

What Went Right. Millwood and Hampton were my anchors all year. But the second halves of Neagle, Guzman, Parris, and Remlinger propped me up. And Chan Ho? Hey, 13 wins are 13 wins no matter how ugly they are.

What Went Wrong. My impatience with Greg Maddux, who eventually won 19. As for strikeouts, there simply is no substitute for lots of innings.

Overheard in the Dugout

If 1999 taught me anything, it's that an owner can recover from bad mistakes. I made my share—more than I deem acceptable for myself. You'll have to come to grips with your own mistakes. Or better yet, your capacity for making them. We're all human here. And even the '98 Yankees lost a few games. Don't let mistakes paralyze you. Fight them off and tango on.

Fumbles

Not every category smelled so rosy (although personally I think roses smell like rotting flesh). Some were quite the belly flops.

Batting Average

I stayed on top of the category for a good 80 percent of the season, but it ultimately did me in.

What Went Right. In the first half, Sean Casey, Kevin Young, Roger Cedeno, and even Tyler Houston powered my charge. And believe it or not, I got nice part-time average boosts from Todd Pratt and Dave Magadan. (Remember what I said about snagging free agent part-timers who can hit?)

What Went Wrong. In the second half, Casey faltered, Young was dealt, and I relied on Chipper Jones, Tony Gwynn, and Craig Biggio, who played with a partially torn labrum in his left shoulder and never really got it in gear. (It says a lot about a player when .294 is a subpar season.) In the end, I couldn't hold on and dropped four points in the final two weeks. That really tagged my toe.

Saves

Finished second to last. We've talked about this before. Wait … do you hear that? It's my stomach acid refluxing.

What Went Right. Not much. Wayne Gomes, as I predicted, took over in Philly when Jeff Brantley suffered his inevitable injury. But Gomes was not even close to enough. The best thing I can say about him is that he brought me prospect Marcus Giles and two reserve picks in trade.

What Went Wrong. Jason Christiansen, Ben Ford, and Guillermo Mota never had a chance. In the spring, all three were pretty good gambles. But I lost. Good thing I didn't try Atlantic City instead.

RBIs and Runs

Finished fifth and sixth, respectively. Thought I'd be much, much higher, especially with the personnel on hand.

What Went Right. Sosa was the man in both categories. Ditto Kevin Young, Sean Casey, and Chipper Jones. Sheffield drove in more than I expected. Drew did not. However, because Drew led off (when he played) he scored a cool 72. Hopefully, that's his lowest total for the next 15 years (a Phillie phan said *that?*).

What Went Wrong. I fell prey to the classic volume trap: not enough full-timers. Throughout the year I relied on Todd Pratt, Tyler Houston, Angel Pena, Damian Jackson, Dave Berg, Dave Magadan, Jeffrey Hammonds, Kevin Millar, and Roger Cedeno. While some of them put up good numbers, not one of them had a full-time gig. I should've taken the same approach I took for strikeouts and wins, but with names like Sosa, Casey, and Biggio in the lineup, I didn't think I'd have to. I was wrong.

What Cost *You* the Points?

How about you? What crushed your hopes and dashed your dreams? Maybe you relied on players who went down for the year. For a while the game was on a "who's next?" roller coaster that left Andres Galarraga, Kerry Ligtenberg, Jason Kendall, Jeff Brantley, Javy Lopez, and Odalis Perez in its wake. (Not a good year to be a Brave, was it?)

There were others who didn't go down for the year, but they seemed to spend more time in the trainer's room than on the field. (Smoltz! I'm looking for John Smoltz! He's where? Playing cards with Reggie Sanders between two gurneys? Thanks!)

Foul Tips

There are so many factors that can make or break you in fantasy baseball. Some you can control. Some you can't. But I believe if you stay on top of the things you can control, it's far easier to cope with the things you can't.

Trash Talk

Don't skimp on the **post-season analysis,** which is basically an autopsy on your season. Like with a real autopsy, don't be squeamish. Be thorough and dig deep. Any information you glean now can be used while prepping for next year's draft.

Maybe you just miscalculated talent. Maybe you were impatient. Maybe you were unlucky. Maybe you were lazy. Maybe you underestimated what it takes to stay competitive in this game.

Even if you've played this game for years, it's still a constant learning process. That's why it's so vital to keep some kind of record on hand. The previous take on my season, which was more a basic overview than an in-depth analysis, could not have taken place if I didn't throw a bunch of stats in a folder every week.

This is not brain surgery, but you will have to pick at the brain a bit. Every piece of useful information gleaned from this postmortem process can be used while prepping for the next draft. And believe me, if you're in an ongoing league, as soon as the World Series is in the can, you'll start having visions of Draft Day dancing in your head. Oh yes. Trust me on that one.

Dwelling on Bad Luck, Bad Trades, and Bad Taste

Yes, analysis is important (as is therapy, but that's splitting semantics). However, dwelling on analysis can be just as harmful as not doing it at all.

I've known owners who talk about stinker trades that happened two or three years ago. I do it, too. (Maddux!) It becomes harmful only when your bad turns start to define you. It's about balance (that word again!). When is this a problem? When you're sitting at the bar crying in your beer about the trade that ruined your '91 fantasy season. "I coulda' been somebody!"

Bad things happen to good people everyday. You're not special. All you can do is take what you can from the situation and *move on*. I will always use my Maddux trade as a cautionary tale to tell myself at bedtime, but I won't torture my friends with it. In fact, to show how dangerous it is to dwell on bad mistakes, I will no longer mention the name Greg Maddux in this book. Happy now? Good, then you see my point.

Did You Learn Anything?

Well, did you? Your first fantasy baseball season—no matter how dedicated a fan or savvy a dealer you are—will always have hard lessons. I don't know any owner who says different.

For every one thing that goes right there are a hundred things that can go wrong. You're fighting odds as well as yourself, your opponents, and time. No matter what the outcome, I hope you'll stick with it—for when there is a next year, there is hope.

If you quit after one year, you're stuck with that performance forever. If you won, that may be just fine. But everyone else will consider you a fluke—or worse, a guy who walks away from the table without giving them a chance to win their money back. Stay and fight. The game becomes far richer when you continue for years. You and some of your players will develop a history, as will you and your fellow owners. You'll always have a place of refuge where you can bury yourself in stats and strategy—and, believe it or not, friendship.

Remember, you fought not just your opponents, but yourself, your players, the odds, and time. And you'll always learn. Just when you think you know all there is to know about the game of ball, something happens to stuff a sweat sock (foot included) in your overworked mouth. The game validates you and humbles you.

The constant learning is the key for me. I've been doing this for a while now, but I still hesitate to call myself an "expert." What exactly makes an expert? I'm writing this book and have some useful experience to pass on, but I'm no Voice From Above.

Lots of sportswriters get paid good money to pen fantasy columns and dole out advice. Are they experts? Not necessarily, because they all thought Chan Ho Park was the cat's nip before the '99 season. So did I. Talent hints at the truth, but performance tells it.

Strike Three

Bad trades and bad luck happen to everyone. Dwelling on them is masochistic, which is fine, but soon your friends will avoid you.

Foul Tips

Whether it's your first or tenth, every fantasy baseball season teaches some hard lessons. Don't be bitter. Be open to learning.

Being paid to write about fantasy baseball does not make you an expert. I hate that word. *Expertise* is a better one, for that is something you can constantly build upon. The learning curve is nasty and breaks hard, folks. Once you start thinking you've got this game beat, it takes a funky hop off a turf seam and pops you right in the kisser.

Take what you've learned and run with it. Try not to make the same mistake twice. And eat more fiber. Short of that, what do we have left to talk about? Lots. Keep 'em turnin'.

Recommended viewing: *Major League*. Again. Just because.

The Least You Need to Know

➤ Keep an ongoing record of your team. Knowing the past will help you plot the future.

➤ After the season is over, do a performance postmortem on your season to see what went right and what went south.

➤ Learn from your mistakes, but don't dwell on them.

➤ If you stay on top of the things you can control, it will be easier to cope with the things you can't.

➤ Stick with the game for more than one year—it becomes far richer the longer you keep at it.

Chapter 19

Keep the Dream Alive (Even on Life Support)

In This Chapter

➤ Will your league continue?

➤ Yet another winter meeting

➤ Reviewing and changing the rulebook

➤ How about winter trading?

➤ When owners walk

Congratulations. You have just entered the fantasy baseball world full-time. The new season begins when the old one ends … and it never really ends. Now you have to worry about a host of things other than your roster. Another winter meeting. New elections. Rule changes. League improvements. Replacing disappearing owners. And yes, finally, keepers.

The whole point of the off-season is to improve your league. You now have the time to really think about it. It's *your* league. You can mold it into any shape you want, be it sensible or obscene. Start by writing down problems and potential solutions. I keep a running list all year, because who can remember anything?

The Winter Meeting

Here we go again. It's hard to believe a year has gone by. The unusual suspects once more must converge on some poor owner's house and turn the mess up to a respectable level. But this time it will be more fun. Why? Because, ta-da, you have awards to give out.

Foul Tips

Let the league kitty finance the end-of-year party/winter meeting as a gesture of goodwill. That way even the losers get something for their trouble.

That's right. Winners won't miss out on the chance to rub victory in the faces of the failures. If you have money to split up, now's the time for the treasurer to cut the checks. If you actually spring for a league trophy, so much the better: The losers will have something to break.

Try spicing up your awards ceremony with some side awards. The actual prize can be anything you want: a token financial award, a six-pack of decent beer, a hunk of pepperoni. Just earmark the money from the league pot before the real winnings are split up.

Here are some side awards to ponder:

➤ Best and Worst Free-Agent Pickup

➤ Best and Worst Trade (could be the same deal)

➤ Owner of the Year

➤ Most Valuable Player (based on price/stats ratio)

➤ Most Insulting Trade Proposal

➤ Best Processed Food Product Brought to Awards Ceremony

Once all the prizes are given out, the real work can begin. But like I said when you convened your first winter meeting: Don't think of it as work. This is your chance to make the league even better. Take it.

I suggest electing new officers first. That way your new or multi-term Commish can dip his toes in the administrative pool by running the rest of the meeting. After that, roll up your sleeves, grab a cold one, and let the screaming begin.

Foul Tips

Change proposals should be collated and distributed before the meeting convenes so everyone has a chance to think them over.

Rulebook as Work in Progress, Revisited

No rulebook is perfect. Now's the time to get it as right as possible until next winter, when you'll have even more changes.

First suggestion: The Commish should have everyone submit their rulebook proposals to the league office a few weeks before the winter meeting. This way, the Commish can collate all proposals, make them coherent, and organize them according to subject. Then he should distribute the complete list to the entire league a few days before the meeting.

There are several reasons for this:

➤ Everyone has a chance to submit proposals without comments from the peanut gallery.

➤ Everyone will be familiar with the agenda; no surprises.

➤ Everyone will have had a chance to think each proposal through.

➤ Debates will be more rational.

➤ The meeting will run smoother.

➤ You won't have duplicate proposals.

➤ Bloodshed will be held to a minimum.

As before, the Commish should mediate, introducing each proposal and allowing each owner a set time limit to make a point. Then vote. Keep things flowing. Your meeting should go a lot faster this time. Everyone will be familiar with the pace, format, and what it takes to get things done.

Now let's look at potential issues you'll face. Forewarned is forearmed, and it's better to be forearmed to the teeth.

What Rules Work/Don't Work

Everyone's point of view will be on full boil during the winter meeting. Meaning they won't care about yours, even if it's the same as theirs. We're back to the old selfishness again, and guys will be guys.

If someone doesn't like a rule, it's usually for one of two reasons:

➤ The rule hurt them; or …

➤ The rule helped someone else hurt them.

Strike Three

Don't change rules without cause. Just because you don't like a certain rule doesn't mean the rule is lousy. In fact, it usually means the opposite.

They will want it abolished/changed/morphed to fit their own selfish needs, using the "if it hurts me, it's just *wrong*" argument. Don't let that happen. Just because an owner doesn't like a certain rule doesn't mean the rule is ineffective. In fact, it usually means the opposite.

Why Rules Are Rules in the First Place

Be objective when evaluating rules. If you question one because it held you back in some way, ask yourself if you would've had an unfair advantage had the rule not been in place. If you say yes, then the rule is probably a good one.

Fantasy baseball rules are designed to keep the playing field level. If you make whole-sale changes, risky frontiers will break open, and owners will use them to full advantage. So be careful. As I've always said, the loudest voices are rarely the right ones.

Foul Tips

Don't ridicule an owner for wanting to change a rule. Let the voters decide.

The majority rule will prevent most of these crybabies from getting a toehold. But the mob mentality can also strike at any time, leaving logic in its wake. That's when your debate time will be well spent. If you know in your heart that something's right or wrong, fight for it.

Issues to Ponder

Listening to the rumblings of my own league, I've already got a good idea what changes will be proposed. I myself have a few ideas, too. To give you a good example of how issues are raised and discussed, here are some on which I anticipate debate in my little corner of the world:

➤ **Salary cap.** At $400, it's still a sticking point with many owners. Naysayers claim it prevents some deals from happening. Advocates say that's precisely why we need it. I predict no change in the cap, but the debates will be lively.

➤ **The number of trades that can be made between two teams in one week.** Some teams dealt with each other way too much in '99. Two teams in particular exchanged nearly every player between them, with some deals including more than 10 players at a time. This made some owners uncomfortable, mostly because these guys rarely dealt with anyone but each other. By limiting the number of inter-team trades, owners will be forced to deal with the rest of the league, which keeps everyone involved.

Strike Three

Don't think your league will ever have a perfect rulebook. That's Utopia, and Utopia doesn't exist, even for Yankee fans.

➤ **Acquiring multiple discount free agents using one injured player.** Our rule is intended to allow only one discount free agent per injured player, but it's not written that way. I, the Commish, was a perpetrator of this dastardly deed. Hey, I saw the loophole and jumped through it headfirst. But I understand how this crack in the rules can be used for evil, so I'll propose we spackle it shut.

See what I mean? Our league has been modifying its rulebook for years and we still have issues every season. Ideally, one would hope that the league will one day reach an off-season where no changes have to be made. But that's a pipe dream. Even the major league rulebook is imperfect. Which is what makes baseball as perfect as any game invented.

What Will Make Your League Better?

Rules aren't the only things that can be changed. Philosophies, amenities, and format can be tweaked to make your league bigger, better, and more fun. Give some of these proposals some thought:

➤ **Expansion.** For my money, the ideal number of teams in any league is 12. That way you get incredible draft depth, but there will still be a worthwhile number of players available as the season wears on. Your opinion may vary, but if you have a few guys who are interested in joining your league, give expansion some thought (more money to take from more rookie owners—yeah, baby, yeah!).

➤ **New categories.** It's definitely time for our league to adopt two new categories and go 6 × 6. That's only my opinion. I don't know if it'll happen. But adding an unusual category can infuse new drama and strategy.

➤ **New stat service.** How was your service? Good? Abysmal? If they were a waiter, how much would you tip them? There are a lot of services out there, so changing yours can alleviate many headaches with very little effort.

➤ **Winter trading.** We'll talk about this in a minute. It's a great tool for maintaining interest during the winter months. It's also great for stocking up on keepers and reserve picks, if you can get a sucker to take your offer.

> **Foul Tips**
>
> Small changes in your league format can greatly affect its dynamic. Don't be afraid to experiment.

➤ **Number of keepers.** Our league currently allows eight keepers. I personally wouldn't go any higher than this, since it would then cut into Draft Day (the more players you keep, the less you have to draft). However, I've heard of leagues that keep as few as four and as many as 15 players. The choice is yours.

➤ **Award breakdown.** Are contenders getting enough money? Maybe you want to spread the wealth a bit. Maybe you want to narrow the payoff. Either way, changing the kitty split is an effortless way to alter the dynamics of your league.

Any one of those changes can provide exciting new strategies.

Strike Three

If you do experiment, always provide the league with an escape clause that will restore the old format. Because experiments can fail.

Foul Tips

Winter trading is a fine tool for preparing for the draft. It is also great for keeping owners involved and interacting during the off-season.

Winter Trading Is a Cold Business

I've long been an advocate of winter trading. Still, for some reason it remains a defeated proposal in our league. I honestly can find no negatives against it. But I guess I'm in the minority.

That doesn't mean I can't recommend it to you. Here is winter trading as I propose it: A period of open trading will be allowed between the dates you decide on, leading up to the league's winter meeting. Within this window, players from the active roster, reserve roster, or minor league roster can be exchanged. Reserve picks can also be dealt. All other trading rules remain in force, including salary cap. Any and all deals will be announced at the winter meeting.

At the winter meeting, you can set up a podium so owners can announce their trades formally. This adds drama to an otherwise banal exercise and makes the occasion seem like the major league's amateur draft: "With the first overall pick, the Philadelphia Phillies select outfielder J.D. Drew … auuuggghhh!"

I can see no disadvantage to winter trading. Instead, I see opportunity:

➤ **Keep talking.** Winter trading keeps owners in touch during the off-season. Believe me, some guys will drop off the face of the Earth come October. This will keep them interested and interacting.

➤ **Stay frosty.** Your negotiating chops will remain sharp. Your killer instinct will remain comfortably chilled and hungry. 'Cause it feels just as good to rake a fellow owner in January as it does in June.

➤ **No no-shows.** Big announcements are one more reason to show up at the winter meeting (there will always be one or two owners who resist).

➤ **A second chance.** If you went hardcore for the title, trading away every prospect and reserve pick in an effort to win, now is your chance to restock. Or perhaps you can keep eight players but you have 11 who are too good to drop back into the draft pool. Dangle three of them to the other owners who are keeper-challenged. They'll be happy to fork over reserve picks and minor leaguers in exchange for some hope.

In all, the more you keep owners interacting and giving their rosters some TLC, the more crazy-sexy-cool your league will be in the off-season. Give winter trading some serious thought. If the other owners in your league haven't sold their souls to fantasy football, it might just fly.

(Note to myself: Photocopy this section to league owners before winter meeting. Attach bribe sheet to get measure passed. Then offer Chan Ho Park for a fifth-round reserve pick.)

Foul Tips

If someone wants to leave the league, let him. Having him around when his heart isn't in it will only hurt the league.

Live Owner Donors and Transplants

Another off-season inevitability: dropouts. Some guys just can't hack it. You'll prod them, coddle them, and cajole them. You'll finally threaten them and call them childish names. Try to refrain from shaking your fists and stomping your feet. On the other hand, maybe a true menace to the league will turn in his draft card, in which case you may want to open the door for him, start his car, and give him a police escort to the county line.

Either way, if someone wants to leave the league, you should let him go without a fuss. Being in a fantasy league is not a love affair. If you set him free, he'll never come back because he never loved you in the first place. Which is a good thing. Let it go. Seriously, persuading an owner to hang around when his heart isn't in it will only hurt the league in the long run.

A Timeline of Disaster

Here's a chronological speculation of what could happen if you try to talk a hesitant owner into staying:

➤ **February.** The guy reluctantly decides to stay in the league.

➤ **March.** Draft Day comes. The guy goes through the motions of filling his roster, fielding a squad that looks more like the call sheet for a John Waters film than a major league fantasy team.

➤ **April.** The new season starts. Already the guy is lax in returning calls and e-mails. Three of his players are injured. He doesn't replace them.

➤ **May.** The owner has an attack of conscience. He apologizes to the league and officially drops out.

Damage Control for Quitters

Now you're stuck with finding a replacement in mid-season—with this new guy inheriting a sickly team. Here's what should have happened:

➤ **February.** The first owner resigns and everyone parts friends. Hey, who knows, maybe one year when he has more time he'll rejoin. Cool. For now, however, you have someone interested in joining up. Even cooler.

➤ **March.** The new guy is approved by the membership. The only stipulation is that he inherits the previous owner's team. There are some good keepers on the roster. If this guy can draft, he'll have as good a shot at the title as anyone.

➤ **April.** The new owner is rabid. He calls and sends e-mails—a little too often for your taste. He begins calling at late hours. He sends you small gifts of candy, fruit, and *Star Wars* action figures. You're puzzled … does he love you, or does he love Mike Piazza on your roster?

➤ **May.** You tell the guy in no uncertain terms, Mike Piazza is *not* available. The phone calls and e-mails end abruptly. Within a few days, you receive a shipment of half-eaten candy, rotten fruit, and the severed heads of Chewbacca, Darth Maul, and Bib Fortuna.

➤ **June.** The new owner swings a deal for Sammy Sosa. He flaunts it whenever you're around, asking rudely how Mike Piazza is working out for you. You mention these episodes to the other owners. But they think he's a really cool guy and you're just paranoid. You show them the severed heads, *but no one is listening …*

Just Play a Lot of Breakup Songs

Well … you get the point. Assuming no one is a psycho, allowing the new owner to take over in the pre-season is far more fair than saddling him with a stinko team in May. Replacing owners should be a relatively painless process. The physical act of replacement should be, that is. If a good friend and even better owner drops out, the league will definitely feel the sting.

Overheard in the Dugout

Between '97 and '99, our league has replaced five owners, three of them in mid-season. The reasons were trifold: lack of interest, lack of time, and lack of stomach. There were some personality conflicts. There were some vanishing owners. But overall, the replacements were enthusiastic, which is a better trade-off any day.

Just be a pro. Do what you have to do to replace them quickly and quietly. Get the new owner wet as fast as possible so the ripples are so small they wouldn't dream of rocking the boat.

After the Race Begins

And if someone drops out in mid-season? That presents its own problems. Here are a couple of suggestions on how to handle it:

➤ Let him go, for the same reasons previously listed.

➤ Get a replacement ASAP. In the meantime, freeze that team's roster (which is easy since no owner will be there to make moves).

Make sure any replacement candidate knows exactly what he's getting into. Show him the frozen roster *before* he commits. There's nothing worse than a new guy coming in with delusions of roster.

If no replacement can be found? You have two choices:

➤ **Freeze the roster for the rest of the season.** This is the easiest and fairest option. All players on the roster would be off-limits for the year, returning to the draft pool next season. However, be sure to delete the frozen team from your stat service. Wouldn't it be embarrassing if an ownerless team beat you?

➤ **Break up the team and redistribute the players.** This allows the rest of the league to benefit from the orphan players. But how do you fairly redistribute the players without stepping on toes? You can stage a supplemental draft, by straight pick, last-place team chooses first, and so on. Or you can make up your own system. Just remember—no matter how you split up the players—that this could really tip the scales for some teams.

Foul Tips

Make sure a replacement owner knows exactly what he's getting himself into: the inherited roster, the level of commitment to the league, and so on.

Personnel changes are part of the fantasy landscape. They can provide shady tree relief or cause rolling-boulder destruction. The best advice is just deal with it quickly. As long as the major leagues stage games, your league will continue.

And if you can't find a replacement? Even after placing personal ads on the seedier Web sites? Don't fret. In fact, you should rejoice: You now have one less team to beat.

Recommended viewing: *Brewster's Millions*. Another great baseball fantasy. Richard Pryor has to spend 30 million bucks in 30 days, so he hires the Yankees to play an exhibition. And he's pitching against them. I mean, Richard Pryor! Run, don't walk, to your local video store.

The Least You Need to Know

➤ Your next winter meeting is a time to distribute awards, celebrate the past season, and legislate rulebook changes that will improve the league for the up-coming season.

➤ All rulebook proposals should be organized and distributed to the entire league by the Commish before the winter meeting. This way everyone has a chance to review them.

➤ Just because you don't like a certain rule doesn't mean it should be changed. Be objective.

➤ Winter trading is a good way to prep for the draft and keep owners interested in the off-season.

➤ If owners want to drop out, let them. A halfhearted owner can hurt your league in the long run.

➤ If you can't find a replacement owner, don't fret. You now have one less team to beat.

Chapter 20

No Rest for the Stupid: Zim's Off-Season, 2000

In This Chapter

➤ Paying attention to the news

➤ Making a keeper list

➤ Who my keepers are, and why

➤ Why it pays to think about the future at all times

Autumn is my favorite season (other than baseball, football, golf, and wabbit). The weather is in constant flux. The leaves change. The sunsets come earlier and more spectacular. At the same time, baseball is winding down—or up, depending on your point of view. The pennant races give way to the playoffs and the World Series. By Halloween, the first trades and free-agent filings sneak between the college football headlines.

November rolls around. Now the trading has begun in earnest. The general managers have their meetings. The post-season awards are handed out. It's a time for appreciation of the previous season's successes. It's also time to figure out what you'll need to make a competitive run next spring.

Are you paying attention? Because now is the time when player values roll with the wind-swept leaves. What happens between now and February will determine who you'll keep, who you'll want, and what it'll take to get them. So let's get ready to rumble. You have work to do.

Unlike Ballplayers, You Have No Off-Season

In fantasy baseball, you are the owner, but you are also the General Manager (GM). GMs work all year 'round. They rarely vacation, and when they do they still have to keep the cell phone by the pool.

Foul Tips

General Managers don't have an off-season. Neither should you. Your preparations for the up-coming season begin with the last out of the World Series.

Strike Three

After the World Series is over, don't wait to start your preliminary player value sheets. Real-life GMs don't wait; neither should you.

So … as GM, what are you going to do to prepare for the upcoming season? Who will you keep? And if your league allows winter trading, who will you deal—and for what?

In many ways, like autumn, this is my favorite part of fantasy baseball. You can think without having to make snap decisions, which allows for more quality of thought. You can formulate a vision as well as a new team.

As I write this, the current off-season has been rollicking. Look at the list of heavy hitters who have already changed addresses by trade:

Juan Gonzalez

Dante Bichette

Shawn Green

Raul Mondesi

Andy Ashby

Pat Hentgen

Vinny Castilla

Jeff Cirillo

On top of that, Ken Griffey Jr. has requested a trade. For cryin' out loud, Santa Claus hasn't even come to town yet. What will the majors look like come February?

The real-life GMs don't wait, and neither should you. You should already have pre-liminary (very preliminary) player value lists drawn up. This will make charting major league moves much easier. All you'll have to do is juggle names and fiddle with dollar values.

Follow the daily news. This is an exciting time, especially if your real-life favorite team pulls off some big moves. It can also be heartbreaking. Players change leagues and you could lose keepers. Or your favorite team could suddenly dump salary and hose down their upcoming season before it even begins. Either way, there is no excuse for not keeping even cursory tabs on what's happening in the majors. A lot of guys use fantasy football as an excuse, but the last time I checked, football and baseball were in the same newspaper sections.

The plan begins now, people. Your first order of business is the toughest: evaluating your keepers.

What Makes a Keeper?

That is the real question, isn't it? There's one easy answer: *price*. There is a myriad of harder answers, too—like player stability, contract status, and draft prediction.

Basically, a *keeper* is any player who is worth hanging on to because his price is way below market value. Keepers are your nucleus. They are the players you build around on Draft Day. They are the bluest of the blue chips.

The more keepers you have for less money, the more money you'll have to spend on Draft Day. Which should translate to a better team (unless you screw up). For instance, if you have $116 worth of keeper salary on your roster, you'll have $144 to spend on Draft Day.

But we're getting ahead of ourselves. First, let's talk about the rules governing keepers.

Foul Tips

The bottom line for any keeper is price.

Trash Talk

A **keeper** is any player who is worth hanging on to because his price is way below market value.

How Keepers Work

Here's how my league does it:

➤ Once he is drafted, promoted from the minor league roster, or acquired through free agency, a player is in his first contract year.

➤ Players may be kept up to three contract years. After the third season, they must be returned to the draft pool.

➤ Players may be kept at their first contract year salary for two seasons. If kept for a third contract year—the option year—their salary jumps $5. For example, I've kept Sammy Sosa for two years so far at $30. His third-year price jumps to $35, and I'd be a fool not to keep him even at that high total.

➤ Each team may keep a maximum of eight players. There is no minimum.

Note: These numbers are strictly for my league. Every league is different.

Overheard in the Dugout

I'm lobbying our league to change the three-year keeper rule. Sometimes you have great players at great prices; naturally you want to keep them longer than three years if their prices dictate it. I and some other owners will try to change the option year clause, allowing owners to keep players for more than three years, though their salaries will jump $5 each subsequent year after two. Eventually, players will be priced out of keeper status, but you get to reap the benefits of drafting the right player at the right price. Will it pass? Hmmm ... tough call.

Applying the Rules

Knowing the rules doesn't make choosing keepers any easier. Some will be no-brainers. You won't have to worry about them. But some choices will be agonizing.

These are the players who are closer to their actual value, but still priced nice enough to ponder. You'll have to play the odds that they will be worth the risk.

Here are some key keeper questions:

Foul Tips

When choosing keepers, keep in mind price and stability. Keepers should be the players you worry about the least.

➤ **Price.** What will the guy go for in the next draft? If it's close, and the guy is true blue, you'll probably want to keep him. On the other hand, if he's going to go for about the same price, why bother? Just draft him again and keep someone else. (See what I mean about tough options?)

➤ **Stability.** Will the player stay put? These days, a long-term guaranteed contract guarantees nothing except that the player will get paid. Big trades happen all the time. If a superstar is going to change leagues on you, you might lose him. Trades can also cause distractions to the player.

➤ **Contract status.** Guys in their final years will have great years more often than not. But these potential free agents are also prone to be traded, especially if their teams won't be able to re-sign them.

➤ **Performance.** Are they on the rise or on the decline? Did they just have a career year? Are they ripe for a crash? Or are they still building toward a talent peak? If you have to question their potential, you might want to reconsider keeping them.

You shouldn't have to worry about your keepers. They're the ones you plug in and forget about. But still … questions will always linger. I know, because selecting my keepers is going to be harder in 2000 than it has been in a while.

Don't wig. Enjoy the inner drama. This is what makes the game interesting … and torturous … and sadistic … and dangerous to your fellow man. Yee-haw!

Overheard in the Dugout

A good example of an "ideal" keeper on my own roster is pitcher Kevin Millwood. He's young, hungry, and plays for a contender. His 18-win '99 campaign was Cy Young–caliber. And I got him at $12, less than half of what he would go for in the 2000 draft. So what makes him ideal? Great price. Great support. Great stability. Barring injury, Millwood is a low-stress, low-maintenance keeper—what every owner desires.

My Keepers

To refresh your memory (and mine), here is my final '99 roster:

My Final '99 Roster

Position	Player	Price
Starters		
C	Javy Lopez	$15 (free agent)
C	Tyler Houston	$2
1B	Sean Casey	$22
3B	Chipper Jones	$32*
CI	Vinny Castilla	$33*
2B	Craig Biggio	$31**

continues

My Final '99 Roster   (continued)

Position	Player	Price
SS	Damian Jackson	$1
MI	Pat Meares	$5
OF	Sammy Sosa	$30*
OF	Gary Sheffield	$20**
OF	Tony Gwynn	$13**
OF	J.D. Drew	$5*
UT	Kevin Millar	$20 (free agent)
SP	Chan Ho Park	$26
SP	Denny Neagle	$21
SP	Bill Pulsipher	$20 (free agent)
SP	Orel Hershiser	$20 (free agent)
SP	Mike Hampton	$15
SP	Juan Guzman	$15 (free agent)
SP	Brett Tomko	$13
SP	Kevin Millwood	$7*
SP	Steve Parris	$5
RP	Mike Remlinger	$5
Reserves		
C	Jason Kendall	$15
C	Angel Pena	$2

* *Up for option year*

** *Player in option year who must return to draft pool*

I'm allowed eight keepers. If you were me, who would they be? I can name seven immediately:

My Definite Keepers

Position	Player	Price
OF	Sammy Sosa	$35 (third-year raise)
1B	Sean Casey	$22
SP	Mike Hampton	$15
C	Jason Kendall	$15 (free-agent keeper salary)

Position	Player	Price
C	Javy Lopez	$15 (free-agent keeper salary)
SP	Kevin Millwood	$12 (third-year raise)
OF	J.D. Drew	$10 (third-year raise)

That's seven players worth a total of $124. All of them are safely below what they would fetch in the 2000 draft. And virtually all of them are untouchable on their respective teams. The only question marks are Kendall and Lopez: How will they rebound from their '99 injuries? I've already read a report on Kendall. He's on schedule. Plus, he has a reputation for being one hard-nosed, driven player. He'll be fine. But Lopez? I've heard everything from "he's on schedule" to "he won't catch again." I'm playing the odds. At $15, it's not a huge financial risk.

What about that eighth slot? You could make an argument for the following players:

➤ **Shortstop Pat Meares, $5.** I drafted him solely on the fact that he drove in more than 60 runs for three straight years. Not many cheap shortstops can do that. The Pirates gave him a better lineup, batting second, which meant more runs scored, too. Unfortunately, he got hurt. But $5 for a shortstop who is stable and consistent (when healthy)? Very nice. But like Castilla, two strikes: the injury (will it hamper his playing time?), and draft prediction (he might even go lower than $5 in 2000). No dice, Pat.

Foul Tips

Some players may be questionable keepers, but if they are relatively cheap, they make nice gambles.

➤ **Starting pitcher Juan Guzman, $15 (free-agent keeper salary).** He was topnotch when he came over to the Reds in '99. And he's still in his mid-20s. Guzman could emerge as a true ace very soon. But he has three strikes against him: price ($15 is probably what he'll go for in 2000, and even that is risky), stability (he probably won't be a Red in 2000), performance (a lot of pitchers dominate on their first tour of a new league; Guzman won't be as good). Three strikes—yer out, Juan.

➤ **Starting pitcher Steve Parris, $5.** At five bucks, Parris is a no-risk investment. Throughout his career, he has pitched well when allowed to start—which is what the Reds will have him doing exclusively. But while he's a fine pitcher and a possible sleeper, he's not a sure thing. Two strikes: health (he hasn't shown durability yet) and performance (I'm not sold on his long-term prospects). Out you go, Steve.

➤ **Outfielder Gary Sheffield, $20 (third-year raise).** Sheffield is a proven performer. He goes out every day. And at $20, he could be a real bargain. But he has a strike against him that I haven't listed: personality. Sheff pouts an awful lot. I believe it affects his performance. Plus, if Raul Mondesi can pout in Dodgertown and get traded, so can Sheffield. Thanks, but no thanks.

➤ **Third baseman Chipper Jones, $37 (third-year raise).** The top candidate for my eighth slot. An MVP-type player. Five tools. The best at his position. Better still, he doesn't get hurt (generally), he won't be traded, and he's still under age 30. Throw him in my lineup with Sosa, Lopez, Kendall, Casey, and Drew, and you have six players with legitimate shots at 100 RBIs. That's big time, baby. His only keeper strike? Price. At $37, he's close to value. In my league, I think he'll top $40 in the draft. Tough call.

➤ **Shortstop Damian Jackson, $1.** The runner-up for the eighth slot. How can you go wrong at a buck? All the man did in '99 was hit nine home runs and steal 34 bases in 388 at-bats. But he also hit a gut-punching .224. He's very young and has a good shot at playing full-time in 2000. Imagine what he could do in 600 at-bats (hit .150?). His only strike is batting average, but that can improve with age. In fact, $1 is so cheap, he could hit anything he wanted as long as he gave me 30 steals. Impossibly tough call.

Those are the possibilities. As I said, Chipper and Damian are the frontrunners. But it's a tough choice. Thankfully, I won't have to make it for a while. A lot of things could happen between now and then. Either way, it's nice to have too many candidates than too few.

How I Plan to Dominate the Millennium

So what's my plan? Well, spelling it out in these pages won't hurt me. No one else in my league can read. And the ones who try would fall asleep by page 10, so I'm not worried. (Those comments are a test to see if they really do read the book.)

Seriously, my strategy will be difficult to thwart even if it is made public. But it will also be difficult to execute. How's that? Let's discuss it and find out.

Milking the Keeper Cow

My keeper list is very strong. They should carry most of my offensive load. Assuming my situation doesn't change between now and Draft Day, I'm still torn between Chipper and Damian. Here's how much my keepers will cost depending on which of the two fill the eighth slot:

Foul Tips

Once your keepers are set, you need to plan the rest of your strategy. Pitching? Hitting? Balance (that word again!)?

Chipper Jones, $37
Keeper Total: $161
$$$ Left for Draft: $99

Damian Jackson, $1
Keeper Total: $125
$$$ Left for Draft: $135

Foul Tips

A good tool to help choose keepers is calculating how much money you'll have left for the draft, per open roster slot (total $$$ divided by open slots).

As you can see, financially, Damian might be the better way to go. But Damian isn't as proven a performer as Chipper. And the .224 average … *ugh*. Let's look at each scenario.

The Damian Gambit

Let's say I keep Damian. The difference between his salary and Chipper's is $36. So that leaves me with $36 extra dollars to make up for the offense I lose by letting Chipper go. While $36 won't get me Chipper, it'll probably get me a Scott Rolen, a Matt Williams, or a Jeff Cirillo. Overall, I'll have $135 to spend on 15 slots (seven batting, eight pitching).

$135 ÷ 15 Slots = $9 per Slot

That's not too bad. I could get some good pitchers for that money, and my offense has a great foundation of keeper power and speed. But Chipper Jones is a five-tool monster …

The Chipper Contingency

Let's say I keep Chipper and every other keeper stays healthy and performs up to his career norm. That's a ton of concentrated offense. But I'll be left with a mere $99 dollars to spend on 15 slots.

$99 ÷ 15 Slots = $6.60 per Slot

That's not so good. The rest of the offense would suffer. I'd have to draft low-average starters and part-timers to fill the roster. And pitching? I'd have Millwood, Hampton, and a crew of cast-off swing men.

Strike Three

Keeping expensive players—even if they are the best at their positions—may not always be the way to go. Players who cost $30+ tie up an awful lot of money on Draft Day.

The advantages of Chipper are obvious: five tools, top of the line. And very, very expensive. Yet I still must consider keeping him down to the last moment.

See what I mean? These are the tough choices an owner has to make. Going strictly by dollars, Damian is, bar none, the way to go. Or is he?

Hmmm. What would *you* do?

Other Strategies

As for Draft Day, I still will overspend for pitching. I'll feel better about it in 2000 than I did in '99 simply because my offensive keepers are so strong. These are the keys to improvement for me:

➤ Assemble a pitching staff as good as '99

➤ Improve offense based on power of keepers

My offense is already off to a better start because of my keepers. But if I do indeed keep Chipper, my draft will have to be inhumanly good. Most of that $99 will go to pitching. Drafting good pitchers is a huge gamble, as has been stated previously. Maybe I'm just a moth to the flamethrowers. Normally I'd say, "It worked for me in '99." But it didn't. The only pitchers I personally drafted that amounted to anything were Hampton, Millwood, and Remlinger. Guzman, Neagle, Parris, and the rest I traded for. Aha. Now that's an interesting point. Maybe I should spend less on pitching this time? Nah!

I don't know why I'm so drawn to pitching. I think it may be because so many other owners disdain it. They don't ignore it, per se, but it's close:

➤ Owners don't pay for pitching.

➤ Owners don't trade for pitching.

➤ Owners don't fight for pitching.

I pay for it, trade for it, and fight for it. If that makes me crazy, I don't never wanna be sane.

Lessons Learned and Other Fallacies

Here endeth the lesson, at least as far as being an owner is concerned.

Of course there is much more to be learned. But that will have to come from your own experiences. I have given you a basic overview of what it takes to make it in a fantasy baseball league. What you do with this information is up to you; however, I'm sure there are fellow owners out there who would be happy to tell you what to do with it.

If you want to go Zen for a moment, fantasy baseball can truly be boiled down to four specific words. They have popped up in this text again and again. Each allows you to open up doors of information, strategy, and victory (three more good words). They are:

➤ Balance

➤ Intelligence

➤ Dedication

➤ Fun

Foul Tips

Remember the four key things to succeeding in fantasy baseball: balance, intelligence, dedication, and fun.

Balance is an easy one. Balance between batting and pitching. Balance between temptation and logic. Balance between good and evil. Every facet of the game needs your attention.

Intelligence you know about. You need information to act. You need smarts to know when to act. You need common sense to know what is worth acting upon. One without the others and you have bubkus.

Dedication is the hardest part. Staying true to yourself. Staying active. Staying interested. Encouraging your fellow owners to do the same. Six months is a long time to concentrate on one thing. If light sabers were legal, we'd all be Jedi by now.

Fun is … well … duh. If you're not having fun, you might as well be doing laundry, mowing the lawn, or spending time with loved ones. You know—the stuff you do out of guilt.

In the end, fantasy baseball comes down to those basic things. Sure, there are other things like luck, money, competition, sportsmanship, and the like. But if it were just about words, we could sit here all day and think some up.

I don't have time for that. You see, I'm in a fantasy baseball league. And I have a roster to fill.

See you on Draft Day.

Recommended viewing: MTV's Rock-N-Jock softball. Pure entertainment. A guilty pleasure. You get to see real stars like Mike Piazza mix it up with the likes of Jennifer Love Hewitt and Foxy Brown. Competition was never so fierce.

The Least You Need to Know

➤ Start preliminary player value sheets as soon as possible. The sooner you begin, the better you'll be able to chart player news.

➤ Keepers are good players priced well below their market value. The point is to have the best players possible for the least amount of money.

➤ Expensive keepers, even if they are undervalued superstars, can be a big gamble. Use caution.

➤ If you're having trouble choosing between two potential keepers, it's usually best to stick with the cheaper one. You'll have more money to make up what you give up.

➤ Remember the key words: balance, intelligence, dedication, and fun.

Part 7

For Your Commish Only

Oh, all right. You can read these chapters if you aren't the Commish. In fact, it'll be helpful. You'll get a good idea what a thankless, brainless, elementary-school principal kind of a job it is. Actually, it's not that bad. But it does take a certain flair for the absurd—and some patience.

These final chapters won't tell you how to win your league. They'll help you run it. So button your jacket, paste on your best smile, and prepare for the rubber-chicken lunches. For you are in for a life of meetings with union reps, concession lobbyists, player attorneys, and marketing teams.

But if that falls through, you should at least be able to keep a straight face during rule debates.

Chapter 21

The Lone Voice of Reason

In This Chapter

➤ The pros and cons of leadership

➤ How to maintain order

➤ How to stay impartial

➤ The temptations of inside information

I was a Commish. Once you do the job, telling people about it makes you feel like Quint in *Jaws:*

"You were a Commish? What happened?"

"A maverick subversive scammed two free agents off the same injured player, Chief. We were just coming back from the island of Manhattan. We just delivered the book, the fantasy baseball book. A dozen men went into a tizzy. The league went down in 12 minutes."

"Didn't see the first owner for about an hour. A loser. You know how you know that in a league, Chief? You can tell by looking from the pitchers to the reserves. Well, we didn't know. 'Course our book mission had been so secret, no distress signal had been sent. They didn't list the transactions overdue for a week. Very first light, Chief, owners come cruisin' …"

Yeah. It's a lot like that. But overall, I do recommend the job. There's a certain lack of nobility to it, which is nice—especially if you have low self-esteem (another plus for fantasy league administrators). So if you're elected Commissioner of your league, don't be afraid. Just pick up this book and read on. You might actually see something that will help you. Imagine that …

The Man and the Maelstrom

Ah, the life of the Commish. What can you expect? You'll calm down screaming children. You'll make sure everyone plays nice. You'll do the spanking. And you'll clean up nasty spills. For no pay. Still sound good?

Seriously, the *Commissioner* is the key role in a fantasy baseball league. He is the administrator, the judge, and the guy who makes things run. A Commissioner's formal responsibilities are as follows:

> ➤ Interpret and make rulings based on the rulebook. This also applies to disputes between owners. Scofflaws and speeders beware.

> ➤ Receive and distribute all roster changes. Owners send their weekly/daily moves to the Commish. He approves them (next bullet), collates them, and sends them to the Secretary for entry into the stat service.

> ➤ Approve roster changes in accordance to the rulebook. To eliminate sneakiness.

> ➤ Award free agents to owners based on FAAB (Budget or Board systems). Very important. The Commish administrates these systems to make sure the correct owner gets the coveted free agent.

> ➤ Plan and mediate Draft Day and the winter meeting. Because someone has to do it.

Trash Talk

The **Commissioner** is the chief executive of a fantasy league. He enforces rules, resolves disputes, and runs meetings.

Foul Tips

The key to being a good Commish is being a good leader. You can fake it, but you can't force it.

This kind of authoritarian position can lead to friction between the Man and the masses. In some ways this is natural. Expect it … to an extent.

The key to being a good Commish is being a good leader. For some, that comes naturally. For others—the intelligent, logical gentlemen out there who finds confrontation as unappetizing as haggis—it has to be learned. Or at least faked.

Be a Good Leader

Leaders of lawless organizations are often portrayed as schmucks: Colonel Henry Blake of *M*A*S*H;* President Hoover of *Animal House;* Judge Smails of *Caddyshack.*

Blake and Smails are two of my favorite characters in modern comedy. Each in his own way just wants peace and tranquility in his respective universe. But the Frank Burnses and Al Czerviks of the world will always be there to push their buttons. As it will be with you. My advice? Make your buttons very, very small.

Strike Three

Do not fear confrontation. Do not fear decisions. If you do, everyone will smell it. Then you'll have a problem.

The problem with organizational leaders is that they will eventually make a ruling that will make someone unhappy. Some people fear this. They don't like confrontation. They don't want to be disliked. Lose this fear immediately. Owners will smell it on you and use it to their advantage—even when dealing with you on more local matters such as trading. Remember, without deterrence, there is anarchy.

If you have a league full of okay dudes, you shouldn't have a problem. But if you have a bunch of buckaroos, watch out. They were genetically encoded to defy the teacher, the principal, and the parent. They won't think much of you.

So how does one be a good leader? Simple. A good leader ...

➤ **Communicates.** Address the league often and update them on the status of pending issues (meetings, problems, parties). If you can make them laugh, so much the better.

➤ **Uses common sense.** It's the best tool in your arsenal.

➤ **Listens to every side.** This is why it is called debate. Just because a guy is riled and screaming to make his point doesn't mean he isn't worthy of being heard. Suppress no opinions, no matter how dumb.

➤ **Keeps a cool head.** Everyone might be yelling. Everyone might be reaching for their throw-down weapon. You're the one who has to pound the table and tell them to shut the - - - - up.

Foul Tips

Lose your fear. Owners will take advantage of you as Commish as well as competitor. (Just try getting a good trade offer out of someone who thinks he owns you.)

➤ **Thinks before he reacts.** Judge Judy doesn't go to her chambers for a smoke. She goes to think. Snap decisions can bite you back. Unless it is a dire emergency, take your time.

➤ **Makes final decisions.** They may not be right. They may not be popular. But they must be final. Take a page from the umps' book. You won't find thicker skin on a T. Rex.

➤ **Knows when he's wrong.** If you do make a mistake, admit it. Reversing yourself is not a sign of weakness when you and everyone else knows it's the right thing to do. You're not God. You're not even Selig.

These are just a few positive traits. There's just no substitute for a patient, fair Commish. Being Patton and smacking your troops around will get you nowhere.

Foul Tips

Formal debates are incredibly useful for arguing points within a large group.

Strike Three

Don't let debates get out of control. Allow one person to speak at a time. Set a time limit and enforce it. Don't let issues drag on. Make the voting process swift and final.

Encourage Debate ... to an Extent

You know what's the problem with today's Congress? I mean besides the boozing, schmoozing, pressing flesh outside of marriage, backbiting, back stabbing, power games, dirty deals, porky proposals, and bad hair? *Too much talk.*

The worst political invention is the filibuster. Good and productive issues literally get talked to death. This is *soooo* useless. I mean, we should respect leaders who can't shut up? A good Commish won't let debates get out of hand.

Formal debates are your best tools for arguing points within a group setting. But they must be controlled.

➤ Allow one person to speak at a time.

➤ Enforce strict time limits.

➤ When someone is done speaking, they are *finished speaking;* no second chances.

➤ Make sure everyone knows how it works beforehand.

When the talking is done, put the issue to a vote. Case closed. The guys on the losing end will always complain. I'd be surprised if they didn't. (See the section in Chapter 22 on crybabies.)

You might think that all this formal structure is stiff. Confining. Even a little geeky. It is. But it has to be that way. Take it from someone with experience: If you don't have a corral, the bulls run free. I learned this as a fantasy baseball Commish and as a fraternity president (where the stakes were higher and the standards lower). Guys are guys. Some lead and some force their leadership on others. It's in the DNA.

Give everyone a chance to speak. Then shut them up and close the issue. Because fantasy baseball leagues are efficient. Filibusters are for the flakes who spend our money in Washington.

The Loudest Voices Are Loudest Because They Are Dumb

Maybe that's harsh. Just because a guy is wrong doesn't make him dumb. But it does make him insecure, belligerent, and prideful. In fact, you'll find the seven deadly sins alive and well in your fantasy league:

1. Greed (for $$$ winnings)
2. Sloth (lax preparations)
3. Pride (saving face)
4. Envy (for your players)
5. Wrath (because of your steal of a deal)
6. Lust (for power)
7. Gluttony (for processed food products)

To paraphrase not one, but two Coen brothers films: "He who is without sin should throw the first stone … *and t'row it hard.*"

Overheard in the Dugout

Lopsided trades—or at least perceived lopsided trades—nearly destroyed our league in '99. I would definitely classify it a crisis. There were accusations of stupidity. There were accusations of collusion. There was enough bad blood flying around to supply a Troma film. As Commish, I stepped in and made everyone explain the rationale behind their deals. When a genuine crisis erupts, you must be standing by, fire hose in hand, to douse the flames.

Don't condemn the sinners. This is just a game, after all. But it is a game whose players take it very seriously. This seriousness spills over as frustration, anger, impatience, and a host of other undesirables. The Commish is the guy who deals with it. Be prepared. You should never, ever be swayed by the loudest voices. The squeaky wheel gets the grease, so they say. Not here.

In this game, the squeaky wheel gets three minutes to make its point. Then someone stops it from spinning.

> **Foul Tips**
>
> A Commissioner must be neutral amid all issues. His vote counts toward the league, of course, but he can show no favoritism.

> **Strike Three**
>
> As Commish, don't risk your integrity. If you're corrupt, you'll be taking a great game and flushing it down the toilet.

Are You Fair and Impartial— Even with Friends?

You're just the Commish, not the RoboCommish. You're human. Which means that you will inevitably like some owners more than others. Some you may have known for years, while others you first met on Draft Day.

Naturally, when it comes time to resolve a dispute, you'll be tempted to side with your buddy. After all, you owe him: He set you up with the blond at the bar last November. You kill wild animals, play paintball wars, and go to ballgames together. How can you possibly side with an owner you hardly know? Because you *have* to.

You are the Commish. You must be the pillar of integrity. If you're corrupt, the league will suffer. It's a great game here, people. Don't screw it up by playing Don Corleone. If you absolutely must use the phrase "I'll make him an offer he can't refuse," at least have the decency to include Mike Piazza and a third-round reserve pick.

If circumstances arise where the Commish is involved with a dispute—or if some conflict of interest is present—the next highest league officer should step in and make the ruling. This could be the Assistant Commish or the Secretary, depending on how you set up your league.

If temptation consumes you, come clean—and pray that you're redeemed faster than a two-for-one coupon at McDonald's. But you probably won't be. Chances are you'll be impeached and maybe even tossed from the league. But hey, you'll deserve it. If you fall off the wagon of honesty, do everyone a favor and hit your head on a rock. It'll save your league a lot of time and anguish.

Inside Information: Use It or Lose It?

Foul Tips

When the Commish is involved in a dispute, or has a conflict of interest, the next highest league officer makes the ruling.

It's time for me to come clean. When I was Commish, I used inside information to my advantage.

The Commish sees and hears everything first. Trades. Free-agent bids. Every transaction, every week. It can definitely give you an advantage. How so? Check it out: If you have weekly transactions, roster changes will roll in by the Sunday night deadline. You, Commish, must sort them and approve them.

Then—unless some safeguard system is in place—you are free to make your own moves afterward, *in reaction to the moves of everyone else in the league.* No one will see it. No one will know it. But I'm blowing the whistle on it. Call Mike Wallace. On second thought, make that Paula Zahn. It's wrong. I'm guilty of it for sure. I'll bet a lot of other Commissioners are, too.

How to Safeguard Against Using Inside Information

The Commish should e-mail all of his roster changes to the next highest league officer *by the same deadline as the rest of the league.* This will prevent him from using transaction info to his advantage.

Here is exactly how I used inside information to my advantage:

> Every Sunday night, the weekly transactions roll in by 8:30. I look them over, type them up, and figure out who put in for which free agent.

> Our league uses the FAABoard system. Two or more owners have to put in for the same player for there to be movement on the Board.

Sometimes, if only one owner put in for a free agent, I'd also put in for the same free agent just to knock that first owner down to the bottom of the Board. Everyone else, including me, moves up a slot.

I would also routinely make all my roster changes well after I'd reviewed everyone else's. That's not an advantage, per se, but I'm still making my roster changes past the weekly deadline, which is wrong.

Does this make me a bad person? Maybe. Does it make me a bad Commish? Not necessarily bad, but definitely corrupt. I plan to propose legislation to close that loophole. My guess is it will pass unanimously.

This is one reason I added these chapters to the book, especially this section on the Commissioner's integrity. Leagues can get so competitive that sharpening yourself any edge, no matter how small, is tempting.

There is a simple solution to this problem: The Commish should e-mail all of his roster changes to the next highest league officer *by the same deadline as the rest of the league.* This will prevent him from using transaction info to his advantage. It will also prevent him from pulling the FAABoard nonsense I described earlier.

So. Now that my credibility is totally shot, let's move on. There is one very important issue regarding commissioners that we haven't talked about yet. Don't know what that is? Read on and find out.

Recommended viewing: *The Fan.* DeNiro and baseball again. Okay, so Bobby D. isn't the player, but Wesley Snipes is believable in any jock role. As is Mr. DeNiro in any psycho role. A hoot.

The Least You Need to Know

➤ The Commissioner enforces rules, resolves disputes, and runs meetings.

➤ The Commish cannot fear confrontation or making decisions.

➤ Formal debates are the best tool for arguing points within a large group.

➤ A Commissioner must remain neutral. He can vote on league issues, of course, but he can show no favoritism.

➤ When the Commish is involved in a dispute or has a conflict of interest, the next highest league officer makes the ruling.

Chapter 22

Wyatt Earp Told Me There'd Be Days Like This

In This Chapter

➤ Eventually, a commissioner has to punish someone

➤ How to deal with crybabies, rebels, conspirators, and jerks

➤ Creating your own penalties

The life of the Commish was nice. I embezzled funds regularly from the league coffers and instituted weekly Roman orgies of food, drink, and Wednesday Night Baseball. But I'd do it on a Tuesday to throw off the cops.

I'd rent out the local palace, turn on the radar gun, and let guests throw baseballs at cardboard cutouts of the Backstreet Boys. At league events, I paid the local paperboy $400 an hour to dress as a gladiator and fan me with a giant peacock feather.

Once a month, I'd use my authority to rent a limo, buy a case of champagne, and club hop all the velvet-roped joints in Orwigsburg. My entourage and I would take over the VIP areas and kitchen. I'd flirt endlessly with famous women, but only those whose first names ended in "a": Winona, Salma, Uma, Fiona, Anna. I was far too busy for the rest of the alphabet.

One time I rented out the local theater and staged a 24-hour marathon screening of *Major League*. Refreshments were served ballpark-style in large trays of ice and heated metal boxes. Wolfgang Puck catered. Spielberg danced on his seat during "Wild Thing." But the Secret Service shut it all down when the President accidentally locked himself in a bathroom stall.

One day it all came to an end. Camelot collapsed, the books were audited, and I was forced to resign—though my lawyers secured no admission of wrongdoing on my part. I now live in seclusion, passing my final days with close friends and an amorous dog named Farfal.

Not!

The Commish and His Dying Wish

The Commish ain't no rock star. Nope. You're just another stiff strapped to his computer chair, doing the work. And the work's fine. It won't kill you.

Foul Tips

The hardest part about being Commish is maintaining order among "friends."

Perhaps the hardest part about being Commish is keeping order. You're Wyatt Earp. Your dying wish is to have a calm, rational group of people who fully understand that they are members of a friendly league. Negotiations run smoothly. Meetings are social occasions where business is quickly resolved so you can move on to the brandy or coffee or what have you.

Ha. Pull this leg and it plays the national anthem.

The Plain Truth

No, your league will probably be populated with a bunch of malcontents. We live in a litigious society where everyone sues everyone for everything. That means that everyone will make a federal case when their rights have been violated.

Strike Three

Beware the ego. It is responsible for more owner resignations and league breakups than any other cause.

One word sums it all up: *ego*. Pick a famous transportation-based disaster—the *Titanic,* the *Hindenberg.* That's the male ego. Big, grand, wonderful, unsinkable. And yet the tiniest hole can pop it. The faintest spark can send it up in flames. When that happens? Hey, you saw the movie. Chaos, hysteria, and outrage at the greedy bureaucrats who ignored common sense and killed everyone.

The male ego is responsible for more owner resignations and league breakups than any other cause. Guys just can't take it. They are never wrong, they never give in, and they never apologize. It's just the way things are. I'm not saying that this territory is exclusive to men. I'm sure there are some women out there who are equally incorrigible. But one advantage that women seem to have, in my experience, is a real nose for male morons. They won't hesitate to knock a guy down a few notches when he deserves it. So to all you ladies playing fantasy baseball out there: give 'em hell.

The faster we all accept this egocentric nonsense, the faster those in positions of responsibility can shed their own egos and make things run better.

The Patience of (the) Job

You, as Commish, must deal with all of it. Sound fun? It can be if you don't take everything too seriously. If you manage that, it's absolutely *hilarious* listening to the guys who treat everything like it's the apocalypse come to their door just for them. Here's where your leadership skills come into play. Patience, especially. You *have* to listen when someone has a beef, no matter how many times he cries wolf. It might just be legit.

Another important aspect of leadership is to check your own ego at the door. You're human, after all. If you think otherwise, you'll end up as surly and argumentative as everyone else— especially when someone accuses you of making a mistake.

But I'd rather take life's lemons and squeeze 'em. Sell the juice at a premium and be a millionaire. To help you do the same, I've split up the worst kinds of offenders and offered idiot-specific advice on how to deal with them. See what you think ...

Foul Tips

Your first job as Commish is to shed your ego. You can't afford to be blinded by pride. You'll just be as surly and argumentative as everyone else. Nothing will get done.

Babies: Kicking, Screaming, Biting, and Spitting

Everyone can be a baby. Hey, if you whine about a bad call against your team in the playoffs, you can be classified as a baby. Remember that the next time Big Blue blows it.

Babies are simple creatures. When they are happy, there are none happier. I have a nine-month-old son at home who smiles to melt the ice caps when he's good to go. He giggles and hops and makes everyone around him happy as well. But the instant something is wrong? Hungry? Dirty diaper? Overtired? Waaaaaahhh! He's not just one squeaky wheel demanding grease, he's a fleet of rusty tricycles looking for a case of WD-40.

Strike Three

Never give in to a baby just to shut him up. You must always do what is best for the league no matter what anyone may think, do, or say.

Foul Tips

Most times, crybabies are crying about another owner's management style, which has nothing to do with broken rules. Disliking another's owner's style is not grounds for complaint.

The guys with the occasional complaints will not be the problem. It's the ones who call or e-mail once or twice a week with beefs of varying magnitude.

"I can't believe you let that trade go through …"

"He can't do that …"

"You shouldn't let him do that …"

"Why did he do that? …"

"Doing that just makes it worse for the rest of us …"

What he's really saying is, "Can you tell I hate my life and myself?"

The litany of can'ts, shouldn'ts, and wouldn'ts from these guys will never end. However, if they want to act like babies, that doesn't mean you should treat them like babies. If you talk to them like they are paste-eating half-wits, they'll just get angrier. You have to be calm and creative. Nine times out of ten, a baby will complain not about a broken rule, but about personal management style. They simply won't like what another owner is doing even though it's perfectly legal according to the rulebook.

This happened quite a bit to me. After a while, it became intolerable. So I came up with a very simple solution. I sent a league-wide e-mail declaring my new complaint policy:

> "From now on, the Commissioner's office will no longer hear complaints that do not have anything to do with a clear and specific rule violation. Complaints about loophole-hopping, gray areas, and personal management style will be ignored."

This strategy basically worked. Guys still called to complain about other guys, but they called as friends, not owners. Giving in to babies is a mistake. They may be the loudest and the most annoying, but they are very rarely right. Remind them that you are a Commish, not a playground monitor. Then quickly move on to the real complaints.

Overheard in the Dugout

In my league, one owner had a real problem with some other owners' habits of drafting injured players on Draft Day, subsequently picking up discounted free agents to replace them. This is a legitimate strategy, but he couldn't stomach it. Personal management style is not grounds for complaint. The complaining owner wasn't happy about this, but there was nothing to be done. No rule had been broken. In fact, the owner who did the most "injury" drafting won the league that year.

Rebels: Where's Yer Cause, Jimmy Dean?

Some guys were born to defy. If they can't be James Dean, they're happy to be John Stamos, Luke Perry, or even David Lee Roth. Maybe it's the leather coats and feather boas. Maybe it's all the hot chicks. But man, there is one thing I will never ever understand about rebels, be they motorcycle gods, tough guys, or punk rockers: If they are so hellbent on being different, why do they all look and sound the *same?*

Purple hair aside, your league may well have a rebel or two. And they will try to outlast the Commish on principle. Authority of any kind is to be defied, after all.

When dealing with rebels, your best weapon is not strength, intelligence or charisma. Rebels won't buy into any load of nonsense you have to offer anyway. All you have are the rules. Break a rule, and there must be consequences. Break enough rules, and the consequences should get very serious.

Foul Tips

When dealing with rebels, your best weapon is not strength, intelligence, or charisma. It's the rules. Break a rule, and there will be consequences.

But many rebels are like bullies: cowards. They'll just *bend* the rules, riding the gray areas to make everyone else mad. I say let 'em. If they aren't breaking any specific rules, you as Commish really can't punish them. So why contribute to your ulcer by worrying about it? What you can do is unleash peer pressure. Quietly encourage the other owners to take matters into their own hands. This will lead the rebel to impale himself on your next-best weapon: the rebel's own rebellion.

Foul Tips

Eventually a rebel will make people so angry that no one will deal with him. Then he will have to make an internal decision: toe the line, or quit.

Trash Talk

Collusion is the act of two or more owners conspiring to manipulate the final results of the league. Methods can include trades, waivers, and point shaving.

If you simply let nature take its course, eventually this guy will make enough people angry that no one will want to deal with him. At which point he will have to make an internal decision: toe the line, or quit. Chances are he'll toe the line. Unless of course he cares more about the act of rebellion than he does about baseball. In which case your league is better off without him.

Sayonara, Dylan McKay. Kiss Brenda for us.

Conspirators: They, Too, Were Honorable Men

Now we are entering a far more sinister and far more serious realm. We'll use words like conspiracy and *collusion*. And if it happens to you, it could threaten your entire league. No crime is dirtier. No betrayal is worse. I'm talking about the owners who deliberately join forces to manipulate the final results of the league.

They can do this a number of ways:

➤ **Trades.** Owners will pass each other players who will optimize their rosters, knocking other owners out of contention. This is the most obvious form, since trades can be lopsided (although owners will always back up their actions with their own logic). A good trade approval system will curtail this.

➤ **Waivers.** Owners will waive a player so the team at the top of the FAABoard can snap him up. Granted, dropping a healthy Derek Jeter in mid-season would look a little suspicious. But dumping a lesser player could indeed pass muster.

➤ **Point Shaving.** Owners can reserve players or otherwise hamper their own active roster to allow another owner to pass them in a certain category.

Let's be realistic for a moment. You probably won't be playing for enough money to make collusion a greed-based crime. It is possible if your Decimal Debate carries team salaries into the three figures, league kitties in the four figures. Not many leagues do that.

However, if there has been repeated internal strife within a league, it is possible for owners to conspire against other owners simply for spite. This is the ol' male ego rearing its cretin head once again. Guys never forget a slight. If this does indeed happen—and it is because of a lingering argument—make sure it's contained. Public disputes between owners, while extremely entertaining, are devastating to league morale.

Overheard in the Dugout

Whenever owners complain publicly about other owners, my first reaction is to tell everyone, "Hey, let's stay off the record with this stuff. If you have a beef, go to that owner personally and settle it privately." Public disputes are rarely helpful to a league unless there is a very specific rule precedent that needs to be set. Whenever you can, keep disputes contained.

This is the stuff that breaks the fantasy spell, reminding everyone that they aren't baseball owners, but just everyday schmucks who thrive on leftover high school athletic adrenaline. As a result, competition becomes all too real. That's when the nonsense starts. That's when two P-O'd owners will get together over beers and plot the downfall of the guy who got them P-O'd in the first place.

My advice is this: When you sense a brouhaha brewing to the haha stage, step in. Insist that the matter be resolved privately between two gentlemen. Offer your services as a neutral arbitrator. You're the Commish. That's your job.

Foul Tips

If two owners can't resolve a dispute themselves, offer to be a neutral arbitrator. Maintaining league peace is part of the Commish's job.

If this helps, great. If not, try to nip the snowballing disaster in the bud by notifying every other team in the league individually and confidentially. (If you do it publicly, the angry owners will only get angrier.) Voice your concerns. Warn them against possible behavioral incidents between the P-O'd guys. And then watch the situation like a hawk.

Obviously, this is no way to live. But if the league is worth saving over a couple of egotistical yahoos, then it's worth risking the wrath of said yahoos. Conspiracies are just plain ugly. I hope you never have to deal with one. But if you do, keep it simple, keep it rational, and if you can, keep it civil. A fantasy league is nothing to lose a friend over.

Jerks: Code Reds and Other Drastic Measures

What's left? The jerks. They come in many forms:

➤ Guys who are always late

➤ Guys who are always misinformed

➤ Guys who are always sure that a free agent is available even though you personally acquired the player three weeks ago

➤ Guys who forget their cash on Draft Day

➤ Guys who let their mid-season tab soar, unpaid

➤ Guys who never answer phone calls or e-mails

➤ Guys who always need to borrow your research materials

➤ Guys who try to cop your value sheets

➤ Guys who love the party but won't help stage it

➤ Guys who will always have a joke but never have a straight answer

➤ Guys who won't take responsibility for their actions

➤ Guys who are inconsiderate, disrespectful, lazy, dependent, demanding, spoiled, needy victims

Foul Tips

"Code reds," or peer pressure, is a great motivational tool. Don't be afraid to ask the other owners to help with a hard case.

In short, guys who are *jerks*. Don't bother making a project out of them. These guys are incurable. Why? *Because they're like this in real life.* Just ask their bosses, their spouses, and their families. They can be the nicest people in the world. They mean no harm. They always apologize, most of them sincerely. But they will always let you down in the end. It's some kind of program malfunction in their genetic makeup.

So what can you do? Did you see *A Few Good Men? Full Metal Jacket?* If not, there is a nice little motivational tool used in the military called a "code red." It basically entails the entire league ganging up on the screw-up to convey one blaring message: *This behavior will no longer be tolerated. Get your act together.*

If jerks have any desire to be in a fantasy baseball league, they'll fly right. If they don't, they'll quit. Either way the league becomes a stronger entity. But if they don't quit and don't come around? Sometimes there's only one thing left to do …

When You're Out of Options

Eventually, the Commish will have to punish someone, whether it's for not paying a tab or conspiring to break Sammy Sosa's knees on his next trip to Chicago. Just remember to make the punishment fit the crime, even if you have to try on a few in the dressing room first.

Benign:

> ➤ **Small fines.** Token penalties worth less than a good cup of coffee at Starbucks.

> ➤ **Gentle public humiliation.** Letting the whole league know what a moron the guy is.

Eyeopeners:

> ➤ **Major fines.** Stiff hits to the wallet that are worthwhile only if you can make the guy pay up. If he just blows you off, what's the point?

> ➤ **Severe public humiliation.** Letting the league know not just what a moron he is, but what he did that night in high school when he drank a whole bottle of cough syrup.

Foul Tips

Fines are good sanctions since they both sting the wallet and pad the kitty.

Face smacks:

> ➤ **Deducting points.** Penalize an owner a point or two. That'll sting.

> ➤ **Deducting future reserve picks.** A man without a future is a man without hope.

> ➤ **Freezing rosters.** Try it for a week. Losing those stats hurts worse than a root canal.

> ➤ **Expulsion.** Too bad, so sad, bye-bye, baby. A last resort, sure, but sometimes there's no other way.

If you decide to invoke a face smack, I recommend putting the issue to a league vote. These penalties directly affect the outcome of your league. They should not be taken lightly, nor should they be used as an idle threat.

To me, the greatest problem with applying sanctions to a lousy owner is that no matter how seriously everyone takes the league, no matter how much it all means to you, no matter how much time you put in ... it's still just a fantasy league. Which makes the threats as make-believe as the game. Sanctions work only if owners take them seriously.

How to Make Fines Work

Levying a fine on an owner is generally a useless gesture because you're talking about pocket change. The owner will be thinking about the fine in real terms. What you need to do is make him think about it in fantasy league terms. Here's how:

➤ Deduct the fine from the owner's remaining FAABudget; or ...

➤ Deduct the fine from the owner's salary cap, either temporarily or permanently.

Either way, the fine is now more threatening.

Why won't an owner be afraid of the Commish? Sanctions don't truly hurt anyone. If it gets really bad, sure, kick the guy out. But he's not going to jail. He owes no community service.

Foul Tips

The Commish is the emotional center of the league. Don't be a wimp. Don't be a tyrant. Just work hard, be positive, and act fairly, and usually people will respond.

It's up to you as Commish to make sure everyone knows that you will not tolerate the bull. They'll test your resolve, especially if egos are on the line. Guys will try to save face and make you out to be the jerk. Don't put up with it. Don't be a tyrant, either. As with anything in this game, it's about balance (that word again!).

My best advice is to take every case as it comes. Base your decisions individually, not cumulatively (unless an owner repeatedly defies the rules). It's a long season for everyone. Battles of will only sap the strength of each owner.

The Commish, ideally, is the emotional center of the group. If you work hard, be positive and act fairly, people will generally respond. Let the jerks fall by the wayside where they belong.

Creative Penalties Not in the Rulebook

Are the usual hardline tactics not working? Try slapping some of these cuffs on the bad guys:

➤ Offending owner sits out the first round of the next Draft Day

➤ No trading for X weeks

➤ No free-agent pickups for X weeks

➤ No releasing players for X weeks

➤ Loss of FAABoard position

➤ Suspension of one or more players from the active roster

➤ Offending owner serves drinks and processed food product to rest of league at next meeting

The point is, be creative. There are many different ways to get to an owner, some serious, some just plain humiliating. The point is to get them to treat you and your fellow owners with respect, and take your league seriously.

If you can do that, you're a better Commish than I. You'll have a happy, calm, enjoyable league. Which, in this day and age, is about as common as sighting the wily pipsquack bird.

Recommended viewing: *Field of Dreams*. I can't think of a better film that sums up what the game of baseball is all about. Watch it whenever you get mad at the game.

The Least You Need to Know

➤ Eventually, a Commish will have to punish an owner. Make sure it fits the crime.

➤ Never give in to a baby just to shut him up. That's what he's banking on.

➤ The only real threat you have against rebels is the rules. Enforce them strictly.

➤ Collusion is the worst of crimes against a league. Conspirators must be dealt with harshly.

➤ Be creative with punishments. And hit 'em where it hurts—in the standings.

Chapter 23

Wrap It Up ...
and Smoke It

In This Chapter

➤ The beginning of a beautiful friendship

➤ If it's not fun, why do it?

➤ In conclusion, we conclude our broadcast day ...

Feels like the end of a really intense movie. Not a poetic ending, like *Casablanca*. An exhausted ending, like *Die Hard* or *From Dusk 'til Dawn*. You emerge from a burning building, clothes sooty and torn, flesh singed and bleeding, psyche hollowed and cold. But you're wired. You've faced a harrowing test—and you survived.

But did you pass? That's up to you to decide. For all I know, you're one of those people who skips ahead and reads the ending first. If that's you, then this tome didn't help you very much. If you did in fact give it an honest read, then I hope everything was clear, concise, and interesting. If so, my job here is finished. And if you even cracked a smile? Just once? Gravy for my humble pie.

But we're not quite finished yet. We have to experience the denouement, if you will. Sort of a literary refractory period where you tie up all the loose ends before you go out and break ground for the world headquarters of your new league.

So without further commercial interruption, I present the conclusion of *The Complete Idiot's Guide to Fantasy Baseball*.

Remember: It's Supposed to Be Fun

That heading sums up this whole book. With all the research, all the memorizing of stats and values and positions, you cannot forget to have fun. In fact, if you have to be reminded, you're probably a lost cause anyway. Believe me, this is where fantasy baseball most resembles real baseball. Why? Because pro players love to pay lip service to the mantra: "It's supposed to be fun."

Foul Tips

Remember to have fun. You may be playing for money or glory or blood. But if you aren't having fun, why waste your time?

We know the truth's a different story. The term professional means you play for money. These guys also play for glory. They play for blood. But fun? You don't have fun unless you win. Which means a whole lot of players didn't have fun last season.

Fantasy ball is the same. Your fellow owners talk about fun, fun, fun. But they're all playing to win, just like you. That's what made those last two chapters on the Commissioner's job so necessary. And so gloomy.

Seriously, I hope I didn't scare anyone off with my endless lists of jerks and how to deal with them. But you need to memorize the whole play even if you're acting in only one scene. How else can you see the big picture?

The Plight of the Quiet Guy

You might be the quiet guy sitting in the corner at the draft. You talk only when bidding and you don't particularly click with the louder guys around the room. Yet you love the game. That's why you're there.

Overheard in the Dugout

Our league has constant ups and downs. We squabble. We argue. We scream. But every year, the same guys keep coming back. Why? Because when it's all said and done, we still have a good time. You should, too.

Suddenly a mid-season eruption occurs that shakes the whole league. Someone cheats, someone says the wrong thing, someone quits. And you—the quiet guy who didn't bother anyone—are left wondering what happened. Is all your hard work going up in smoke? Down with the ship?

With any luck, you now have a better idea of how to deal with problem owners. And there are many things to be dealt with. The sheer number of layers in this game still staggers me, more so as I look back on what filled this book. It's like peeling an onion. Hopefully, if you have a familiarity with those last two Commish chapters, then you can get a better read on what the rest of the league is doing—and perhaps contribute a meaningful suggestion to resolve the problem.

Strike Three

You'll experience a complete run of the emotional spectrum during a fantasy baseball season. Some guys don't know how to cope with their emotions. The result: They disguise them with a thick grizzly bear coat of aggression.

Peeling a Baseball

Here's the bare minimum of what you have to do to set up a fantasy baseball league:

Setting up a League

➤ Assemble owners

➤ Deliberate rules

➤ Confirm owners

➤ Adopt a stat service

➤ Execute the draft

➤ Collect all fees

Keeping a League Running

➤ React to news

➤ Maintain rosters

➤ Negotiate trades

➤ Acquire free agents

➤ Watch the salary cap closely

➤ Enforce rules

➤ Remember deadlines

➤ Stay active

➤ Determine winners

➤ Award prizes

Perpetuating a League

➤ Continue in the off-season

➤ Announce keepers

➤ Replace resigned owners

➤ *And much, much more!*

That list might leave some scratches on the surface of fantasy baseball. But there's more underneath. As you go, you'll experience the nuances, quirks, and traps that each facet has to offer. I'm talking full immersion here. Bring a scuba tank.

Your Off-Season Prep Work Begins *Now*

In this game, timing is everything … and nothing. You could be reading this two months or two days before the season opens. It doesn't matter. You still have the same amount of work to do to prepare.

Foul Tips

You'll be surprised how little you will have to memorize. Much of your strategy will flow from your mind naturally.

I won't rehash the specifics of earlier chapters. But you're finished reading this book. Which means that you now know what's expected. Don't be frightened by the workload. If you love the game, it's not work at all. It'll fly by, and the next thing you know, you'll have a handful of pages detailing a draft plan that is uniquely your own. You won't have to memorize it: It'll flow from your mind naturally.

Don't procrastinate. The beauty of fantasy baseball is its year-round relevance. Baseball may take a break, but you don't have to. There's always news. Trades. Free-agent signings. Off-season surgeries. They may not make headlines, but each affects players' value in its own way.

So off you go. Get to work. Install that seatbelt on your computer chair. Give the straitjacket to someone you trust, someone who will know when it's time to use it. Another helpful hint: Have someone check in on you once a month to make sure that the smell coming from your workspace is that of a living person. If you're prone to naps at the keyboard, buy this person a small mirror so they can check your breathing without waking you.

Other than that, there isn't much more for me to say. I could give you some Yoda line like "no more training do you require," or a Sean Connery *bon mot* like, "here endeth the lesson." How 'bout Mr. Myagi? "Best baseball still inside you."

What I will do is send you off with something everyone's mother said to them at one time or another. A simple request, yet tinged with so much deeper meaning: "Stop being a pain in the - - - and go play!"

Our Game, Your Game, It's All the Same

Ah, the game of ball. It makes madmen of us all. Whether we reach the pinnacle of ability or never play a single inning, the game belongs to all of us. Whether we favor the majors, the minors, or Legion ball, we can buy a couple of tickets at any time and watch. You don't even have to follow the action on the field. You can sip a beer and soak up the sun. You can watch everyone else. You can even catch 20 winks. The beauty of the game is its total acceptance of any fan at any level.

But for the serious fan, the rabid fan, there is fantasy baseball. It allows this special class of maniac to access the inaccessible, even if it's only through the imagination.

We always ask ourselves ... what would it be like to be in the owner's box? What would it be like to be in on the conference call that executed the trade of the year? What would it be like to have access to the finest talent the same way the managers do? Fantasy baseball is the answer.

Strike Three

Don't procrastinate. You can begin preparations for your up-coming season in October or March. There *is always* news.

Foul Tips

Fantasy baseball answers all our questions about what we would do if we owned a major league baseball team.

It's More Fun Than ...

Still, with all its heartbreaks, teases, and obsessions, this game is the most fun I've ever had for an extended period of time since I discovered girls and beer. It makes Braves fans out of Phillies fans, makes enemies out of friends, adds a bold-faced "in" where "sanity" once stood alone. Bitterness. Spite. Antagonism. Vendettas. Sabotage. This is what is best in men.

Our Camelot is a dream to us, a nightmare to others. And yet, no matter how much internal strife your league has, there is a kinship. When some outsider intrudes on your hit parade, mocking your devotion, stabbing at your sacred hearts, watch as your entire league joins together in a verbal carpet-bombing so complete and devastating that all that will be left of this interloper is a smear.

Hmmm. Maybe that does make it a little like *Casablanca*, after all. You know, "the beginning of a beautiful friendship." But then even the bitterest enemies will stand together against a common foe—if it serves their purpose.

Fantasyland is a dangerous place. No Mickeys, Goofys, or Plutos here. Only fans and their self-created wasteland of crumpled stat sheets, half-burned scouting reports, and suicide prevention literature. It's a place where someone doesn't exist unless his name appears on a 40-man roster. A place where inner-children become spoiled, vicious little memorabilia hounds who will sell their autographed balls as easily as they sold their souls to whichever dealer will fork over the bill with the highest number on it.

Strike Three

Don't forget, it's only a game (yeah, right).

It's a place of agitated e-mails, subversive sub-adult humor, and run-on sentences longer than the bathroom line during the eighth inning at Wrigley. Where else can so many enjoy the feats of so few by doing so much?

The Changing Fan

Once upon a time, being a baseball fan was about sitting in a recliner with a cold beer, wondering if this was the pitch, this was the inning, this was the game of the week of the year that was finally going to send your favorite team to the Series.

Now it's about sitting in the home-office chair with a stale coffee wondering is this is the at-bat, the game of the week of the year that Rey Ordonez turns into a .250 hitter.

What have we all become?

As a denizen of this tenth circle of Hell, pain and pleasure have never been so plainly explained to me. You could take away my wife, my son, my dog, and my 401(k) plan as long as Sosa hits two more off Schilling tonight. As long as Smoltz isn't out for the year. As long as Jack McKeon stays with LaRue at catcher.

Every winter is long and cold. Until that glorious day when the annuals arrive. The thick, rich books that hold scouting reports and stats and projections. Until then your only planning for the upcoming season is based on a well-worn copy of last year's final stats, tea leaves, and not much else.

What pathetic, inkless squids we all are.

But the off-season does afford one key function: forgiveness. All your failures are forgotten. The mistakes. The misjudgments. The misdemeanors. In their place will grow a fresh new flower of optimism, a burst of color and style and strategy designed for only one purpose: victory. Well, victory and her cousins, domination, annihilation, and humiliation.

Overheard in the Dugout

In the process of writing this book, I've had to review my previous fantasy seasons like I never had before. There's a lot to digest. But I'm here to tell you that it's worth it. All of it. The surges, the setbacks, the total insanity that rages within this game. Take fantasy baseball and run with it. I promise, you'll wake up at the end of the season and say, "Holy cow, that's one of the most intense experiences of my life."

Then again, maybe you won't.

And finally ... at long last ... if you've done your job, made your list, checked it twice for lice, you'll arrive at your draft sporting a master plan to build one of the most potent statistical machines ever put to paper.

The rest is up to you ...

Recommended viewing: Nothing. Go spend some time with your family.

The Least You Need to Know

➤ Remember to have fun.

➤ Off-season preparations can begin any time—whether it's October or March.

➤ Fantasy baseball will remind you why you fell in love with the game in the first place.

A Sample Rulebook

As I've said throughout this book, your league is your league. You can ultimately do whatever you want. However, the rules I present here are tried and true. I recommend trying them before changing them. I've included various options where appropriate. It's up to your league to decide which are right for you. Good luck.

The Object of the Game

The object of the game is to assemble a lineup of major league baseball players whose cumulative statistics during the regular season exceed those of all other teams in the league.

The Active Roster

A team's active roster consists of two catchers, four outfielders, one first baseman, one second baseman, one shortstop, one third baseman, one corner man (either first baseman or third baseman), one middle infielder (second baseman or shortstop), a utility player (any position except pitcher), and 10 pitchers.

Players may be added to or removed from the active roster throughout the season. Any transaction that increases the size of the active roster beyond 23 players (such as a trade or waiver claim), must be accompanied by another transaction that returns the active roster to its maximum 23 players.

In addition, after the completion of these simultaneous transactions, the roster must consist of 23 players who are eligible to play the roster positions (two catchers, four outfielders, and so on).

Options: Try adding a fifth outfielder and an 11th pitcher. Just be sure to bump up your Draft Day budget accordingly.

The Reserve Roster

A team's reserve roster consists of those players acquired through the reserve draft, through trades, through demotions from the active roster, or through free-agent claims.

Any transaction that increases the size of the reserve roster beyond 13 players must be accompanied by another transaction (such as a trade, promotion, or waiver) that simultaneously reduces the size of the reserve roster to its maximum of 13 players. There is no minimum number of players that can be on the reserve roster.

Options: The number of roster slots. Thirteen works for my league. I don't recommend going any higher than 13 slots, however, as that might encourage stockpiling of players.

The Minor League Roster

Each team also controls a minor league roster of no more than eight players. To be eligible to be placed on a minor league roster ...

1. The player must never have had more than 75 at-bats in a major league season, or pitched more than 25 innings.

2. The player did not appear on any Opening Day major league roster in the year he was drafted, nor has he appeared on any Opening Day roster during any year since he was drafted.

3. The player must never have been on any fantasy team's active roster or reserve roster.

Options: You can fiddle with the minimum at-bats and innings-pitched numbers. It all comes down to how long you think it's fair for an owner to hold his players on the minor league roster even though they have been called up in real life. These minimum requirements have sparked many a debate in our league, but this is where they stand for now.

The Auction Draft

A major league player auction draft is conducted on a date to be determined before the start of the regular season. Each team must acquire 23 players for its active roster at a total cost not to exceed $260. A team need not spend the maximum.

The league by general agreement determines the order in which teams may nominate players for acquisition. The team bidding first opens with a minimum bid of $1 for any eligible player. The bidding then continues around the room at minimum increments of $1 until only one bidder is left. That bidder acquires the player for that amount and announces the roster position the player will fill.

The maximum salary allowed for any one player is $52.

The process is repeated, with successive owners introducing players for bid, until every team has a squad of 23 players, by requisite position. Only players who begin the season on an Opening Day roster, disabled list, suspended list, or restricted list for the appropriate league may be selected in the auction draft (for example, NL may select only NL players).

Players with multiple position eligibility may be shifted from one position to another during the course of the auction draft. No team may make a bid for a player who qualifies only at a position that the team has already filled.

For example, a team that has already acquired two catchers and whose utility slot is occupied may not enter the bidding for any player who qualifies only at catcher.

No team may make a bid for a player that it cannot afford. At least $1 must be kept available for every roster slot that the team has remaining to fill. Each owner may pass his/her turn one time.

Options: You can opt for the straight pick style and forego the auction. As for the numbers involved, they will change depending on your Decimal Debate. (See Chapter 1, "Get Into the Game.")

The Reserve Draft

After the conclusion of the auction draft, teams may successively draft up to five additional players in five separate rounds of selection. Players acquired in this fashion comprise a team's reserve roster.

Any person anywhere in the world is eligible to be selected in the reserve draft. The order of selection is determined by the previous season's standings, last place to first place (or by lottery in the initial season).

The salary of each player taken in the reserve draft is $5. These salaries do not count against the $26 auction draft budget. However they do count toward the overall $40 salary cap. Teams may decline their pick in any round if they choose.

Options: The number of reserves you draft can be adjusted.

The Minor League Draft

After the conclusion of the reserve draft, teams may successively draft up to eight players with little or no major league experience (no more than 75 at-bats for hitters, 25 innings pitched for pitchers) to occupy their minor league roster.

The order of selection is the same as in the reserve draft. The cost of a player acquired in the minor league draft is $5 (to be deposited in the league kitty); however, these salaries do not count against the $260 auction draft budget or the $40 regular season salary cap.

These players are owned in rights only, and thus will not have a contract with their affiliated fantasy team until they are promoted to the active roster, at which time their $5 salary will count toward the $40 salary cap. Teams may decline their pick in any round if they choose.

If a team has retained some minor league players from the previous season, that team may draft only as many players as they have openings on their minor league roster.

Options: The number of minor leaguers you draft can be adjusted.

Free Agents (FAABoard System)

Any player remaining undrafted or unclaimed after Draft Day is eligible to be acquired as a free agent during the regular season.

All free-agent acquisitions must be made through the Commissioner by 8:30 P.M. on Sunday of each week. The cost of a player acquired as a free agent is as follows:

Before the All-Star Break

> ➤ General acquisition, $20
> ➤ Player acquired to replace injured player (must be same position), $15

After the All-Star Break

> ➤ General acquisition, $25
> ➤ Player acquired to replace injured player (must be same position), $20

Free agents must be assigned to the active roster. If the acquisition increases the active roster beyond 23 players, a currently active roster player must be reserved or waived to make room. If this demotion increases the reserve roster beyond 13 players, the team must waive a player to reduce the reserve roster to 13 players.

Any player waived by another team automatically becomes a free agent and is eligible for acquisition. Once an owner waives a player, that owner must wait eight days before re-acquiring the same player (this is to prevent the guy holding the #1 slot on the FAABoard from waiving Larry Walker at $40 one week and picking him up the next week for $20).

If two or more owners attempt to acquire the same player in the same week, the player in question will be awarded to the owner listed first on the Free Agent Acquisition Board (or FAABoard). The FAABoard will be created on Draft Day each season, and its positions can be included in a trade between owners.

Once an owner receives a player based on his FAABoard position, that owner is moved to the bottom of the FAABoard. No owner can acquire a free agent by bypassing use of the FAABoard due to player injury or a player lost due to trade to the American League (which means if that happens, you're hosed).

Options: The weekly deadline can vary (or be daily). Or you can forego the FAABoard system and use the FAABudget system (see Chapter 13, "The Replacements [Not the Band]").

Free Agent and Minor League Freeze

Any players acquired through free agency or promoted from the minor league roster must remain on the active roster for at least two weeks before being placed on the reserve roster.

If a player is acquired before Opening Day (but after Draft Day), he must remain on the active roster for the first two weeks of the regular season. The last day teams may acquire free agents is two weeks before the final Sunday of the regular season.

Position Eligibility

A player may be assigned to any position at which he appeared in 20 or more major league games in the preceding season.

A player may be eligible for any number of positions by this measure. If a player did not appear in 20 games at any one position, he may be assigned only to the position at which he appeared most frequently. If a player appeared at two positions an equal number of times, but at each less than 20 games, then the player is eligible at either position.

These totals are used to determine the position or positions at which a player may be drafted. After the reserve draft, the player retains all eligibility granted to him by the above rules for the remainder of the season, and he also becomes eligible for assignment to any position at which he has appeared at least five times during the current season.

Variables

➤ Players selected for the utility slot may qualify at any position.

➤ A rookie with no major league experience will be eligible for the position at which he played predominantly in the minor leagues, and/or the position he is expected to play during the upcoming season.

Options: You can play with the eligibility requirements, but they work pretty well as is.

Trades

The following commodities may be traded:

➤ Players on active rosters, reserve rosters, and minor league rosters

➤ FAABoard positions

➤ Future reserve picks

"Players to be named later," "future considerations," money, and gifts are not allowed.

Each owner reserves the right to protest a trade that they consider to be particularly unfair. If an owner feels that a trade is unfair, the owner may, within one week, submit a formal protest to the Commissioner (or next most-qualified league officer). The Commissioner may overturn a trade if he feels the transaction is working "against the best interests of the league."

Options: Pretty cut and dried. I wouldn't mess with players to be named and future considerations. You're just asking for trouble.

Statistics

The fantasy season ends on the last day of the regular season. The transaction reporting deadline is Sunday at 8:30 P.M. The effective date of any transaction is each Monday, before commencement of play on that Monday.

Performance stats of a player count only while that player is on the active roster. Any stats a player accumulates while on a fantasy team's reserve or minor league roster do not count.

Pitcher's offensive stats are not counted, nor are the pitching stats of the occasional position player called in to pitch in an emergency.

The Ruthian Clause. If a player is a regular pitcher as well as a regular positional player (like Babe Ruth while with the Red Sox, who would pitch one day and then play the outfield or first base for the next three days), the fantasy team must choose one or the other.

Standings

The statistical categories (batting and pitching) used by the league shall be determined before the start of each season. As it currently stands, the following criteria are used to determine team performance:

Batting

- ➤ Runs scored
- ➤ Batting average
- ➤ Runs batted in
- ➤ Home runs
- ➤ Stolen bases

Pitching

➤ Wins

➤ Earned run average

➤ Walks + Hits per Innings Pitched (WHIP)

➤ Saves

➤ Strikeouts

Teams are ranked from first to last in each of the 10 categories, and are awarded points for each place. The first-place team in each category receives as many points as there are teams in the league. The second-place team receives one point less than the first-place team; the third-place team receives one point less than the second-place team, and so on, so that the last-place team in the category receives one point.

The points scored in all 10 categories are then added together. The team with the greatest total number of points at the end of the regular season wins the League Championship.

In cases of two or more teams tied in an individual category, the total number of points between the teams are divided by the number of teams and split among them evenly.

Options: Play with categories. (See Chapters 2, "Going Batty," and 3, "The Perfect Pitch.")

Movement Between Rosters

A team may demote a player from the active roster to the reserve roster, or promote a player in the opposite direction at any time. Such promotions and demotions will take effect for statistical purposes each Monday.

At no time may the active roster have more or fewer than 23 players. There is no minimum number of players that must be on the reserve roster or the minor league roster.

A team may promote a player from the minor league roster to the active roster at any time. Once a player's first promotion out of the minors occurs, however, he becomes ineligible to ever again be placed back into the minors. A player may not be promoted from the minor league roster directly to the reserve roster.

Fees

The following fees are levied and in force at all times:

➤ Draft budget: $26

➤ Reserve draft salaries: $5 per player selected

➤ Minor league draft salaries: $5 per player selected (This salary does not count toward the regular season salary cap until the player is promoted.)

➤ Any movement of a player between the active, reserve, or minor league rosters: $2.50

➤ Trades: $2.50 per player

➤ Free agents: see free agent clause discussed earlier for a price list

➤ Waivers: no charge

Which team pays charges incurred during a trade transaction is subject to the negotiations of the trade.

Options: Tweak any and all fees.

Winter Rosters

Between the conclusion of the regular season and a date to be determined, the players on the active and reserve rosters of each team will be reduced to a maximum of eight players. There is no minimum. These are the team's keepers.

At the following year's auction/draft, each team must deduct the total salary of the keepers from their $26 draft budget. The remaining money will be used in the auction to fill out the open roster slots.

The keeper salary of players acquired by free agency in the previous season is $15.

In addition to the players kept on their active/reserve rosters, each team may (but is not required to) keep any or all of the players on their minor league roster.

Options: You can change the number of keepers, but remember that the higher the number of keepers, the lower number of players you have to buy at auction (which could diminish the importance of your draft).

Player Contracts

A player who has been under a standard contract during two consecutive seasons and whose service has been uninterrupted must, following the conclusion of his second season, be given his outright release or be signed for his option year.

Uninterrupted service means that he has not been a free agent at any point during that time. He may have been traded.

If signed for an option year the player's salary is increased by $5. The player automatically returns to the draft pool at the end of the upcoming (option) season unless he is waived and acquired by another team as a free agent.

Options: As mentioned in Chapter 20, "No Rest for the Stupid: Zim's Off-Season, 2000," you can eliminate the mandatory return to the draft pool after the third (option) year and continue to keep players indefinitely. I strongly suggest you bump their salaries each extra year, however. (Five dollars is a nice round number.) You have to give them back eventually.

Salary Cap

The total salary for each team shall not exceed $40. If a trade or free-agent acquisition causes a team to exceed this salary cap, the team must immediately make adjustments to its roster to insure the total team salary is below the cap.

It is the sole responsibility of each owner to insure that his team is in compliance. Any team that fails to comply with the cap will be sanctioned as per the judgment of the Commissioner.

Options: As I mentioned in Chapter 23, "Wrap It Up … and Smoke It," sanctions can be creative and cruel. Make 'em count.

Team Ownership

The following rules apply to team ownership:

➤ An owner may not transfer ownership of his team in the middle of the baseball season unless approved by a majority vote.

➤ All primary owners must be present on Draft Day.

➤ An owner can have an interest in only one team in any given league.

➤ The last day for an owner to announce his intention to join or drop out of the league is January 30 of each year.

➤ If the number of teams drops below nine, the continuation of the league is contingent upon a majority vote by the remaining owners.

➤ The league may expand with the approval of at least half of the current owners.

➤ Team owners can be expelled with a 4/5 majority vote of all other owners.

➤ Each owner can designate an alternate owner (who does not own another team in the same league) to handle his team's affairs during periods of unavoidable absence.

Options: All numbers and dates are open to discussion.

League Officers

League Officers' duties are as follows:

Commissioner

➤ Interpret and make decisions based on the rulebook

➤ Receive, approve, and distribute all roster changes made by owners

➤ Administer the FAABoard (or FAABudget) system and award free agents to owners

➤ Plan and mediate all meetings

Assistant Commissioner

➤ Approve all trades

➤ Review disputed trades

➤ Reserve the right to overturn trades or send involved owners back to the table to improve the deal

➤ Assume the responsibilities of the Commissioner as required

Secretary (Statistician)

➤ Review roster changes as distributed by the Commissioner

➤ Insure compliance with position eligibility and other roster issues

➤ Process weekly transactions into the stat service

➤ Act as liaison to the stat service to resolve problems and disputes

Treasurer

➤ Review roster changes as distributed by the Commissioner

➤ Insure compliance with the salary cap

➤ Maintain records of and collect all fees, penalties, and debts from owners

➤ Provide a weekly report showing outstanding balances and salary cap compliance

➤ Assess sanctions for deadbeat owners

Options: You can add or subtract offices and/or responsibilities as you see fit.

Prize Money

The balance of all league funds shall be divided among the first six teams in the final standings as follows:

➤ First place: 50 percent

➤ Second place: 25 percent

➤ Third place: 10 percent

➤ Fourth place: 7 percent

➤ Fifth place: 5 percent

➤ Sixth place: 3 percent

In addition, other cash prizes will be awarded for exceptional performances by individual players. The following situations assume nine inning games only (unless otherwise noted) and that the player is on his team's active roster during the game played.

Seasonal (Assumes that the player played for the same fantasy team for the entire year)

➤ Batter hits .400 or better for the year (minimum 400 at-bats): $10

➤ Batter hits 50 or more home runs in a season: $5

➤ Batter has 50 or more stolen bases in a season: $5

➤ Pitcher has an ERA under 2.00 for the season (minimum 125 innings pitched): $3

➤ Pitcher has WHIP under 1.000 for the season (minimum 125 innings pitched): $3

➤ Pitcher records 300 or more strikeouts for the season: $3

➤ Pitcher records 45 or more saves in a season: $2

Single Game

➤ Batter hits for cycle: $5

➤ Batter hits three or more home runs in one game: $3

➤ Pitcher throws a perfect game: $10

➤ Pitcher throws a no-hitter: $5

➤ Pitcher strikes out 16 or more batters: $3

Options: Wide open. You can spread the wealth any way you like.

A Final Note

As I've always said, these are basic rules that work and will allow you to start and maintain a fantasy baseball league right away. But there are many other versions of rulebooks/constitutions/charters out there. Read as many as you can find. Make sure your league understands that it has options.

With a little research, some elbow grease, and patience, you'll be able to forge a rulebook that is unique to your league, functions on all levels, and let's everyone have a good time.

Useful Web Sites

The following Web sites are endless sources of news, analysis, and information. As in-depth as I've tried to make this list, it no doubt leaves out many great sites. My advice is to surf like you've never surfed before!

Official Major League Baseball Sites

The official major and minor league baseball Web sites are basically billboard sites (available at a ballpark near you … baseball games!). But if you dig, you can find some interesting information. Hey—you have a question on the rules of real baseball? The official rules are in there (and much, much more!):

Major League Baseball
www.majorleaguebaseball.com

Minor League Baseball
www.minorleaguebaseball.com

Official Team Sites

These sites, while good at hawking season tickets, are also the first and last word on official team statements. Schedules, scores, and news are all available. Plus, some sites have fan chat areas and other curiosities. Check 'em out:

Anaheim Angels
www.angelsbaseball.com

Arizona Diamondbacks
www.azdiamondbacks.com

Atlanta Braves
www.atlantabraves.com

Baltimore Orioles
www.theorioles.com/index.htm

Boston Red Sox
www.redsox.com

Chicago Cubs
www.cubs.com

Chicago White Sox
www.chisox.com

Cincinnati Reds
www.cincinnatireds.com

Cleveland Indians
www.indians.com

Colorado Rockies
www.rockies.com/baseball

Detroit Tigers
www.detroittigers.com

Florida Marlins
www.flamarlins.com

Houston Astros
www.astros.com

Kansas City Royals
www.kansascity.com/royals

Los Angeles Dodgers
www.dodgers.com

Milwaukee Brewers
www.milwaukeebrewers.com

Minnesota Twins
www.wcco.com/sports/twins

Montreal Expos
www.montrealexpos.com

New York Mets
www.mets.com

New York Yankees
www.yankees.com

Oakland Athletics
www.oaklandathletics.com

Philadelphia Phillies
www.phillies.com

Pittsburgh Pirates
www.pirateball.com

St. Louis Cardinals
www.stlcardinals.com

San Diego Padres
www.padres.org

San Francisco Giants
www.sfgiants.com

Seattle Mariners
www.mariners.org

Tampa Bay Devil Rays
www.devilrays.com

Texas Rangers
www.texasrangers.com

Toronto Blue Jays
www.bluejays.ca

News, Scores, Standings, and Updates

All of these sites are great sources for up-to-the-minute news. Some have extra features such as columnists, live chats, and regular features on fantasy sports. To paraphrase Yoda: "Decide you must which serves you best."

Baseball America
www.baseballamerica.com

Baseball Newsstand
(Includes links to many other news sites)
www.baseballstuff.com/newsstand/index.html

Baseball Notebook
(Includes useful fantasy baseball essays)
www.baseballnotebook.com

CBS Sportsline
www.cbssportsline.com/mlb/index.html

CNN/SI
www.cnnsi.com/baseball

ESPN
www.espn.go.com/mlb/index.html

Fastball
www.fastball.com

Fox Sports
www.foxsports.com

MSNBC
www.msnbc.com/news/mlb_front.asp

Sport Server
(Many links to NCAA, Japanese, Korean, and other baseball leagues)
www.sportserver.com/sportserver/baseball/noframes.html

The Sporting News
www.sportingnews.com/baseball

USA Today
www.usatoday.com/sports/mlb.htm

Yahoo!
www.sports.yahoo.com/sports/bbm

Local Papers

These are the sites for every major league team's hometown paper. These are the reporters who know the teams best. These are the best sources for specific team information. You heard it here first.

Anaheim Angels and Los Angeles Dodgers
Los Angeles Times
www.latimes.com/home/news/sports

Atlanta Braves
Atlanta Journal-Constitution
www.accessatlanta.com/sports/braves

Arizona Diamondbacks
Arizona Republic
www.azcentral.com/sports/diamondbacks/dbacksindex.shtml

Baltimore Orioles
Washington Post
www.washingtonpost.com/wp-srv/sports/orioles.htm
Baltimore Sun
www.sunspot.net/sports

Boston Red Sox
Boston Globe
www.boston.com/globe/sports/redsox

Chicago Cubs and White Sox
Chicago Tribune
www.chicagotribune.com/sports/cubs
www.chicagotribune.com/sports/whitesox
Chicago Sun-Times
www.suntimes.com/index/sports.html

Cincinnati Reds
Cincinnati Enquirer
www.reds.enquirer.com
Cincinnati Post
www.cincypost.com/sports
Cleveland Plain Dealer
www.cleveland.com/sports/tribefan

Colorado Rockies
Denver Post
www.denverpost.com/rock/rock.htm
Rocky Mountain News
www.insidedenver.com/rockies

Detroit Tigers
Detroit Free Press
www.freep.com/index/tigers.htm

Florida Marlins
Miami Herald
www.herald.com/content/today/sports/baseball/content.htm

Houston Astros
Houston Chronicle
www.chron.com/content/chronicle/sports/baseball/index.html

Kansas City Royals
Kansas City Star
www.kcstar.com/sports/royals/royalspg.htm

Montreal Expos
Montreal Gazette
www.montrealgazette.com/pages/default.html

Milwaukee Brewers
Milwaukee Journal Sentinel
www.onwisconsin.com/sports/brew

Minnesota Twins
Minneapolis Star-Tribune
www.startribune.com/stonline/html/sports.shtml

New York Mets and Yankees
The New York Times
www.nytimes.com/library/sports/baseball
New York Daily News
www.mostnewyork.com/most/sports/sports.htm
New York Newsday
www.newsday.com/sports/sports/htm
New York Post
www.nypostonline.com/sports/sports.htm

Oakland Athletics and San Francisco Giants
San Francisco Chronicle
www.sfgate.com/sports
San Jose Mercury News
www.sjmercury.com/sports

Philadelphia Phillies
Philadelphia Inquirer
www.sports.phillynews.com/phillies/main.asp

Pittsburgh Pirates
Pittsburgh Post-Gazette
www.post-gazette.com/pirates

St. Louis Cardinals
St. Louis Post-Dispatch
www.postnet.com/postnet/stories.nsf/sports/cards?openview

San Diego Padres
San Diego Union Tribune
www.uniontrib.com

Seattle Mariners
Seattle Times
www.seattletimes.com/mariners

Tampa Bay Devil Rays
Tampa Tribune
www.tampabayonline.net/rays/home.htm

Texas Rangers
Dallas Morning News
www.baseball.dallasnews.com

Toronto Blue Jays
Toronto Star
www.thestar.com/thestar/editorial/mlb/index.html
Toronto Sun
www.canoe.ca/torontosports/home.html

Fantasy Baseball Sites

These sites specialize in fantasy baseball. Some require you to subscribe, but most are free and brimming with info, rumors, advice, and bells and whistles so loud you'd think you were in the USC marching band. I've made notes where I thought they would be helpful.

NOTE: These sites were going concerns at the time of this writing.

Baseball Central
www.baseballcentral.net

**Baseball Headquarters: The Homepage for Baseball Analysts
and Fantasy Leaguers**
(Subscription)
www.baseballhq.com

Baseball Think Factory
www.baseballstuff.com/btf

The Closer
www.thecloser.com

Fantasy Baseball Central
(Information service)
www.fantasybaseballcentral.com

Fantasy Baseball Index
(Subscription newsletter)
www.fantasybaseballindex.com

The Fantasy Sports Corner
www.thefantasysportscorner.com/baseball.html

The Hot Corner
www.thehotcorner.com

Masters of Baseball
www.mastersball.com

Player Projections
www.playerprojections.com

Rob's Fantasy Baseball Heaven
www.rotoheaven.com

Roto Junkie
(News, advice, and "The Bull Pen," a very active message board
that is good for feedback)
www.rotojunkie.com

RotoBall
www.rotoball.com

Rotoguru
www.rotoguru.com

Rotonews
(Free stat service and news)
www.rotonews.com

Rotoworld
www.rotoworld.com

Sandlot Shrink
(Advisory service)
www.sandlotshrink.com

Stathead Consulting
www.stathead.com

Stats, Inc.
(Various fantasy sports services)
www.stats.com

TQ Stat Projections
www.tqstats.com/_baseball/_projections

Books and 'Zines

The following books and magazines are, like their online counterparts, fantastic sources for information. Unfortunately in this livid, light-speed Digital Age, the printed word is often the obsolete word.

A Note on Usefulness

News travels fast, leaving weekly sports publications writhing in the wake of the stampede for split-second knowledge. What weekly 'zines can offer better than the online chaps is *depth*. Having a few days between deadlines allows for some thought, analysis, and useful conclusions. I recommend all of the following …

For In-Depth Reporting and Analysis

Sports Illustrated (weekly magazine). You can't beat the king for quality of writing, depth of journalism, and sharpness of commentary. Plus, the swimsuit edition arrives just in time for your draft prep.

Baseball Weekly (weekly newspaper). *USA Today* is behind this one, which offers great columnists, team-by-team updates, and John Hunt's informative, entertaining fantasy baseball section. Required reading.

The Sporting News (weekly newspaper). Sort of a middle ground between *SI* and *BW*. *TSN* covers all sports, but has long been known for its extensive baseball coverage, especially during the season.

ESPN: The Magazine (monthly). A slick brand, a big size, and access to the biggest names in sports. Unfortunately, its schedule prohibits any timeliness.

For Draft Prep

Note: Magazines and their publication schedules are specified. All other entries are annual books appearing in time for Spring Training.

Rotisserie League Baseball (Diamond Library). Written with panache and authority, this is the official guide to Rotisserie Baseball by the men who invented the game. All offshoots of fantasy sports can be traced to these guys. Geniuses, all of them. This book offers the official rules to pure Rotisserie Baseball and more individual player values and predictions than you can shake a 34 oz. stick at.

STATS Scouting Notebook. One of the best sources out there. Offers player-by-player talent analysis, statistical breakdowns, and predictions. Also provides a basic overview of each team's minor league prospects.

STATS Minor League Scouting Notebook. Offers the same priceless information as the *Scouting Notebook,* but on every minor league player out there. Indispensable for the minor league draft.

Preview Sports Fantasy Baseball (annual magazine). Arrives just in time for draft prep. It offers thorough player values and projections, but because of its format, space is limited. But for the price, it's a great source.

Fantasy Sports (monthly magazine). Calls itself "The Only Magazine Devoted Exclusively to Rotisserie and Fantasy Sports." This also is a nice source and is published monthly. The problem is exactly that. Their info doesn't change much from month to month—at least not the three issues I bought. Still, it can be very useful for draft prep.

The Sporting News Baseball Register. Another great source. Comprehensive stats and information on every active major leaguer.

The Sporting News Baseball Guide. Calls itself "The Ultimate 2000 Season Reference."

STATS Major League Handbook. Offers lifetime records for all current major leaguers, including left/right splits, leader boards, and projections.

STATS Minor League Handbook. Like the *Major League Handbook,* but for minor leaguers.

STATS Player Profiles. Virtually every kind of statistic you can think of for every current major leaguer.

If You're Still Looking for a Stat Service

I'm not going to help any stat services with their advertising. I've mentioned before the benefits of scouring the chat rooms for good recommendations. Another great source? The fantasy sports magazines I mentioned earlier. They have advertising out the wazoo.

Advertising does not always equal quality, but it's a good place to start your search. But I still recommend going to the people who play the game for advice. Those chat rooms and message boards are meccas for sports talk and everyone is usually eager to help out.

Good luck.

The "Trash Talk" Glossary

auction-style   A draft style in which owners bid on players in $1 increments. Players go to the highest bidder.

bid-up value   How many dollars above a player's perceived value the league can get one owner to pay. Five-tool fantasy studs and over-hyped rookies are the easiest players to bid up—and someone will *always* pay.

ceiling price   The absolute limit to what you will pay for a given player. When the bidding hits the ceiling, walk away.

collusion   The act of two or more owners conspiring to manipulate the final results of the league. Methods can include trades, waivers, and point shaving.

Commissioner   The chief executive of a fantasy league. He enforces rules, resolves disputes, and runs meetings.

crickets pick   A player's name called out during the draft that elicits total silence—except for crickets chirping—from the other owners, followed by cursing if the player is any good.

draft mole   An owner who shows up for Draft Day, has a blast, assembles a good team, and then burrows into the ground, not to be heard from again until next spring. Other names exist for this kind of person, but decorum prohibits listing them here.

draft-pick style   A draft style in which owners select players one-by-one in turn until rosters are full. This is a simpler and quicker draft style than any other.

dump   When an owner trades away all his star talent in favor of keepers and draft picks in preparation for next season. Also known as "quitting."

earned run average (ERA)   The average of earned runs a pitcher allows every nine innings. It is calculated by multiplying earned runs by nine, then dividing by innings pitched.

fantasy baseball   A game that allows an "owner" to draft his or her own baseball team using real players and their real stats from the upcoming season. Whoever has the best overall stats in the league at the end of the regular season wins.

five-tool baseball player   A player who excels in every aspect of the game. In real baseball, he runs, throws, catches, hits for power, and hits for average. However, in fantasy baseball, the five-tool player dominates the five major offensive categories.

free agent   Any player who was not taken in the normal draft, and who remains unclaimed. During the season, a free agent can be claimed to replace injured players or players lost in a trade to the other league.

keeper   Any player who is worth keeping because his price is so far below market value.

max-out   Occurs when an owner puts every salary cap dollar into the active roster, "maxing out" both the cap and his production.

minor league draft   A supplemental draft that allows owners to select a certain number (depending on your rules) of minor league players for the upcoming season—and beyond.

on-base percentage (OBP)   How many times a player reaches base divided by his total at-bats. This includes hits, walks, and hit-by pitches, but not bases reached on errors.

orphan stats   Statistics produced by players who aren't owned by anyone in your league, or who are owned but are not on an active roster. Orphan stats usually cause great feelings of disgust, frustration, and helplessness—and spur beer sales.

performance category   A category that is mathematically calculated such as batting average, earned run average, and on-base percentage, as opposed to a category of stats that represent simple volume, such as total wins, RBIs, saves, and so on.

pre-emptive bid   See scare bid.

reserve draft   A supplemental draft that allows owners to select a certain number (depending on your rules) of supplemental players as reserves for the upcoming season.

reserves   Players who are selected in the supplemental reserve draft, or any players on a team's reserve roster.

scare bid   The same as a pre-emptive bid. An owner throws out a bid so high that no other owner will dare top it. Also known as a nuke bid.

sleeper picks Players who are drafted at bargain-bin prices, yet break out to have incredible years. Every owner tries to predict them. Few owners actually get them—and they are never who you think they will be. They're the winning lottery tickets of fantasy baseball.

swing man A pitcher who can start or relieve. He can be an incredibly good—and cheap—fantasy player.

tell An unconscious action that gives away what cards a poker player is holding—or what a fantasy owner is planning to do.

ten dollar theory Says that, as the draft progresses, a player's actual price will most likely fluctuate five dollars up or down from your price list. If this happens consistently, you've done a good job establishing values.

throw-in A marginal player included to help balance a nearly completed trade.

trading deadline The date that cuts off league-wide trading for the season. It's an optional rule, but one I recommend.

volume category A category based on the accumulation of statistics such as total home runs, RBIs, runs scored, wins, saves, and so on, as opposed to stats that are calculated by formula, such as batting average.

vulture wins and saves (a.k.a. **vulching**) Stats amassed by the dozens of middle and long relievers populating major league staffs. These athletes rarely have Draft Day value, but can be very useful when one of your starters gets hurt and the pickings are thin.

WHIP (Walks + Hits per Innings Pitched) Measures how many batters a pitcher allows on base per inning, either by base-on-balls or hit.

Index

305

311

313